M000087559

Europe and the
Rise of Capitalism

Edited by

*Jean Baechler, John A. Hall and
Michael Mann*

Basil Blackwell

Copyright © Basil Blackwell Ltd 1988

First published 1988
Reprinted and first published in paperback 1989

Basil Blackwell Ltd
108 Cowley Road, Oxford, OX4 1JF, UK

Basil Blackwell Inc.
3 Cambridge Center
Cambridge, MA 02142, USA

All rights reserved. Except for the quotation of short passages for the purposes of criticism and review, no part of this publication may be reproduced, stored in a retrieval system, or transmitted, in any form or by any means, electronic, mechanical, photocopying, recording or otherwise, without the prior permission of the publisher.

Except in the United States of America, this book is sold subject to the condition that it shall not, by way of trade or otherwise, be lent, re-sold, hired out, or otherwise circulated without the publisher's prior consent in any form of binding or cover other than that in which it is published and without a similar condition including this condition being imposed on the subsequent purchaser.

British Library Cataloguing in Publication Data

Europe and the rise of capitalism.
1. Europe—Economic conditions   2. Asia
—Economic conditions
I. Baechler, Jean   II. Hall, John A.
III. Mann, Michael, 1942–
330.94′02   HC240
ISBN 0–631–15006–4
ISBN 0–631–16942–3 Pbk

Library of Congress Cataloging in Publication Data

Europe and the rise of capitalism.
  Based on papers from a symposium organized in September 1985 at Emmanuel College, Cambridge, under the title of "The European miracle", sponsored by the Economic and Social Research Council in co-operation with the Centre national de la recherche scientifique, Paris.
  Includes bibliographies and index.
  1. Capitalism—Europe—History—Congresses.
2. Capitalism—Asia—History—Congresses. 3. Europe—Economic conditions—Congresses. 4. Asia—Economic conditions—Congresses. I. Baechler, Jean. II. Hall, John A., 1949– . III. Mann, Michael, 1942– .
IV. Emmanuel College (University of Cambridge)
V. Economic and Social Research Council (Great Britain)
VI. Centre national de la recherche scientifique (France)
HC240.9.C3E97 1987   330.94   87–12293
ISBN 0–631–15006–4
ISBN 0–631–16942–3 (pbk.)

Typeset in 10½ on 12 pt Ehrhardt
by Hope Services, Abingdon, Oxon, UK
Printed in Great Britain by T. J. Press, Padstow

Contents

Preface

In September 1985 we organized a symposium held at Emmanuel College, Cambridge, under the provocative title of 'The European Miracle'. This title – borrowed from E. L. Jones's book *The European Miracle* (Cambridge, 1981) – indicated our interest in explaining the massive and, perhaps, unique development of medieval and early modern Europe towards capitalism, the Industrial Revolution and modernity. To that end we gathered a group of distinguished, international scholars from several academic disciplines. The Economic and Social Research Council generously provided funds for the symposium under its programme of Anglo-French co-operation with the Centre National de la Recherche Scientifique, Paris.

All but two of the chapters here presented were given in earlier form in either English or French at the symposium – the exceptions being invited contributions from Ernest Gellner and Chris Wickham. (Chris Wickham's chapter has also appeared in the *Journal of Peasant Studies*.) We would like to thank all those who participated in Cambridge for their contributions to our lively and stimulating discussions.

The French contributions have been translated into English by W. D. Halls.

Jean Baechler, Maison des Sciences de l'Homme, Paris
John A. Hall, University of Southampton and Harvard University
Michael Mann, London School of Economics

Acknowledgements for the illustrations in chapter 5

Figure

3a Reproduced by kind permission of Mark Elvin.

3b Diderot, *Encyclopedie*, vol. XXVIII, plate VIII Sig. H, fol. Bs 459–486 (K.5.221), is reproduced by kind permission of the Bodleian Library, Oxford.

3c Diderot, *Encyclopedie*, vol. XXVIII, plate XII Sig. M, fol. Bs 459–486 (K.5.221) is reproduced by kind permission of the Bodleian Library, Oxford.

4a The Mansell Collection.

4b Reproduced by kind permission of Mark Elvin.

5a Reproduced by kind permission of Glasgow University Library.

Introduction

Ernest Gellner

The conference on which this collection of essays is based was originally called 'The European Miracle', and the idea of the miraculousness of the European experience continues to haunt much of the argument. The European Miracle sounds like an extraordinary example of European vainglory and vanity. We are the miracle. *Le miracle, c'est moi.* It is all a bit like the man who explained his failure to take part in the war by saying – '*I* am the civilization you are fighting to defend. The rest of you simply exemplify the ordinary condition of humanity, unblessed and unhallowed by any miraculous intervention.' *We* need to be explained; *you* constitute a kind of unproblematic and unexciting baseline, a moral null hypothesis, which invites no intellectual exploration, and contains no valuable lesson.

That is what it sounds like. The truth of the matter is exactly the opposite. The phrase should not be read – the *European* miracle. It must be read – the European *miracle*. We know not what we do, and we do not know what hit us. We cannot take credit for it. Economic, social and cognitive development, like thought itself, cannot properly be spoken of in the first person. Just as one should always say 'it thinks' and never 'I think', so one should also say that *it* developed, and not that *we* developed. The underlying puzzlement, the perception of a problem which inspires the question, is not any kind of Europocentric vision of history, but on the contrary, a sense of proportion, of the general and pervasive obstacles to progress, and a humility in face of the occasional rare surmounting of those impediments.

Europeans had indeed once been vainglorious and Europocentric. Then they equated their own history with human history as such, and lacked a sense of any specific miracle. They had only received what was their due. Their own fate was what was intended for humanity. Life or history itself had intended them to be the beneficiaries of what had come their way. They were and deserved to be at the head of the queue. Thus the new humanist faith in work was a covert glorification of one kind of man.

The period stretching roughly from the end of the eighteenth to the beginning of the twentieth century, the age of the faith in progress, was, of course, also the time of an awareness of fundamental social and intellectual change. It was linked, in most cases, to an optimistic conviction that this change was for the better. Global change was endowed with a systematic direction, and it was underwritten by some persistent mechanism or force which guaranteed that this overall direction should remain beneficial and operative. Basically there was but one principle and one mechanism of change. It manifested itself, in its most striking and best developed form, in European or Western history. The age whose thought had fused history and philosophy, which saw historic change as the manifestation of our collective salvation and as the clue to human destiny, focused on Western history. What of the rest of mankind?

The question was not always asked with very much insistence. What did the rest of the world matter? But for those who did ask the question, the answer was obvious. The rest of the world exemplified the same principles, the same mechanisms, the same destiny, as did the West. But these other cultures or races or civilizations exemplified them in feebler, slower and retarded forms. They could see their future in us. We could see our barbarous past in them. That indeed constitutes their scholarly significance. As late as the second half of the twentieth century, Claude Lévi-Strauss could point out that for the *Marxisant* Jean-Paul Sartre, backward races could only enter history proper by courtesy of incorporation in the European dialectic. This was *la mission civilisatrice* in Marxist language.

So the Europocentric nineteenth-century philosophies of history tended to assume that the recent dramatic transformations, which had disturbed the earlier certainties and seeming stabilities of Europe, were firmly inscribed on a universal human agenda. These were issues facing mankind, not Europe as such. Their solutions were valid for humanity, not just for Europeans. These problems and solutions had been ever present, latent in the destiny of mankind. Europe attained them first, but they were not specifically European. Europe was the avant-garde model. It was through the European situation that the human condition as such was to be understood. The principles of human society were the same everywhere, but Europe, being most advanced, provided the norm.

Philosophy had become historical when it became manifest that radical social change was not an aberration, but was inherent in the human condition. Change ceased to be seen as part of social pathology, as it had been for Plato, and became, instead, the central theme and device of a new, secular soteriology. But the vision did still assume that the turbulence of European history revealed human destiny as such.

This assumption, so often tacitly accepted, has now been abandoned. The historical nature of philosophy (though repudiated or ignored by the academic trade) continues to be valid: change is the law of all things, and we cannot understand ourselves without understanding the patterns of change. But we no longer constitute the model which explains all else. We are an aberration, which can only be understood by investigating the other, more typical social forms. What has disappeared is the supposition that the changes which occurred here – if only we can pick out their crucial features and their underlying principles – were inscribed into the order of things, into the very essence of human society, requiring nothing but time and maturation to reveal themselves generally.

Of course, nothing can happen unless it is possible. But a great deal can happen without being necessary. The emergence of a society without poverty, a society blessed with perpetual economic and cognitive growth, an egalitarian and/or fraternal society which incorporates everyone in a shared moral citizenship and a high culture, a society without oppression or arbitrariness – whichever of these or similar features you consider to be central to an optimistic vision of social development – is not inscribed into any historic plan. On the contrary, it is plausible to argue that agrarian society as such is a trap, and moreover one from which it was almost impossible for mankind to escape. A stored surplus needs to be guarded and its distribution enforced. No principle of distribution is either self-validating or self-enforcing. Conflict is inevitable, and victors have no interest in permitting a return match. They have every reason to prevent it by pre-emptive action. Herein lies, as Plato amongst others saw, the root cause of political coercion. Few agrarian societies escape this coercive destiny.

The consequences of the codification and storage of knowledge, in other words of the discovery and use of writing, are no better, as David Hume noted: the guardians of a centralized and codified doctrine are less tolerant than the priests of traditional, non-scriptural religion. Codification makes possible the definition of orthodoxy and hence of heresy, and hence the extension of social control to belief as well as of practice. The monopolists of truth are as jealous as the monopolists of power, and have as good reasons for eliminating competition. So oppression and dogmatism which is, in diverse forms, the shared lot of agro-literate societies, is not an accident but a fatality.

How then did we manage to escape the dreadful regiment of kings and

priests? Certainly not because we were any better than those who failed
to escape. The miracle occurred, not in the West as such, nor even in
Europe, but in one small part of Europe, and on one occasion only. It did
not occur in other parts of the same continent, and was often suppressed
when attempts were made to spread it. Those who achieved it once had
not been able to perform it on earlier occasions. Had this one instance
been suppressed, as it very nearly was, there is no evidence that they
would have been able to repeat it later. Of course we cannot be sure
about this, as we do not know what would have happened: but that is
what the evidence suggests.

So the sense of miracle is not inspired by the vainglory or self-
congratulation of those who were its first beneficiaries, but, rather, by a
sense of its precariousness. This sense springs from a vivid perception of
the difficulties of diffusing the benefits of the new order, but also from an
awareness of its fragility, and of its mysteriousness in its original
homeland. Looking at those caught in the agrarian trap, we know that but
for the Grace of God, that would be our condition,. This is the switch
from the entelechy, acorn-to-oak tree vision (exemplified, for instance,
by Marxism), to the fortuitous, contingent opening of a normally shut
gate, to the accidentally open gate model (exemplified by Max Weber).

When a great deal of twentieth-century philosophy turned its back on
history and on any preoccupation with historic patterns, it did not do so
because its nineteenth-century predecessors had been Europocentric. It
did so because it claimed that history as such, whether ethnocentric or
not, was irrelevant. In so doing, it became, in effect, essentialist, whether
or not this was recognized. It assumed, or affirmed, that human nature,
society, institutions, could be understood and/or evaluated by somehow
approaching their given, inherent essences, which were independent of
the historically revealed transformations. R. G. Collingwood saw the
absurdity of this clearly, but he was not heeded.

Nowadays, there is a variety of such fashionable von Münchhausen
philosophies, whose practitioners would lift themselves, and the rest of
us, by their own breeches from the ditch of contingent reality to the
heights of normative essence. These trans-historical essences are
allegedly approached by diverse patented methods – linguistic, phenom-
enological, formal–logical, contractarian and other. In fact, their
trascendence of history is spurious. Philosophy must become historical
again, but it may not absolutize any one condition or pattern of change.
It must explain how, against all odds, a dramatic transformation became
possible – not why it was necessary. It can illuminate options, not
prescribe any one of them.

If we now return, as we must, to a concrete investigation of the historic
constraints which define the range of our options, the manner in which

we do so is radically different from our nineteenth-century predecessors. We also differ from our anti-historicist or history-blind contemporaries, who suppose they can work out the moral or conceptual answers first, and only then turn to social fact, when it comes to the merely technical problems of implementation. In practice, they naïvely use a supposedly abstract model, which, however, covertly incorporates and absolutizes highly specific and favoured historic idiosyncracies. They feed their own illusions back to themselves, as putative conclusions of supposedly neutral trans-historical premises.

We differ from the historicist predecessors who supposed that history was a palimpsest, which, once deciphered, gave us the answers. It does nothing of the kind. What we do claim is that certain assumptions and values which are absolutely central to our style of life and thought – the assumption, for instance, of a unified orderly and manipulable nature, and correspondingly, of a generic reason, capable and alone capable of attaining truth in a symmetrical way, allowing no cognitive privilege – have historic roots. These roots neither vindicate nor de-validate those ideas. They only give us a realistic account of our predicament, of our options, and of their cost. The essays assembled in this volume are, I think, basically inspired by such a desire, and aim to provide us with an effective mirror which will help us to understand ourselves.

1

European Development: Approaching a Historical Explanation

Michael Mann

The 'miracle' of massive economic development occurred 'spontaneously' in Europe, and nowhere else. There are two main types of possible explanation: the comparative and the historical. John Hall's chapter attempts a predominantly comparative explanation; I will complement him by attempting an explanation based largely on European history. As I wish, above all, to be brief, much of this will appear as rather general assertion. I provide fuller documentation for my assertions in chapters 12–15 of Mann (1986). But my intention is to introduce rather than to settle arguments.

Establishing the Chronology and Overall Character of Development: Extensive and Intensive Power Achievements

The greatest contribution of the historian to the methodology of the social sciences is the date. As an undergraduate, I found it useful to mug up date-lists when revising for my examinations. Twenty years later I cannot remember what the Compromise of Avranches was, but I know it was in 1172. *When* things happened is essential to establishing causality, especially in such a complex causal chain as European development. So when, exactly, did it happen?

Of course, it never 'exactly' happened; it was a long drawn-out process. It culminated in the Industrial Revolution in England where, in only 50 years from about 1760, human society liberated itself from the age-old energy constraints provided by animal and human muscle power. But the previous century also saw an 'agricultural revolution' in which the agrarian surplus virtually doubled. The two centuries before that also witnessed sustained agricultural growth and massive trade expansion which we can push back to the 'navigational revolution' at the end of the fifteenth century.

At that point some theorists stop. They compare the barbarism of Europe with the contemporary civilizations of Asia, particularly China, and the Middle East. It follows that the point at which Europe 'overtook' Asia must have been around 1450, the period of European naval expansion and the Galilean revolution in science. For example, Joseph Needham (1963): 'the discovery of the basic technique of scientific discovery itself, then the curve of science and technology in Europe begins to rise in a violent, almost exponential manner, overtaking the level of the Asian societies.' So we search for our explanation in the period immediately prior to this overtaking, in late medieval Europe.

But only a few societies can be simply placed above or below each other on a single developmental scale measuring their collective powers. More frequently societies differ in their achievements. This was so in the case of medieval Europe and China. European self-denigration comes from its obsession with 'extensive power' – the ability to organize social co-operation and the exploitation of nature over large territories and populations. Extensive power is sustained by a technology capable of co-ordinating a large number of inputs to produce an output. Measured by this standard, Europe lagged until after 1500. Prior to this, Marco Polo could rightly boggle at the splendour and the military and political power of Kubla Khan: no European monarch could appropriate such riches, pacify such spaces, mobilize such a number of troops. Furthermore, the Christian rulers of the northern Mediterranean fought a long, retreating struggle against Islamic states over many medieval centuries. Europe was often inferior, never superior, in extensive powers until after 1500. Most innovations which proved to have great implications for extensive power (notably gunpowder, the mariner's compass and printing) came from the East. 'Extensive technology' seems to have lagged in Europe before about 1450. Europeans were generally content with the communications technology bequeathed by the Romans. No major innovations were made in the medieval period in the communication of messages or, with two exceptions, in transport technology (see Leighton, 1972, for a detailed discussion) – these two concern the use of horses, developed primarily to improve ploughing rather than communications, and Viking-derived ship rigging.

But now let us look at 'intensive' power and technology – the ability to use a few inputs 'intensively', that is to mobilize a few people, animals and tools over a small area so as to increase the productivity of the inputs. Productive efficiency, not massive co-ordination, is the key. On this criterion a European–Asian comparison would probably give different

results, especially in agriculture, especially in north-west Europe. For the
whole of the medieval period, European agriculture was using intensive
technology which increased its productivity well beyond the ancient
world's, and probably that of Asia. This was achieved locally, predominantly in villages and manors. Though it presupposed long-distance
trade, there was very little extensive co-ordination of this. Economic
power achievements were massive but locally, intensively organized.

Four major technology inventions were made in agriculture: ploughing,
shoeing and harnessing of draught animals, field rotation, and the water-
mill. All were widespread by about AD 1000; all disproportionately
increased the yield from wetter, heavier soils, that is from northern and
western Europe. Cipolla (1976: 159–60) summarizes their development
as:

a.   from the sixth century: diffusion of the water mill.
b.   from the seventh century: diffusion, in northern Europe, of the
     heavy plough.
c.   from the eighth century: diffusion of the three-field system.
d.   from the ninth century: diffusion of the horseshoe: diffusion of
     a new method of harnessing draught animals.

Lynn White (1963: 277) summarizes their effect: 'Between the first half
of the 6th century and the end of the 9th century Northern Europe
created or received a series of inventions which quickly coalesced into an
entirely novel system of agriculture. In terms of a peasant's labor, this
was by far the most productive the world has seen.' Bridbury (1975)
Duby (1974) and Postan (1975) have all argued that economic revival
occurred well before AD 1000. Elsewhere in this volume, Karl
Ferdinand Werner argues for a similarly early date for a more general
revival.

Let us consider the character of these innovations. The heavy plough
had an iron coulter knife to incise a furrow, an iron share to cut it deeper,
and an angled mould-board to tear loose and overturn the sliced earth
towards the right-hand side. It could turn over deeper, heavier soils,
raise them up and provide them with drainage furrows. The waterlogged
plains of northern Europe could be drained and exploited. But the
plough needed more energy to pull. This was provided by improved
shoeing and harnessing of bigger teams of oxen or horses. Field rotation
is more complex. But the very complexity and unevenness of the
diffusion of 'two-field' versus 'three-field' systems indicates that farmers
were aware both of the richer potentialities of heavier soils for grain and
some vegetable yields and of the specific fertilizing problems raised by
such soils. The interdependence of arable farming and animal husbandry

tightened, and this, too, shifted power to the north-west, to areas like south-eastern England or Flanders where zones of good pasture lands and cornfield interpenetrated. In global terms it probably gave western Europe a decisive agricultural edge over Asia, particularly over Chinese intensive rice cultivation techniques. Energy and manure from animals gave the European 'a motor more or less five times as powerful as that possessed by Chinese man' according to Chaunu (1969: 336). None of these were merely technical innovations; they also involved intensive social organization. An economic unit of about the size of the village or the manor was useful for equipping an oxen or horse team, arranging its co-operative use (which encouraged the characteristic long strips of early medieval agriculture), and organizing field rotation and manuring. Such organization could increase the yield of heavy soil grains. The watermill could efficiently grind them.

Nothing indicates more clearly the character of early medieval agricultural dynamism than the water-mill, invented during the Roman period but not widely diffused until then. Here we have a statistic. The Domesday Book records 6000 mills in England by 1086 (Hodgen, 1939), a figure Lennard (1959: 278) considers an understatement by at least 10 per cent, but which averages out at two per village and about one per 10–30 ploughs. Some of these water-mills were under the control of the local lord, others were independent. But all showed that economic power and innovation had passed to the now thoroughly decentralized locality.

When did it begin? We cannot say exactly because of the Dark Ages of the records, but probably before AD 1000. By contrast, many popular explanations begin much later – with the twelfth-century town, the struggles in the thirteenth and fourteenth centuries between peasants and lords, fourteenth-century capitalist accounting methods, the Renaissance of the fourteenth and fifteenth centuries, the fifteenth-century navigational revolution, the scientific revolutions between 1400 and 1600, sixteenth-century Protestantism, seventeenth-century Puritanism, English capitalist agriculture of the seventeenth and eighteenth centuries – the list could be continued.

These may be important contributors, but they form only a later part of an extraordinarily long and almost continuous process lasting from before AD 1000 to 1800. The continuity can be glimpsed through two attempts at quantification, of population and of the yield ratios of crops. Obviously they are both crude estimates, relying on very imperfect data, but, viewed in the long run, both increase right from before 1200 to 1800, with only one pronounced slump in the fourteenth century (for yield ratios see Slicher van Bath, 1963: 16–17; population accounts tend to conflict, though not in the overall continuity of growth – for England, see Russell, 1948; Postan, 1975: 30–5; see McEvedy and

Jones, 1978, for overall European graphs). Both also reveal the steady shifting of growth towards the north-west.

So, development began before or around AD 1000, was extraordinarily continuous and shifted steadily towards the north-west. Its character centred on 'intensive' local power relationships, though after 1450 or so it also began to develop 'extensive' power techniques. This leads me to believe that local European institutions had within them from a very early stage the fundamental preconditions of growth. How were these institutions able to withstand all obstacles – Malthusian cycles, plagues, wars and so on – and stimulate economic creativity and growth over a very long period?

Theoretical Redescription of the Problem: Autonomous Local Power Networks, Extensive Normative Regulation

The conventional wisdom of our age was produced by the capitalist culmination of the development. It purports to give us a clear answer, in terms of neo-classical economics. Land, capital and labour interact as factors of production on competitive markets across given ecologies. As Jones (1981) argues, part of 'the European miracle' when compared to Asia resides in its ecological contrasts. This produces a 'dispersed portfolio of resources' whereby bulk, utilitarian goods – such as grains, meat, fruit, olives, wine, salt, metals, wood, animal skins and furs – were exchanged right across the continent. The high proportion of coastlines and navigable rivers kept transport costs low. Then, Jones continues, consequences flow from economic rationality: states had no interest in pillaging bulk subsistence goods traded as commodities, only in taxing them; in return, states would provide basic social order. Europe avoided the state 'plunder machine', hence economic development. As a neo-classical economist who believes that markets are 'natural', Jones paraphrases his mentor, Adam Smith – if you have peace, easy taxes and a tolerable administration of justice, then the rest is brought about by 'the natural course of things' (1981: 90–6, 232–7).

But such a model has essential preconditions whose emergence we must explain. Why is 'Europe' to be regarded as a continent in the first place? This is not an ecological but a social fact. It had not been a continent hitherto: it was now created by the fusion of the Germanic barbarians and the north-western parts of the Roman Empire, and the blocking presence of Islam to the south and east. Its continental identity was primarily Christian, for its name was Christendom more often than it was Europe.

Europe was undoubtedly a place where competition flourished, but why? It is not 'natural', nor is it the kind of state mentioned by Smith. In fact, competition presupposes two further forms of social organization. First, autonomous actors must be empowered to dispose of privately owned resources without hindrance from anyone else. These actors need not be individuals, or even individual households, enjoying what in capitalist societies we call 'private property'. From Alan Macfarlane's (1978) work we know that this process was quite well developed in medieval England. But collective institutions also qualify, as long as they have a responsible authority structure empowered to dispose of its resources for economic advantage, without interference from others or from custom – then the laws of neo-classical economics can begin to operate. The etymology of 'private' is 'hidden' – hidden, in this case, from the interference of the state and other plunderers, as well as from the inertial control exercised in many agrarian societies by the combination of overlapping lineages and custom.

Second, competition among actors on a market requires normative regulation. They must trust one another to honour their word. They must also trust each other's essential rationality. These normative understandings must apply not only in direct interaction but right across complex, continental chains of production, distribution and exchange. Ethical and normative solidarity also results in more tangible results such as the routine pacification of trade routes without costly coercion.

Now we can see that European social structure supplied these requirements. The social structure which stabilized in Europe after the ending of the barbarian migrations and invasions (that is, by AD 1000) was a multiple acephalous federation. Europe had no head, no centre, yet it was an entity composed of a number of small, cross-cutting interaction networks. These, based on economic, military and ideological power, each differed in their geographical and social space and none was itself unitary in nature. Consequently no single power agency controlled a clear-cut territory or the people within it. As a result most social relationships were extremely localized, intensely focused upon one or more of a number of cell-like communities – the monastery, the village, the manor, the castle, the town, the guild, the brotherhood and so on. These collectivities had a power autonomy guaranteed by law or custom, an exclusivity of control over 'their' resources. They qualify, therefore, as 'private' property owners.

In agriculture the two main actors were the village community and the manor. Thus monopolistic power organizations rarely existed in the local economy. Formidable as were the powers of the lord, they were usually restrained by the fact that even the serf could find support from the village community and from customary law. The two power networks were also interpenetrating – peasant and lord were partly independent of one another, partly implicated in each other's organization, as the distribution of their strips of land reveals. Interpenetration was most pronounced along the old Roman frontier provinces where the German free village and the Roman estate mixed – in England, the Low Countries, northern and central France, West Germany, and eastern and northern England. But a similar balance between organized collectivities existed in the political, military and religious realms. No one ruled Europe.

Whatever this extraordinary multiple, acephalous federation would achieve, it was unlikely to be organized stagnation. Historians over and over again use the word *restless* to characterize the essence of medieval culture. As McNeill puts it, 'it is not any particular set of institutions, ideas or technologies that mark out the West but its inability to come to a rest. No other civilized society has ever approached such restless instability. . . . In this . . . lies the true uniqueness of Western civilization' (1963: 539). But such a spirit need not induce social development. Might it not induce other forms of stagnation: anarchy, the Hobbesian war of all against all, or *anomie* where the absence of social control and direction leads to aimlessness and despair? We can marry the insights of two great sociologists to guess why social development, not anarchy or *anomie*, may have resulted.

First Max Weber, who in noting the peculiar restlessness of Europe, always added another word: *rational.* 'Rational restlessness' was the psychological make-up of Europe, the opposite of what he found in the main religions of Asia: rational acceptance of social order by Confucianism and its irrational antithesis in Taoism; mystical acceptance of social order by Hinduism; other worldly retreat in Buddhism. Weber located rational restlessness especially in Puritanism. But Puritanism emphasized strands of the Christian psyche which had been traditionally present. Salvation to all in return for ethical individual conduct; and judgement of all by an Apocalypse. Christianity encouraged a drive for moral and social improvement even against worldly authority. Though much of medieval Christianity was piously masking brutal repression, its currents of dissatisfaction always ran strong. We can read an enormous literature of social criticism, visionary, moralistic, satirical, cynical. Some is laboured and repetitious, but its peak includes some of the greatest works of the age – in English: Langland and Chaucer. It is pervaded by the kind of psychological quality identified by Weber.

But to put this rational restlessness in the service of social improvement probably also required a mechanism identified by another sociologist: Emile Durkheim. Not anarchy or *anomie* but normative regulation was provided at first primarily by Christendom. Political and class struggles, economic life and even wars were, to a degree, regulated by an unseen hand, not Adam Smith's but Jesus Christ's. Let us remember that the village, the manor and the other interpenetrating communities required also a more extensive exchange of commodities, in which a geographical area other than the village–manor core, the northern shores of the Mediterranean, was at first the leader. The community depended on the general recognition of norms regarding property rights and free exchange. These were guaranteed by a mixture of local customs and privileges, some judicial regulation by weak states, but above all by the common social identity provided by Christendom.

Let us try a little hypothetical reconstruction of the case of England. If we were able to travel back to England around 1150, armed with questionnaires, tape-recorders and the necessary linguistic skills, to ask a sample of the population with all due circumspection to what social group they belonged, we would get rather complex answers. The majority would not be able to give one sole identity. The lords, whom we would interview in Norman French (though we could try Latin), might indicate that they were gentlefolk – Christians, of course; they might elaborate a genealogy indicating also that they were of Norman descent but linked closely to the Angevin king of England and to the English baronage. They would think that, on balance, their interests lay with the lords of the kingdom of England (perhaps including its French possessions, perhaps not) rather than with, say, the lords of the kingdom of France. I am not sure where they would place 'the people' – Christians, but barbarous, unlettered rustics – in their normative map. The merchants, whom we would interview in a diversity of languages, might say that they were English or citizens of towns from the Baltic coast to Lombardy; if they were English they would probably show more anti-foreigner 'nationalism' than anyone else, out of sectional interest; they would naturally say that they were Christians; and their interests lay in a combination of guild autonomy and alliance with the English crown. The higher clergy, whom we would interview in Latin, would say Christians first and foremost. But we would then usually find both a clear, kin-based, class solidarity with the lords, and an overlapping identity with some lords and merchants, but definitely excluding the people, centred on the possession of literacy. The parish priest, with whom we could try Latin – or failing that, Middle English – might say Christian and English. Some would claim, perhaps dubiously, to be *literati*. The peasants, the vast majority of our sample, we would interview in the various Middle English dialects and amalgams of Saxon, Danish, Celtic and Norman French (of which we only have the vaguest outlines). They were *illiterati*, an abusive term denoting exclusion, not membership of a community. They would say Christian, and then they might say English, or they might say they were Essex or Northumbrian or Cornish

folk. Their allegiances were mixed: to their local lord (temporal or
spiritual), to their local village or other kin network and (if they were
freemen) to their king.

The main conclusion is unmistakable. The most powerful and
extensive sense of social identity was Christian, though this was both a
unifying transcendent identity and an identity divided by the overlapping
barriers of class and literacy. Cross-cutting all these were commitments
to England, but these were variable and, in any case, included less
extensive dynastic connections and obligations. Thus, Christian identity
provided both a common humanity and a framework for common
divisions among Europeans. Class struggles were perceived and organized
in religious, sectarian terms. Christians were not aliens but persons with
a common rationality among whom normatively based understandings
and disputes might circulate.

I use the term 'transcendence' for this identity quite deliberately, for I
wish to suggest that it was capable of conquering geographical distance.
Apart from trading activities, the most frequent type of movement
around Europe was probably religious in nature. Clerics travelled greatly,
but so too did lay people on pilgrimage. Pilgrimage has been called 'the
therapy of distance'. Most people able to afford it would, at some point in
their lives, expiate the blessing conferred by holy relics. Cynics said there
were enough splinters of the True Cross scattered across all the shrines
to build a battle-fleet to retake the Holy Land. But Europe was
integrated by the scattering, the constant journeying and the carefully
cultivated, culminating experience of *praesentia*, the supposed physical
presence of Christ or saint at the shrine (Brown, 1981). At the ethical
level, the church also preached consideration, decency and charity
towards all Christians: basic normative pacification, a substitute for costly
coercive pacification normally required in extensive societies. The main
sanction the church could provide was not physical force, but exclusion
from the community, in the last resort, excommunication. *Extra ecclesiam
nulla salus* (no salvation outside the church) was widely accepted. Bandits
were wary of excommunication, wished to die forgiven and paid the
church (if not always to modify their behaviour) to receive absolution.

If we wished to eye this community more materialistically or cynically,
then we would add two qualifications. First, the *ecumene* was infrastructure
as well as superstructure. Until the thirteenth century it monopolized
education and written communication and provided the *lingua franca*:
Latin. Thus state bureaucracies, manorial estates and trading associations
had access to generally useful knowledge through Church infrastructures.
The network of churches, abbeys, monasteries and shrines also provided
the major staging-posts of extensive communication and many of the
most technologically advanced agrarian economies. Second, the church

also led the nastier side of medieval society. The darker side of normative pacification was the savage treatment meted out to those outside the *ecumene*, to schismatics, heretics, Jews, Muhammadans or pagans. Indeed, let us not look at this religious community in modern, pious terms at all. It was also bawdy folklore, satirizing the common religion, carried by travelling players and mendicants whose plays and sermons would strike modern church congregations as blasphemous, as in parodies of all the major religious rituals. Preachers drawing audiences of thousands were conscious of their tricks-of-the-trade. One, Oliver Maillard, wrote marginal notes to himself like 'sit down – stand up – mop yourself – ahem! ahem! – now shriek like a devil' (quoted by Peter Burke, 1979: 101, cf. 122–3). But in all of this – ritual, ethics, technology, barbarity and the grotesque – the common culture *was* Christianity (as, indeed, Werner also argues in his essay in this volume).

The Christian achievement was the creation of a minimal normative society across state, ethnic, class and gender boundaries. It did not in any significant sense include the Eastern Byzantine Church. It did, however, integrate the two major geographical areas of 'Europe', the Mediterranean lands with their cultural heritage, their historic and predominantly *extensive* power techniques – literacy, coinage, agricultural estates and trading networks – and north-western Europe with its more *intensive* power techniques – deep ploughing, village and kin solidarities and locally organized warfare. If the two could be kept in a single community, then European development was a possible consequence of their creative interchange.

Medieval Europeans were primarily concerned with intensively exploiting their own locality. They penetrated deeper into heavier, wetter soils than any previous agrarian people. They harnessed more effectively the energy of their animals. They struck a more productive balance between animals and crops. The image is of small groups of peasants and lords standing looking at their fields, tools and animals, figuring out how to improve them, with their backs to the world, relatively unconcerned with more extensive techniques and social organization in the secure knowledge that these were already available at a minimally acceptable level.

This gave rise to an intellectual environment conducive to what we understand by the natural sciences – penetrating beneath the phenomenal appearance of nature in the secure expectation that its physical, chemical and biological properties will be ordered, but by dynamic not eternal laws. Medieval agriculture fostered dynamism and the penetration of nature: Christian natural law theory provided the security of natural order. In both we find the same combination of intensive concern and extensive confidence.

Explaining Origins: Accidents and Patterns

I have redescribed what I feel to be the core of the medieval achievement
in relatively systematic terms – intensive local power autonomy, extensive
normative regulation. But I have not explained it. How did it get there?
Its origins lie in a great diversity of times and places. We can simplify
some of this. Peasant strip-farming and village communities descended
primarily from the Germanic barbarians, manors and major trade-routes
mostly from the late Roman world. Many economic, military and political
practices recognizably fused these two traditions. Anderson (1974), for
example, uses the term 'mode of production' so broadly that we can
partially concur with him when he says that the 'feudal mode of
production' fused the 'Germanic tribal mode' and the 'ancient mode'.
But even this idea overpatterns what happened. It is not good at dealing
with other types of regional contribution to the eventual pattern: for
example the distinctive Scandinavian inputs of sea trade, navigation
techniques, and small but cohesive warrior kingdoms. Also it fits
Christianity too easily into this pattern as the transmitter, through Rome,
of the classical legacy. Yet Christianity, though it had come through
Rome, was also bringing the influence of the eastern Mediterranean and
the Near East – of Greece, Persia, Hellenism and Judaism.

Further, if we look inside these Germanic or Roman 'patterns' we find
them less than cohesive, themselves composed of influences from
different times and places. We could chart over a very long time-
spectrum the gradual growth of Iron Age peasant agriculture. This
steadily enhanced both the economic power of the wet-soil peasant
cultivator and the military power of the peasant infantryman. These two
carried their joint power northwards into Germany during the Roman
Principate. Later they returned together in the form of Germanic
invasions. But then they separated. The economic trend continued, and
economic power continued slowly shifting north-west to the medium-
sized farmer. But the military trend was reversed, as the conditions of
defensive warfare against non-Germanic barbarians, and available
Eastern models of heavy cavalry, enabled noble knights to elevate
themselves above the free peasantry. Frankish feudalism, in many ways
proto-typical of later feudalism, was thus a mixture of the very, very old,
deep-rooted drift of 'European' peasant society and of the brand new,
the opportunistic, the 'un-European'.

For all these reasons it is difficult to avoid the conclusion that the
origins of European development lay in a gigantic series of coincidences.
Many causal paths, some long-term and steady, others recent and
sudden, others old but with a discontinuous historical growth (like

literacy), emanating from all over the European, Near Eastern, and even central Asian civilization areas, came together in a particular time and place to create something unusual.

But there was also something of a pattern embedded in all this: over several millenia there had been a drift of 'the leading edge' of power in the Near Eastern/Mediterranean/European cultural area to the west and north, gradually privileging areas of heavier soils and open-sea navigation. This was partly the consequence of geopolitical blockage to the east, where far more powerful states generally existed.

Two geopolitical processes were still consistent with the historical norm. First, Europe was blocked eastwards. It never remotely threatened to overpower Islam in its heartlands nor the Huns, Mongols or Tartars in the steppes. If Europe were to expand, it would not be eastwards – and ecology and climate ensured that it would not be to the north or south either. Second, it was quite likely that if the easterly parts of this civilization, whether or not they were its 'leading edge', did successfully defend the eastern frontier, they would in so doing drain themselves. In the long run the east European kingdoms, Byzantium, the Norman adventurers, Venice and Genoa committed so much of their resources to this unproductive struggle that they would be unlikely to make a major contribution to the European dynamic. Only much later, when the tide turned, could powers such as Spain, Austria and finally, and most spectacularly, Russia, gain from the struggle against Islam and Tartary.

Now this says nothing about whether the 'leading edge' *would* proceed further westwards. For this to occur, a quite separate set of conditions were necessary. Power potentialities were also required in the west, so that those looking westwards, or those in the western marches, could exploit them. They would *want* to do so, because all other directions were blocked. But whether they *could* do so was entirely contingent on what lay there capable of exploitation.

Western opportunities came in two main forms. First were the agricultural opportunities presented by deeper, wetter, fertile soils and by a local social structure (described above) capable of exploiting them. These opportunities began in the Dark Ages and continued intermittently until the eighteenth-century 'agricultural revolution'. Second were navigational opportunities presented by the Atlantic and Baltic coastline, and by appropriate local social structures. These opportunities were exploited in two distinct phases: the early Viking-to-Norman expansion, and the expansion between 1400 and 1600 of medium-size sea-coast states from Sweden to Portugal. At the end of all these processes stood one medium-size, wet-soil island state, perfectly situated in the geoeconomics and geopolitics for take-off: Great Britain. Accident or macro-historical pattern? The broad answer is a combination of both.

The European dynamic was the accidental conjunction of two macro-patterns, long antedating the medieval experience of Europe, acting upon the unique but internally patterned power networks of Europe. The two macro-patterns were political blockage to the east and agricultural-cum-trading opportunities to the west. In the medieval era, agricultural-cum-navigational opportunities were exploitable by a historically conjunctural, but internally patterned, set of overlapping power networks. These were (1) the normative pacification of Christendom, later largely replaced by a diplomatically regulated multi-state civilization; (2) small, weak political states, growing in centralized-territorial, co-ordinating and organic powers, but never internally or geopolitically hegemonic; and (3) a multiplicity of partly autonomous and competitive, local economic power networks – peasant communities, lordly manors, towns, and merchant and artisan guilds – whose competition gradually settled into that single, universalistic, diffuse set of private property power relations we know as capitalism. By 1450 these power networks were developing into their simpler, modern form: a multi-state, capitalistic civilization capable of transforming the world. Such a conjunction of patterned processes and historical accidents seems to me to be as close as we can come to an overall theory of European development using historical forms of explanation.

References

Anderson, P. 1974: *Passages from Antiquity to Feudalism*, London.
Bridbury, A. R. 1975: *Economic Growth: England in the Later Middle Ages*, London.
Brown, P. 1981: *The Cult of the Saints*, London.
Burke, P. 1979: *Popular Culture in Early Modern Europe*, London.
Chaunu, P. 1969: *L'expansion européenne du XIIIe au XVe siècle*, Paris.
Cipolla, C. M. 1976: *Before the Industrial Revolution*, London.
Duby, G. 1974: *The Early Growth of the European Economy: Warriors and Peasants from the 7th to the 12th century*, London.
Hodgen, M. T. 1939: Domesday Water Mills. *Antiquity*, 13.
Jones, E. L. 1981: *The European Miracle*, Cambridge.
Leighton, A. C. 1972: *Transport and Communication in Early Modern Europe*, Newton Abbot.
Lennard, R. 1959: *Rural England 1086–1135*, Oxford.
McEvedy, C. and Jones, R. 1978: *Atlas of World Population History*, London.
Macfarlane, A. 1978: *The Origins of English Individualism*, Oxford.
McNeill, W. 1963: *The Rise of the West*, Chicago.
Mann, M. 1986: *The Sources of Social Power*, vol. I, *A History of Power from the Beginning to 1760 A.D.*, Cambridge.

Needham, J. 1963: Poverties and triumphs of Chinese scientific tradition. In A. C. Crombie (ed.), *Scientific Change*, New York.

Postan, M. 1975: *The Medieval Economy and Society*, London.

Russell, J. C. 1948: *British Medieval Population* Albuquerque.

Slicher van Bath, B. H. 1963: Yield Ratios, 810–1820. *A. A. G. Bijdragen*, 10.

White, L., Jr 1963: What accelerated technological progress in the Western Middle Ages. In A. C. Crombie (ed.), *Scientific Change*, New York.

2

States and Societies: the Miracle in Comparative Perspective

John A. Hall

Samuel Johnson believed that the prospect of hanging would concentrate the mind of a condemned man. I offer a model of the European miracle in comparative perspective in order similarly to focus attention. Obviously, I do not have sufficient space to offer a full explanation, and I shall concentrate on raising salient questions. I offer a complete account of the rise of the West in comparative perspective elsewhere (Hall, 1985a). Focus is limited to state/society relationships in each of the major world civilizations, and within this field mostly to the character rather than the origins of such relationships.

One preliminary point must be made about the notion of 'strength' of a state. The point at issue can be highlighted by a brief consideration of imperial rule. The image to the forefront of our minds when we think of empires is that of great power. But even a cursory reading of modern historians on various empires quickly shows a series of ways in which the powers of the emperors were limited. In the later Roman Empire, for example, the emperor was quite incapable of seeing every paper sent to him. In consequence, he threatened all administrators who prepared or submitted illegal rescripts, but 'he openly admitted his impotence by declaring invalid in advance any special grants in contravention of the law, even if they bore his own signature' (Jones, 1973: 410). Those who have written about empires have tended to stress either strength or weakness. But *both* were present, and the paradox (for it is not a contradiction) of empires is that their strength – that is their monuments, their arbitrariness, their scorn for human life – hides, is based upon and reflects social weakness. They are not able to penetrate deeply, change

I should like to thank Patricia Crone for characteristically incisive comments on an earlier draft of this chapter.

and mobilize the social order. It is important to be clear at this point. I have distinguished two faces of power, that is arbitrariness and the capacity to mobilize, and will continue to do so. Hereafter a state will be considered to be strong only in so far as it has the capacity to penetrate and organize social life. With this in mind, we can turn immediately to Imperial China.

Imperial China

The Chinese empire was bounded to the north by the Great Wall manned by troops whose supplies came to be sent up the Grand Canal from the fertile, double-cropping rice lands of the south. What is implied by this simple statement? The extensive area of the empire was created and held together by military might, just as the legions had created and maintained the *Pax Romana*. In contrast, it seems likely that culture was passive, secondary and certainly *not* larger than the state. The examination system which encouraged intellectuals to serve this civilization as bureaucrats rather than as priests was clearly created by the state, first under the Han and much more decisively under the Tang. Does the presence of an imperial state manned by bureaucrats schooled in a Caesaropapist creed give evidence of a strong state? Was the mandarinate a bureaucracy of great efficiency? There were never enough mandarins to form an efficient governing class. The first Ming emperor in 1371 sought to have as few as 5488 mandarins in government service, and by the sixteenth century there were still only about 20,400 in the empire as a whole, plus another 50,000 minor officials (Huang, 1981: chapter 2). A local official might well have managed 500–1000 square miles with the aid of only three assistants. So the Chinese state did not have the means of total control envisaged in Wittfogel's fantasy of *Oriental Despotism*. Of course, it sought, as did other imperial states, to gain such autonomy, but arbitrary action against individuals was counterbalanced by an inability of the state fundamentally to go against the gentry class as a whole. The state sought to improve the economy but had very limited means with which to push through any plan of its own. Reformer after reformer tried to establish a decent land registry as the basis for a proper taxation system, but all were defeated by the refusal of landlords to co-operate. The empire as a whole witnessed a power standoff between state and society which led to the inability to generate a large total sum of societal energy.

This stalemate can be seen at work in the dynastic cyclical pattern. A newly established dynasty sought to create a healthy peasant base both for its tax and military potential. Yet even without internal or external pressures, the state tended to lose control of society. The power of the gentry locally enabled them to increase their estates and to avoid taxation. Other pressures on the empire were usually present as well. Internally, an expansion of population, by no means discouraged by the gentry, eventually caused land hunger and peasant rebellions. Externally, the nomads on the borders found the empire more and more attractive as its prosperity waxed in front of their eyes. Such nomads were often employed as mercenaries by empires in their later days; as a result they learnt military techniques which, when allied with their inherent military resource of great mobility, made them a formidable force. The imperial state was, of course, forced to increase taxation rates, and it was at this moment that the power stand-off between state and society proved to be important. For many landlords chose to shelter peasants who refused to pay such increased taxation, and thereby increased their own local power. The combination of feudal-type disintegration and overpopulation led to a constant decrease in the number of taxpaying peasant smallholders. Rodinski cites the census of AD 754 which showed that there were only 7.6 million taxpayers out of a total population of 52.8 million (1984: 78). In such circumstances the state was forced to tax even more heavily where it could and this in turn fuelled peasant unrest. Breakdown ensued. A new dynasty was, however, established in the long run, either by nomads or by leaders of peasant revolts, forced eventually to co-operate with the gentry.

None the less, the Chinese empire was restored time and again. The mandarins, unlike the Latin Christian church at the fall of Rome, held together and remained true to the imperial deal. On a number of occasions barbarians tried to rule without them, partly because the mandarins were wont to stay away from a dynasty that did not respect the fundamentals of Confucianism. Any consideration of the rather small numbers of the elite shows that an enormous confidence trick was played on the gentry. They remained loyal to the state, but the paucity of their numbers is evidence that they did not do all that well from it. Furthermore, there was great insecurity attached to the holding of office. This is not, it must be stressed, to resurrect the notion of totalitarian strength on the part of the state. This did not exist, and in most matters and for most of the time, the scholar–gentry class could block imperial initiatives. But *individuals* amongst its number did suffer in one way or another. The argument being made is that there was a definite autonomy of the state, of the political, in Chinese history because the state *was* strong enough to force class relations into a particular pattern. This makes us consider the key question: in what ways, if any, did the imperial form affect the Chinese economy?

Medieval China witnessed considerable economic advance of a

broadly capitalist type. Interestingly the greatest expansion took place during a period of *disunity*. The northern Sung did rule China from 960–1127, but even they were faced with the militant, nomadic Jurchen. Disunity encouraged the southern Sung to build a navy in order to man all waterways which stood between them and their northern competitors. More generally, the markets and cities gained autonomy during this period of disunity in Chinese history. The quality of coinage provided by states tended to improve during disunity because traders would not themselves return to or trust governments which manipulated the coinage (Elvin, 1973: chapter 14).

How did the empire, when it was reunited, react to capitalist forces that had flourished previously? The state controlled the autonomy of cities. Little is known about the collapse of the iron and steel industries of Sung China. However, we can explain the collapse of the Sung naval strength. The foundation of a native dynasty which improved the Grand Canal (so no longer necessitating ocean-going transport from south to north) undermined the navy; most obviously, between 1371 and 1567, all foreign trade was banned. *The* most spectacular way in which politics could affect the economy concerned the fate of the explorations undertaken by the eunuch admiral Cheng-Ho in the 1430s. The mandarins were always extremely jealous of the emergence of sources of power alternative to their own. They were naturally opposed to Cheng-Ho precisely because he was a eunuch, whose cause was promoted by the eunuchs at court. The centralization of political life mattered. Although the bureacracy was not able to penetrate far into society, it could and did prevent other forces from gaining much autonomy. Another classic instance of this had been the suppression of Buddhist monasteries.

Chinese imperial government deserves the appellation *capstone*. The Chinese elite shared a culture, and sat atop a series of separate 'societies' which it did not wish to penetrate or mobilize; it feared that horizontal linkages it could not see would get out of control. This capstone government blocked the fully fledged emergence of intensive capitalist relationships. The concern of the mandarinate was less with intensifying social relationships than in seeking to prevent any linkages which might diminish its power. This can be seen particularly clearly in an analysis of Ming taxation.

> As the Ming administrators saw it, to promote those advanced sectors of the economy would only widen the economic imbalance which in turn would threaten the empire's political unity. It was far more desirable to keep all the provinces on the same footing, albeit at the level of the backward sectors of the economy. (Huang, 1974: 290)

This is *not* to say that the impact of the state upon capitalism must always be negative. A different type of state, the European organic state, was capable, once capitalist relationships were established, of providing crucial services for capitalism. The Chinese state was incapable of so doing:

> It must be pointed out that in the late Ming most of the service facilities indispensable to the development of capitalism were wholly lacking. There was no legal protection for the businessman, money was scarce, interest rates high and banking undeveloped. At the same time merchants and entrepreneurs were hindered by the frequent roadblocks on the trade routes, government purchase orders and forced contributions, the government's near monopoly of the Grand Canal and active involvement in manufacturing. On the other hand, the security and status of land ownership, the tax-exemption enjoyed by those who purchased official rank, and the non-progressive nature of the land tax increased the attraction of farming to the detriment of business involvement. (Huang, 1974: 318–19)

Politics and culture in China tended to have the same extensive reach, and this pattern was crucial to China's fate. Centralized power allowed for the blocking of capitalism whilst the absence of any real competitors made this sort of low-intensity rule a viable proposition. The three remaining agrarian civilizations also had extensive cultures. But they differ in having, for crucial periods, cultures more extensive than polities. Michael Mann has described the Durkheimian normative integration of Christianity; in all these three cases social identity was achieved and maintained without benefit of state regulation: ideology created and did not 'reflect' a society. (Mann makes this case in his chapter in this volume. See also Mann, 1986; Hall, 1985b.) The absence of a single political centre suggests that capitalism might well prosper, free from bureacratic interference. This was, as we shall see, a part of the reason for the rise of the West, but India and Islam have to be considered first. They demonstrate that the absence of an empire was not enough in itself to ensure the triumph of capitalism. Political fragmentation was a necessary, not a sufficient condition, for the 'miracle'.

The Land of the Brahmans

The *Rig-Veda* makes it clear that Aryan invaders were not able to rest easily in the land they had invaded. Warfare with the native population, possibly different in colour, was continuous. This situation contrasts with those that faced nomad invaders elsewhere. Those who invaded the Roman Empire rapidly bowed before Christian monotheism, and most nomads in history tend to be absorbed into the larger world they conquer. The Islamic nomad conquerors of the Middle East were completely different in having their own monotheistic religion, which made them feel superior to those they conquered: they were not absorbed by a civilization but rather imposed their own. Perhaps the situation of the Aryan invaders was in the middle of these extreme positions.

> There were a few cities with a little writing, there was agriculture, there were other ruling people and the earliest records of the conquerors show that they were neither much superior nor inferior in civilisation to the people among whom they came. The only advantage they possessed was a greater mobility. . . . the Indo-Aryans were neither submerged nor were able completely to dominate . . . they accommodated themselves to a life which allowed a certain separateness together with a certain independence. (Karve, 1961: 40)

This is to offer the beginnings of an explanation of the caste system that the combination of specialization of occupation, social hierarchy enforced by the control of marriage and social and dietary laws designed to prevent the devated pure from being polluted by contact with the lowly filthy brought about. It is necessary to say something about the origins of this extraordinary system if we are to understand the character of state–society relations in this civilization.

The social and religious organization of the early Aryans was in no way as strict as the classical caste system. With the passing of time, however, a more complex social order did emerge, and the *Brahmanas* show an increasing hold over religious power on the part of the Brahmans. In China, intellectuals at the behest of the state produced a type of Caesaropapist doctrine, and such fusion of religious and political power occurred elsewhere. In India a *division* took place between secular and religious power from very early times. Yet it is as well to remember that the *Brahmanas* are a claim to power quite as much as a description of actual social practices. Ideas do not always translate into reality, as we can see by turning to two challenges to Brahmanical power that emerged in the later Vedic period.

Firstly, the Brahmans were anchored at this time in the countryside and were not able to keep pace with developments in urbanization and trade. In particular, the individualism and discipline encouraged by urban life seem to have created some sort of demand for a more rational type of religion, capable of offering the individual a route to salvation. This intellectual challenge can be seen surfacing within the orthodox Vedic tradition. Secondly, Brahmans' claim to speak for the social order was attacked by the Nandas and Mauryans who united India under a single imperial umbrella. Interesting efforts were made to produce an ethic suited to the empire as a whole. Asoka introduced and generalized the idea of *Dhamma* which stressed, as did Confucianism, social responsibility and service to the state.

What does all this amount to? The imperial drive tried to create loyalty to the emperor rather than to the social order. Power and hierarchy were to be reconciled, and the emperor, as the fount of law, was to become leader of the community. An elective affinity was established between the political and the religious threats to Brahmanical control. Asoka became a Buddhist. It seems likely he was attracted by the universalism of a salvationist religion to combine with the universal political order of the empire.

The elective affinity between Buddhism and empire never gelled sufficiently to create a stable imperial system. But why, at some later date, was the creation of a universal empire, backed by Buddhism, not achieved? Perhaps Buddhism did *not* neatly fit with the rule of emperors and kings. Crucially, rulers in India may have become suspicious of Buddhism's relation to the political realm for altogether more material reasons. In time the Brahmans were welcomed:

> as a counterpoise and a safeguard. The Buddhist monasteries were incessantly enriched by pious donations, and, thanks to their longevity, stability and organisation were powerful institutions, the lords of souls and of vast estates. They checkmated temporal authority and threatened to destroy it. The Brahman gave it less to fear: he had taken no vow and was bound by no contract; he was free, independent and alone; he could move with the times and he founded no order; he did not live in a community. . . . He did not dream of human brotherhood or universal salvation; he aimed only at his own supremacy, and, as the basis for it, the caste system; he carried his institutions, beliefs and laws within himself. (Lévi, 1905, vol. 1: 30)

A further reason for the failure of Buddhism to triumph over its rivals lay in its concentration on salvation. Buddhism simply turned its back on the Durkheimian aspect of religion: it offered no real guidance, until the modern period, for as basic a social need as the regulation of marriage! Nevertheless Buddhism's concern with soteriology had a fundamental impact on Brahmanism: it was only as the result of a serious fight that the Brahmans were able to cement their claim to power.

One part of the Brahmans' response concerned soteriology. Neo-Brahmanism proved capable of integrating within the bounds of Hinduism movements which had started out avowedly critical of the Vedic tradition as a whole. Neo-Brahmanism arranged the Gods monotheistically. This monotheism was not *jealous*, as are Christianity and Islam. Neo-Brahmanism stressed inclusion rather than exclusion;

there are many ways to God, and nobody should judge between these routes. The secret of this religion lies in its capacity to tolerate differences rather than in any desire or ability to organize or police belief. However, the greatest achievement of neo-Brahmanism lay in its capacity to organize social relationships. The Brahmans fought back by extending and regularizing the services they performed on every occasion of the life-cycle, and their presence became firmly anchored in the locality. The *Laws of Manu* show Brahmans providing laws to organize every aspect of social life. The Brahman-dominated social order did the work of an empire not just in opening up new lands but in the most fundamental way of all: it brought peace and social order. Its achievements were real and significant, and it is not surprising that the place of the Brahman in Indian civilization came to stand so high.

Brahmanical organization of society distanced itself from both wealth and power. This withdrawal affected political life very markedly. Kings are recognized as individuals rather than as representatives of longer-lasting states, and few expectations are held of them. Their duty in life is simply to fight, and they have no other secular duty than that of protecting the social order: the state is *custodial*. Politics had very shallow roots in society. Kings could not gain regular taxation, but were offered tribute on an irregular basis. That was the cause of constant instability of political rule in traditional India.

So the Brahman blocked the emergence of powerful polities, by withdrawal from political power. But even the strictest co-operation between ruler and priest was unlikely to lead to a new social system:

> if one seeks to understand Hinduism in relationship to the political sytem, that is, as an aspect of ideology, then it must be recognised that it often provided for considerable instability. The power of political legitimation was vested with local Brahmans responsible to no superiors, and the religion was characterised by a basic discontinuity between relatively high caste (Brahman and non-Brahman) participants in Vedic sect activities and the mass of Hindus involved in highly localised, non-Vedic, folk religious affiliations. The discontinuity in Hinduism considered as a morally binding force – the gulf between high and low – is a factor which historians have neglected. The other side of ritual exclusiveness is a discontinuous moral order. (Stein, 1976: 86)

The price of the relativism of Hindu religion was that a single community of equal individuals was not even sought. For all the services that the Brahmans provided, they were not 'powerful' enough to react to Buddhism by organizing society in terms of any jealous monotheism of their own. Their power was negative, being based on endorsement of what was already in place rather than creation of something altogether new. Nevertheless this form of triumph was not without consequences for economic relationships.

In the first place, caste proved debilitating to economic life because of its hierarchical conception of social life. Trade expanded during the Gupta period, but so too did caste regulations, and these made its salience more limited. Further, caste did not allow for a flexible division of labour (Hutton, 1946: 123–4). This divisiveness of caste played a deleterious role as far as the advance of knowledge was concerned. The great advances made by the Brahmans in mathematics and astronomy were treated as their secret knowledge; obstacles were placed in the way of the diffusion of knowledge.

This first point deserves summary. Hinduism organized more social relationship by withdrawing from power than could Islam and Christianity, despite their greater monotheistic drive, since they were irredeemably involved in politics. There is, however, a great difference between Hinduism and these other two world religions. Our very notion of society implicitly contains conceptions of universality and reciprocity. The sense of community created by Islam and Christianity was one in which, at least in principle, all human beings could participate. Fundamental spiritual equality was written into the society by the promise of salvation held out to everyone. Indian society was not universalist in this sense. It had no sense of brotherhoood. Its society was a community based on division rather than the possibility of shared experience. This must have had adverse effects upon the intensity of social, and therefore economic, interaction.

It is important not to exaggerate this first aspect of caste since there *was* more flexibility to the system than is often allowed. However, there is a second impediment to economic life for which caste was held responsible. Brahmanical organization of social life by means of caste created unstable polities. Instability made for predatory rule. Kings had power for such a short period that they simply took what they could: as the state was not long-lasting, there could be no conception of nurturing merchant activities with a view to long-term tax revenue. Grants to temples could not be touched by kings, and the temples consequently grew incredibly rich (Stein, 1960). When states changed hands, so too did land ownership, and tax farming rights. This discouraged investment in the land which was to be exploited as much as possible whilst it was possessed, a situation in which peasants had no reason to invest. The economic cost of weak polities can be highlighted in a most dramatic way. It proved impossible to protect the north-west frontier, even though a Great Wall here would have been extremely effective; in consequence, India suffered a whole series of invasions, some of them hugely destructive.

Islam and Pastoralism

Hindu India stepped back from China in two ways: its extensive culture was not universal, whilst its states were transient, predatory and therefore completely incapable of providing social infrastructure. Islam boasts a culture which is both extensive and highly universalistic, and this can be seen as an advance not only on the Indian but also on the Chinese situation. But Islam had weak polities, resembling, albeit for different reasons, those of India, and in this matter it is less advanced than the admittedly weak Chinese political form. We can proceed by characterizing Islamic culture, seeing how this fitted with pastoralism so as to produce weak states and then establishing how this pattern affected economic life.

A religious vision united the Arab tribes and thereby allowed them great military capacity. As noted, the Islamic conquerors brought a monotheism with them; they possessed 'force *and* value' – a term coined by Cook and Crone (1977). This inheritance presented problems when rule over conquered lands had to be consolidated and regulated. The Umayyads were able to rule for some time on the basis of traditional kinship cohesion, but such politics were far removed from original Islamic purposes. The Arabs did not 'feel at home' in their conquered lands. They were unable to integrate with the settled population; since they were the carriers of their own religious vision they scorned and did not wish to be absorbed by 'civilization'. Tribesmen had not bargained for, nor were prepared to accede to, taxation, and they hankered for the simplicity and egalitarianism that had marked the earliest period of Islamic history. It is in these Umayyad years that the experts in the word 'codified' Islam. The *ulama* were not integrated into the first caliphate and the codification they made harked back to a simpler tribal past, a past in which there was little room for the necessities of power (Crone, 1980: 62–3). Mainstream Islam, in other words, came to have a distrust for the exercise of political power. Shari'a law was neither a Caesaropapist doctrine supporting imperial power nor one like Christianity, which said that the purpose of religion was purely spiritual, and that accordingly power relations did not matter and could be left to proceed on their own course. Government thus has very slim roots in society, and stability came to depend upon such solidarity as the rulers of society could themselves achieve, as is true of most conquest societies. As such social solidarity tends to be evanescent, government in classical Islam tended to be highly unstable.

Possession of the sacred norms of society did not, however, enable the *ulama* to turn their backs on political power as had Indian intellectuals.

The reason for this divergence lies in the nature of pastoralism. Power was needed because nomads were militarily powerful. Islamic civilization was not just made in the image of tribal simplicity, but also had to contend with the continuing presence of tribes. Pastoralism combined with the rigour of Islamic ideology in a manner first fully spelt out by Ibn Khaldun.

Nomads are not completely independent. Ibn Khaldun noted that the city is necessary for them: certain craft work, such as tanning and heavier metalwork, requires static equipment which would *per se* invalidate nomad existence. It is much easier to obtain such material by trading, especially as this brings in wealth. Cities require a government so that market transactions can be reliable and regular, but its control is limited to the cities and their surroundings. The essential contrast, to use a Moroccan expression, is between the *Bled el Makhzen*, the area of order, and the *Bled el Siba*, the area of tribal dissidence: it should be noted that the third party, the peasantry – thin on the ground in North Africa but of great historical importance in Egypt, Iran, Iraq, Syria and Anatolia – plays no active role in this picture since tribes, rather than peasants, have military force.

The dynamics of Ibn Khaldunian sociology result from the inability of cities to govern themselves. In European society such self-government ultimately depended upon the ability of cities to raise their own troops or to provide mercenaries able to defeat organized armies operating over a relatively pacified terrain. Muslim society in the arid zone was not at all like this. Urban citizens faced a land of dissidence capable of great military surges. Those who could not defend themselves looked for a defender, and they found it in *one* tribe, capable of fighting off tribal incursions and of providing order for markets. But a tribe, as soon as it became the ruler of a city, automatically began to suffer moral degeneracy. The quality that had allowed the tribe to come to prominence in the first place was social solidarity, but the ease and luxury of city life undermines this. So although citizens support the tribal rulers at first, they become restive, typically by about the third generation of the ruling dynasty. The *ulama* begin by serving the ruling house as administrators and judges; yet they possess the sacred norms of Islam which, because of their precise codification, are not nearly as much at the mercy of secular power as was the relatively spiritual doctrine of Christianity. Some *ulama* become discontented with the ruling house as it becomes corrupt. In time, they declare the ruling house to be impious, and invite in one of the tribes from the area of dissidence. It is here that the presence of an ideology shared with the tribesmen matters. This manner of accession to power probably explains why Islamic culture, more extensive than any state, was maintained: a ruling house coming to power as the result of a religious spasm was unlikely to turn against Islam and never had the time to do so.

This Ibn Khaldunian circulation of elites suggests the term *cyclical polity* for the state in classical Islam. This polity was as transient as the custodial state of India, and its effects upon economic relationships were similar. The universalism of Islam did make this a great trading civilization, but the transient and predatory polity had debilitating effects upon economic life in general. Two types of landholding deserve special attention, the *iqta'* and the *waqf*. The former of these were land-grants given to the supporters of the ruling dynasty. Crucially, as dynasties changed, so did the landholders. This partly explains the character of the *waqf*, formally a religious endowment and therefore typically not touched by a new ruling house, but often in fact a means whereby a family could draw a certain income from the land in covert form. This dual type of landholding proved inimical to agricultural advance. Insecurity of tenure encouraged a predatory use of land, and there was little genuine investment in the land (Cahen, 1970). Equally importantly, Muslim society did not allow for the autonomous city: the burgher was less important than the military governor (Lapidus, 1967). The presence of government made political favours more important than the market.

The argument deserves to be summarized. The cyclical state in Islam was unstable, and this affected the economy in two ways. It was arbitrary and predatory enough to interfere directly in the market, with the workings of justice and the autonomy of cities. On the other hand, the government was weak. Land went out of circulation with a corresponding loss of tax revenue and a limitation upon the number of state servants it was possible to recruit. Few services could be provided by the state. The situation is reminiscent of that in Indian states, although the mechanisms at work were different in each case. But in both civilizations there was no unitary empire covering the whole culture, and some of the bureaucratic effects of the capstone state of China were thus ruled out. Such differences are important when we seek to capture the specificity of these civilizations. However, all three systems seem very similar when they are compared to the organic state of Europe. All had weak states, and the form of their arbitrariness, either predatory or bureaucratic, does not matter from this perspective. All blocked, albeit in different ways, the emergence of capitalism.

The Rise of Christian Europe

In order to avoid any repetition or overlap, I shall take as background Michael Mann's description of the acephalous but intensive agrarian civilization that grew up after the fall of Rome under the umbrella of normative pacification provided by the Latin Christian church. (See Mann's chapter in this volume; also Mann, 1986.) Jack Goody (1983) has added to this the impact of the church upon kinship, and further points about monasticism could be added. But the focus here is on state – society relations, and the question to be addressed is correspondingly simple. Why was it that market relations, once in place, were not later so controlled by states as to destroy the European dynamic? The argument to be made has three parts: a counterfactual proposition, a characterization of the *organic* state of north-west Europe and an appreciation of the role of state competition. All of these parts are mutually supporting, and all centre on the undoubted fact that European society did not, despite the attempts of Charlemagne, Frederick Barbarossa, Napoleon and Hitler, develop an imperial structure after the collapse of Rome.

At first sight some of the statements in the preceding paragraph may seem slightly overblown. Surely, it might be objected, the church did seek to establish a real imperial papacy? But did it manage to establish a new primacy sufficient to give it something like an imperial status? The answer to this question must be a definite negative. The papacy never possessed its own army, whilst the various kings of Europe very plainly did. Perhaps the greatest symbol of papal weakness was the loyalty of the French bishops to their king when Boniface VIII challenged him at the start of the fourteenth century.

If the drive to an imperial papacy was defeated as much by the presence of diverse states as by anything else, how did those states come into being in the first place? Specifically, what role did the church itself play in the creation of such states? Several sets of barbarians came into Europe at the end of the Roman empire, and this was an initial condition in favour of a multi-polar system. But we can add to this that the church played a very notable role in making a secular empire impossible. Most obviously, it welcomed the rise of states which were able to give more secure protection to its own property. But there is a more important point to be made: the church refused to serve as second fiddle in an empire equivalent to those of China and Byzantium, and thus did not create a Caesaropapist doctrine in which a single emperor was elevated to semi-divine status. This whole process was symbolized in 1312 when the Emperor Henry VII asked Pope Clement V to send Robert of Sicily, the pope's vassal, to the imperial court at Pisa. Clement issued the bull *Pastoralis Curia* in which he argued that a king owed no duties to the emperor, and was instead master in his own realm. And this was not the only way in which Christianity provided the best shell for the emergence of states. The church provided the numinous aspects of kingship – the coronation and the singing of the *Laudes Irae* for example – that made a king more than one amongst equals. Even more importantly, its attack on extended kinship systems was vital. In other civilizations, perhaps above all Islam, the lower classes could often rely upon kinship systems as a means of protection and mutual aid. The removal of the weapon of the lower classes made the European peasant that much better fodder for state formation. This is the political consequence of weak kinship.

With these background comments in mind, the first and most obvious argument can be presented. Imagine what European history might have been like had the Roman Empire somehow been reconstituted, or had any empire taken its place! Pre-industrial empires are too centralized for their logistical capacity, and thus have produced capstone government based on their accurate knowledge that secondary organizations are dangerous. Such empires sought to encourage the economy, but this form of government never ultimately allowed sufficient leeway to the economy for it to gather self-sustaining momentum. Why should an imperial Europe have been any different? This can be put in a rather different manner. Mann and Werner contend in this volume was that a decentralized market system came into place during those years in which there was no government which could interfere with its workings, but an organization which nevertheless made medieval men realize they belonged to a single civilization. An imperial form would very probably have sought to control such 'natural' processes. The point is perhaps best illustrated by a consideration of the European city. All historians agree that Max Weber was correct in the more materialist part of the theory concerning the rise of the West, namely in his contention that only in Europe did the city gain full autonomy. This autonomy provided a space in which the merchant was king, and in which bourgeois values could gell and solidify. We live in the world created by this civilization. With a matter of such import it is essential to ask how this autonomy occurred. The more satisfying answer is that the north Italian cities were themselves the creation of the absence of a single centre of power in Europe. Specifically, they gained their autonomy as the result of a power vacuum between pope and emperor, such that they were able, as is often the case in Third World countries today, to get the best for themselves by opportunistically chopping and changing their allegiance (Burke, 1986). How much they owed to their freedom from interference and freedom to experiment is simply seen: once they became part of the Spanish mini-empire they contributed virtually nothing new to European civilization. And much the same point could be made by indulging in a 'thought-experiment': had Philip II created a long-lasting empire based on his new Spanish possessions, what would have happened to the social experiments taking place in Holland and Great Britain? Had an empire been established at any time it seems likely that social innovations at the peripheries would have been ruled out.

This first point amounts to reiterating that political fragmentation was a necessary condition for the autonomy of the market. But the Indian and Islamic cases have demonstrated that such fragmentation is not sufficient by itself to encourage economic dynamism. What else was involved? It might at first sight seem contradictory to say that the organic state helped economic development after the largely negative comments made up to now about state interference. But there are *different* types of state in different historical and social circumstances. Two general principles about the relations of government to the economy can be maintained. Firstly, the absence of all government is disastrous since it encourages disorder and localism, and thus prevents trade. The insistence that Christianity held Europe together shows that no anarchist vision is encouraged here. Secondly, bureaucratic and predatory governments *were* indeed hostile to economic development. As noted, it is mistaken to consider such government strong since it was based on weak infrastructural penetration of the society; indeed its arbitrariness results, in part, from that weakness. This gives us the clue to the distinctiveness of the European state: a limit to arbitrariness combined with – indeed, in part caused – considerable and ever-increasing infrastructural penetration. Two such limits are important.

The first limit is straightforward. The European state evolved slowly and doggedly in the midst of pre-existing social relationships. One uniqueness of the West is the role that parliaments played in its history: indeed so unique has this role been that German historians have considered the *Standestaat* – the representation of the three functional estates: church, noble and burgher – a distinctive stage in world history (Myers, 1975). It is quite clear that the prominence of such assemblies owes a great deal to the church. Since it owned so much land it was as jealous as any noble of the powers of the crown to tax. Hence it generalized two tags of Canon law: 'no taxation without representation' and 'what touches all must be approved by all', and these became crucial to these estates. But 'liberties' were widely diffused throughout society, and churchmen had allies amongst nobles, burghers and yeomen. This deserves to be called a civil society. The monarch's only way of gaining money was to co-operate with this society. European pluralism, in other words, has an extremely long history.

The paradox of this situation is that restraint on government in the end generated a larger sum of power in society. Perhaps the most important mechanism in this process was the making of money via the provision of a certain infrastructure to the society. This is most clearly seen in the provision of justice. Fees were charged for every legal transaction, and these came to provide an important part of the revenue of most monarchs after about 1200. This is not to say that the law was equally open for all to use; but it *was* available. European states provided other sorts of infrastructural help. They became good at managing disasters of various sorts; by the eighteenth century, for example, considerable help was available to the victims of earthquakes, whilst disease was quite rigidly controlled by quarantine laws (Jones, 1981). Furthermore, the internal colonialism whereby Scots, Irish and Welsh were integrated into a single community – a process repeated elsewhere in Europe – created a single market. In the more advanced European states (that is, not France until post 1789) this process went hand-in-hand with the removal of internal tariff barriers, and this was an incentive to trade. These policies were not designed with the improvement of the economy in view, but rulers had consciously encouraged trade for a long time. They did so because a disproportionate bulk of their revenues came from customs and excise. They sought to attract traders; a typical piece of legislation in this matter being Edward I's *Carta Mercatoria* of 1297. And what is apparent as a whole is that large sections of the powerful were prepared to give quite high taxation revenues to the crown because they realized that their own interests were usually being served. Tocqueville was right to note that the English aristocracy and gentry manned local government and taxed itself. The level of infrastructural support and penetration was correspondingly high. A Confucian bureaucrat moved every three years simply could not know enough about local conditions to serve a particular area well. Representation to a central assembly by local aristocrats created a different result.

The second general restraint on arbitrariness is also the third general point to be made about the European polity. The complete 'formula' of the European dynamic is, then, that competition between strong states inside a larger culture encouraged the triumph of capitalism. Individual states did not exist in a vacuum. They were rather part of a competing state system, and it was that system, particularly the military organization it engendered, that played a considerable part in determining the character of individual states. Why was this?

A state system leads to a high degree of emulation. This emulation can be very clearly seen in artistic matters, but it extended to the establishment of various scientific clubs in eighteenth-century France in conscious imitation of their English rivals. Such emulation is ultimately only possible between states which recognized each other as of more or less similar standing; empires do not tend to copy the culture of small neighbours – mere barbarians! And the reference to empires brings out other facts about a state system that prove beneficial for economic growth. A state system always had an in-built escape system. This is most

obviously true in human matters. The expulsion of the Jews from Spain
and the Hugenots from France benefited, and was seen to benefit, other
countries, and this served in the long run as a limitation on arbitrary
government. Very importantly, capital was equally mobile. Thus Philip
II's abuse of Antwerp led within a matter of years rather than decades to
the rise of Amsterdam. In a brilliant passage making this point, McNeill
(1982) has shown that time and again Philip II *wanted* to behave like an
autocrat but the mobility of capital defeated him. This was particularly
true of his relationship with Liège, the foremost cannon producer of late
sixteenth-century Europe. When Philip pressurized them too hard,
artisans and capitalists simply went elsewhere. A certain measure of
decent and regularized behaviour was ensured by these means. However,
perhaps the fundamental mechanism at work was that of military
competition. The positive impact of competition on European society can
most dramatically be seen in the modern world. The revelation of
German industry applied to war in 1870, for example, sent a ripple of
anxiety and countermeasures throughout European capitals; states were
forced to rationalize their societies to survive. Yet state competition was
responsible for rationalizing European societies *prior* to the age of
industry. Consider again the German case. Dramatic defeat by Napoleon
was not ascribed to greater industrial development, but to the impact of
an ideologically motivated citizen army. The reform group around
Hardenburg (including Scharnhorst and Gneisenau, and with Clausewitz
as their greatest intellectual figure) realized that serfs could not provide
such an army; the reforms of 1807, 1811 and 1818 changed the Prussian
social structure at a stroke. The purpose of such changes was military but
the commercialization of agriculture that resulted was economically
beneficial. This mechanism was at work in Europe roughly from 1100
when the multi-state character of Europe finally crystallized. Throughout
the middle ages there was a breeding race to provide heavier, more
effective cavalry, and other great changes were associated with the rise of
bowmen and pikemen, the adoption of gunpowder and the consequent
need for new Italian defences, the vast increase in army size in the
seventeenth century, and the creation of a citizen army during the
French Revolution. Each of these changes necessitated money, and it
was the search for funds that necessitated the king calling his estates, and
raising funds by providing the infrastructures mentioned.

   As noted, the European state became able to generate far more power
than its imperial rivals: thus the France of Louis XIV probably had as
large an effective army as Ming China even though her population was
only 20 million, not about 150 million. This raises an interesting and
important question. The organic quality of the European state arose
from its having to accept and co-operate with other elements in civil

society. Why was it, however, that the more powerful European state did not turn inwards in order to establish something more like an imperial system? Roughly speaking, European absolutism represents just such a move, and it is important to stress how unsuccessful it was. It is conventional to compare absolutist France with England in order to give the impression of greater strength in the former case. This is mistaken since English society generated more power *without* an absolutist façade; it proved this in defeating France in war on every occasion bar one in which they met in the eighteenth century. This returns us to the question of competition. No state could afford to go it alone without risking defeat. It is hugely significant that by the middle of the eighteenth century France was sending its intellectuals to England, and was in other ways trying to copy her secrets. All this suggests that there must be a prime mover amongst the states in order to get competition to work in the first place. In fact, there were several prime movers in European history, the torch of progress being passed from Italy, to Holland and to England. The latter played a highly significant part as such a torch bearer, and it seems no accident that this state possessed a powerful and, crucially, *centralized* estates system which insisted on the state remaining organic during the absolutist period. (See Macfarlane's chapter in this volume.) It is important to stress this since the reaction to the discovery that imperial strength hides feet of clay has been to say that the European state was always more powerful (Turner, 1981). Put like this the statement is misleading. Power operates on two dimensions and the real contrast is between arbitrary capstone government generating little power and civil society/organic government generating a great deal.

Conclusion

The argument can be summarized. For market relationships to gain autonomy, extensive social interaction networks are needed. In China, such extensive networks were provided by the polity. However, imperial rule was, perhaps could only be, based upon the negative tactic of preventing horizontal linkages that it could not control, and it was because of this that bureaucratic interference eventually proved deleterious for the economy. In the non-imperial civilizations, extensive networks were guaranteed by ideological organizations without the presence of a central polity. But in both India and Islam the state was weak, and had no more capacity to penetrate and organize social relationships than had the Chinese imperial state. In addition, the state in India and Islam was short-lived, thereby predatory, and this accounts for their negative effect on economic relationships. Only when long-

lasting states were forced by military competition to interact strongly with
their civil societies was economic progress possible.

A final reflection is in order. Is the account offered a product of Mrs
Thatcher's Britain? That is, does it amount to a paean of praise for
laissez-faire on the part of the state? Competition, both military and
economic, *did* play a crucial role in the rise of the West. But I have also
argued both that competition took place within a larger arena of
normative regulation and that the organic state provided positive services
to nascent capitalism. The third book of Adam Smith's, *The Wealth of
Nations*, was perhaps the greatest attempt to understand the 'miracle',
but it need modification in these two ways (Hall, 1986).

References

Burke, P. 1986: City States. In J. A. Hall (ed.), *States in History*, Oxford.

Cahen, C. 1970: Economy, society, institutions. In P. M. Holt, A. S. Lambton
    and B. Lewis (eds), *The Cambridge History of Islam*, vol. 2, *The Farther Islamic
    Lands: Islam, Society and Civilisation*, Cambridge.

Cook, M. and Crone, P. 1977: *Hagarism*, Cambridge.

Crone, P. 1980: *Slaves on Horses: the Evolution of the Islamic Polity*, Cambridge.

Elvin, M. 1973: *The Pattern of the Chinese Past*, Stanford.

Goody, J. 1983: *The Development of the Family and Marriage in Europe*,
    Cambridge.

Hall, J. A. 1985a: *Powers and Liberties: the Causes and Consequences of the Rise of the
    West*, Oxford.

   1985b: Religion and the rise of capitalism. *European Journal of Sociology*, 26.

   1986: States and economic development: reflections on Adam Smith. In J. A.
    Hall (ed.), *States in History*, Oxford.

Huang, R. 1974: *Taxation and Governmental Finance in Sixteenth-Century Ming
    China*, Cambridge.

   1981: *1587*, New Haven.

Hutton, J. H. 1946: *Caste in India*, Cambridge.

Jones, A. H. M. 1973: *The Later Roman Empire*, Oxford.

Jones, E. L. 1981: *The European Miracle*, Cambridge.

Karve, I. 1961: *Hindu Society: an Interpretation*, Poona.

Lapidus, I. M. 1967: *Muslim Cities in the Later Middle Ages*, Cambridge, Mass.

Lévi, S. 1905: *Le Népal*, 2 vols, Paris.

McNeill, W. H. 1982: *The Pursuit of Power*, Oxford.

Mann, M. 1986: *Sources of Social Power*, vol. 1, *From the Beginning to 1760 AD*,
    Cambridge.

Myers, A. R. 1975: *Parliaments and Estates in Europe to 1789*, London.

Rodinski, W. 1984: *The Walled Kingdom*, London.

Stein, B. 1960: The economic function of a medieval south Indian temple.
    Journal of Asian Studies, 19.

   1976: The state and the agrarian order. In B. Stein (ed.), *Essays on South India*,
    New Delhi.

Turner, B. S. 1981: *For Weber*, London.

3

The Origins of Modernity: Caste and Feudality (Europe, India and Japan)

Jean Baechler

It can be maintained that the social sciences in general, and sociology in particular, arose, from the eighteenth century onwards, in an attempt to understand and explain the innovations that were emerging in European societies – what we are pleased to call modernity. Since the occurrence was unique and it is impossible to explain its uniqueness, a pole of comparison has spontaneously been produced, so that we speak of 'traditional societies' in contrast to 'modern societies'. Events have shown that it was imprudent to use so vague a category as 'traditional societies', in which were confused tribal societies, ancient cities, the empires of history and the *anciens régimes* of Europe. Despite lavish effort, the mystery of the origins of modernity remains almost intact, whether it is defined in terms of the Industrial Revolution, the scientific era, the impulsion towards democracy, or secularization . . .

Comparison remains the sole possible approach because, by searching out what Europe has in common with the rest of the world and what distinguishes it from it, the relevant factors of modernity might be revealed. Two precautions must be taken, however: we must compare what is comparable, and not embark upon the comparison at a time when the situations are already so different that it would be futile to hope to find the factors of differentiation; there is a danger of simply emphasizing again what needs explanation. For example, it would be fruitless to compare the Europe of today with Africa South of the Sahara. It would be preferable to juxtapose the barbarous Europe of the Hallstatt period or La Tene and Africa on the verge of colonization in the nineteenth century. We must take into account not modern, but pre-modern Europe, and compare it to other pre-modern societies, while taking a second precaution. Points of comparison of the same order of size must be selected – not pre-modern Europe on the one side and the rest of the world on the other, but Europe and a particular historical episode that occurred in a spatial and temporal framework of the same dimensions.

The present situation itself dictates our points of comparison. Leaving aside those modernities whose provenance was directly European, and those that were able to develop in the *emporia*, Japan is the only country that has modernized itself in the space of one or two generations. Since history does not, any more than does nature, 'make a jump', the hypothesis can be formulated that pre-Meiji Japan had developed endogenously all the conditions for the possibility of modernization. As the histories of Europe and Japan run a danger of being *too* parallel, in order to isolate these conditions with certainty it is appropriate to pick out a third case, one of modernization that, if it did not fail, was at least difficult. India seems destined to fit the bill. It would be indispensable to bring China into it as well, and the Middle East, but we must be able to confess our ignorance and to keep some tasks for the morrow.

Europe, Japan, India: each case is an infinitude. How may the infinite be reduced to the finite, in order to try to find an explanation? As always, by starting from a theory that has been deduced. This may be summarized in the few propositions that follow. Modernization is the transposition into economic, technical, scientific, religious and aesthetic terms . . . of a political democratization applied to societies that are demographically counted in millions; democratization cannot be carried out unless certain conditions of possibility are present together; these conditions have been gradually brought about, over a thousand years of history, the significance of which is only revealed in retrospect (Baechler, 1985: part III, book IV). These conditions can be reduced to four main ones: the consistency of the polities; the existence of a cross-political system of an oligarchical kind; the presence within each polity of autonomous decision-making centres, powerful enough to contain the expansion of political power; specific qualities developed by the social actors – self-control, individualism and altruism. To seek to grasp the historical emergence of this fourth condition in the three regions selected would take us too far. We shall aim at considering only the three preceding conditions. We can hope, if not to obtain definite answers, at least to identify the most important ones, by focusing the comparison upon four massive realities: polities, morphologies, stratifications and political regimes.

Polities

I mean by polity that very special kind of human grouping characterized by the fact that, if one looks inwards, there exist procedures that should in principle allow conflicts to be resolved peacefully, whereas, looking outwards, such procedures are missing and conflicts can at any time develop into wars. Since humanity has so far never been united in one single grouping that acknowledges the same procedures, it has always been split up into polities.

We have decided to take castes and feudality as the guiding thread in our analyses. This choice assigns to the study of European and Japanese polities a very narrow range of dates: from the fifth to the thirteenth century for Europe, from the ninth to the seventeenth century for Japan – note the chronological disparity but the identical duration. For India it is difficult to designate the *terminus a quo*. As regards the morphology we will make clear that the analogy of feudalism is the *jāti* and not the *varṇa* caste. It is practically certain that the regime of the *jāti* did not exist during the Maurya era. If, in fact, the Vedas, the Brahmanas, the Upanishads, the Jatakas and Greek sources allow us to follow the outlining, emergence and consolidation of the *varṇa*, they do not make the slightest reference to the *jāti*. In fact the rare indications of their existence, preceding the testimony of Arab and Western sources, are on the one hand the notion of 'mixed castes' developed in the *Dharmaśāstras*, in particular in Manu, and, on the other hand, the use of the word in the *Arthaśāstra*. Unfortunately we cannot date exactly either Manu or any other classical Sanskrit text. We are forced to content ourselves with *termini* that are curiously distant, and to place everything between the third century BC and the fourth century AD, that is, between the Mauryas and the Guptas. If one set out to resolve the problem of the origin of the regime of castes, this length of time of almost a thousand years would not be an unsurmountable obstacle, for it is unthinkable that the regime was conceived, so to speak, ready-made, and immediately imposed itself upon the whole subcontinent. It is plain that there was a long gestation, proceeding by trial and error and adapting to an infinite variety of local conditions.

The comparsion of the polities in the three cases, over periods of time that are very precise – for India, up to the British conquest in the nineteenth century – reveals a fact that weighs heavy and is common to all three: everywhere the process of imperialization failed and brought about a long period of inconsistency in the polities. Yet, whereas Japan and Europe only experienced this situation transitorily, it became the norm in India for over two thousand years. It is Japan which, from this viewpoint, experienced the most favourable situation. It is *one* polity from the beginning of the fifth century onwards, when Yamato emerged from a political tribal dispersion of a very classical kind. Whether it was to imitate China or, which is more likely, follows upon internal movements that sought and found in China a model that clarified what they were obscurely aiming at, the end of the seventh and the eighth centuries sees an attempt to impose upon Japan an imperial regime *against* local aristocracies. Nara sought to substitute for Japanese aristocratic society one with ranks, in the Chinese style, in which all the social elites would constitute manifestations and delegations of the imperial power. Nara was a failure, so utter a failure that Japan was to know eight centuries of progressive dissolution of the central authority and to have to discover a morphological solution to this break-up: this solution was feudality, which was to flourish between the fourteenth and sixteenth centuries. Yet, and this is in several respects the decisive point, never at any moment did the Japanese polity threaten to explode into several polities: unity was always not only maintained, but was always the successful goal. One can conceive that the various provinces that had lasted more or less intact for over fifteen centuries might have set themselves up as independent polities – all the more easily because Japan is an archipelago. It is not enough to argue that Japan owed the preservation of its unity to the radical political disqualification of its emperors from Heïan onwards, and to their being confined to a strictly religious and symbolic role within the framework of the court of Kyoto. For why did all the powerful always deem it good to receive from them a legitimacy that arms were not sufficient to confer upon them? The sole explanation is a very strong sense of identity, backed up by a cultural unity that had been very quickly acquired and never called into question. It is probable that the insularity and immunity that had preserved them against any invasion are the ultimate factors.

Whatever it may be, Japan remained a unity, but this single polity was, up to the turn of the seventeenth century, stretched to breaking point. The various provinces always conserved or have acquired an autonomy, so that the reality of the whole rested almost entirely upon the agreement of the various elements to acknowledge themselves as parts of that whole. Japan has never made up a trans-political system, but it has never either succumbed to a unification imposed by a strong, levelling imperial power. The Japanese polity has found a middle position, one that is original and unique, between the two most common solutions. That solution has had far-reaching consequences, to which we shall have to return.

Europe met with a very different solution: the installation of a trans-political system, grouping together less than ten polities, which were more or less firmly established. This system was only installed from the fourteenth century onwards, reaching its full flowering in the eighteenth century. Before arriving at that point, Europe passed through a very lengthy phase in which polities were almost dissolved. The nadir was reached when, after the extravagant attempt of Charlemagne to reconstitute the Roman Empire, the ninth and tenth centuries saw the polities descend to the level of principalities, countships and seigneuries, with war becoming endemic. It is very remarkable that such a situation did not lead ultimately to an imperial restoration, but to the concert of European nations. Logically, the system of action in Europe in AD 1000 should rather have led to the former solution. When very many actors are in a permanent state of violent competition the system of action leads to the successive elimination of the weakest and the emergence of an ultimate victor. It was in this way that, over thousands of years, empires succeeded tribes.

In Europe the elimination of the weak did indeed take place, but halted at a position of oligarchy, where a limited number of actors, five at least and twenty at the most, are always capable of forming instant coalitions in order to neutralize any attempt at hegemony on the part of any one of them. I remain convinced that in the last analysis this blocking at the point of oligarchy resulted by chance and that it would have become unjammed if the number of decisive actors had been reduced to four or three. But the eventuality had been prepared for by a fact that recalls the Japanese situation. The polities set up by the Barbarians to succeed the Roman Empire remained *virtually* remarkably stable. Cases of usurpation of the throne are astonishingly few, which indicates a very deep faith in the idea of monarchical legitimacy: no king without a kingdom. In vain were the kings reduced to the political role that was allowed them in their power as lords: over all their rivals they benefited from one decisive advantage. Whereas the conquered are eliminated from the game, the kings can lose every battle. In terms of games theory Europe was not a unified, homogeneous system of action; it was segmented into several subsystems corresponding to the former kingdoms, which were not abolished, but reduced politically to skeletal entities. Two games systems were juxtaposed, among the subsystems and within each one of them, with interference constantly occurring between the two systems. The situation was one of immense complexity, as is attested by political events between the ninth and the thirteenth centuries. Yet, beneath the appearance of chaos and irrationality, one can, in retrospect, discover two kinds of logic at work: one leading to the restoration of firmly based polities; the other to the installation of a balanced trans-political system.

The first kind of logic was more or less realized early on, and indeed according to local conditions, which posed for Europe its great problem: the political inconsistency of German central Europe. This complex history of European polities explains the specific factors in their sense of political identity. Whilst the Japanese identify with Japan, Europeans lived with a dual allegiance. On the one hand they wished to be and felt themselves European in their capacity as Latin Christians, as against the Greek Christians, and above all as against the Moslems. On the other hand, they felt themselves, and wished to be, Frenchmen, Spaniards, Englishmen and Germans . . . and increasingly so from the fifteenth century onwards. According to whether this sense of identity coincided to a greater or lesser extent with real polities, it was more or less felicitous – and this is another way of grasping the singularity of the German situation.

The case of India is distinguished completely from those of Japan and Europe, inasmuch as the collapse of the empire determined a definitive inconsistency in the polities. The Indian dilemma seems to have been: either an empire, or nothing. Since the empire, in spite of the renewed attempts of the Mauryas, Guptas and Moguls, has always failed very rapidly, politically 'nothing' has always carried the day. As humanity cannot do without living in polities, India has had to seek out and find a mixed solution. This consisted of a four-level political organization which is very well documented for the Mogul era (Cohn, 1962). At the lowest level there are chieftainships, of which the most important group together cover perhaps a hundred villages. They are ruled either by a dynasty, a fortunate adventurer, a tax-collector designated by a higher level, or even by a tribal chief. Above this there exists what one might call the super-chieftainship, dominated by an individual or a family, openly undergoing competition from other candidates. The level above would be that of the kingdom, a great historical, cultural and linguistic region, such as Bengal. Finally the imperial level in principle groups together the entire subcontinent, with the exception of the extreme south which has always eluded it. This Mogul structure is certainly very ancient. The *Mahābhārata* explicitly proclaims the ideal of 'the king of kings' – the fourth level – which is expounded within the framework of a kingdom – the third level – whose sovereign dominates the regional and local chiefs – the second and first levels. In the same way, light is thrown upon the theory of the 'circles' in the Arthaśāstra by this general configuration.

The remarkable fact is that each level is characterized by an extreme inconsistency and fluidity. At every moment in time, the Indians have always lived in polities, but over the course of time these were never the same. The imperial level has always been the most fragile one. It is only present from 320 to 185 BC – the Mauryas – from AD 320 to 500 – the Guptas – and from 1526 to 1707 – the Moguls. The kingdoms never ceased to fluctuate over time, much more so in the south than in the north. The super-chieftainships are made and unmade. Even at the local level, the chieftainship loses and gains villages according to the fortunes of war. In a word, the polity is a limited area, subjected to a political power that is permanent, and inhabited by people who feel themselves to be, and want to be, members of this grouping – the polity, defined in this way, is not a reality in India. The Indian polity is nothing other than the instant transposition in space of an armed power. Properly speaking, there is no trans-political system, there is a continental area promised to the empire of the strongest, which shows itself very quickly as too feeble for this task: meanwhile one contemplates the confused rise and fall of powers, defined temporally and spatially in every kind of way.

If we can relate the constant failure of imperialization to the vastness of the cultural area that had to be unified, to the continental nature of the whole, to climate, hydrography and hydrology, to the excessive geo-graphical heterogeneity between the Indo-Ganges plain and the Deccan plateau, it would be more difficult to find a satisfactory explanation for the absence of a solution on European lines: a plurality of stable kingdoms, sharing an entity between them and constituting a system in equilibrium. Let us merely note the fact. It explains why the sense of identity in India could never be political. It has merely been capable of being either a cultural attribute, through adherence to certain common religious and ethical beliefs, or of being projected upon a grouping that was non-political: the *jāti*. Indeed the political failure led to the invention of a morphological solution – the most original ever – the regime of the *jāti* castes. In Europe as in Japan, the failure of the empire also imposed a need to improvise, and to invent feudality, but there the solution was transitory and was to lead to something different, whereas in India the definitive political failure forced a solution to be adopted definitively, and a dissimilar society to develop.

Morphologies

By morphology I mean the organizational principle that allows people to live in society. The clan is a morphology grouping four or five nuclear families, i.e. some twenty-five individuals, in a clan in the narrow sense, and a score of such bands, i.e. some 500 persons, in a demographic and cultural cluster. The 'city' brings peoples together in a group centred on a village or a town, the whole being identified with a polity, with all the features attached to it. The empire and the nation are other morphologies. We can also locate segmentary morphologies, whose distinctive characteristic is to construct or break up wholes with the help of basic segments that can be added or taken away. The genus has three species: the tribe, the feudality and the regime of castes. Whilst the tribe is to be met with on every continent, only two cases of feudality are known – Europe and Japan – and India is the only one that has produced the regime of castes.

In designating by the word *casta* – 'pure' – the phenomenon that they observed on the West coast of India, the Portuguese discovered both an essential characteristic and also wrought a confusion of which Indian studies have not yet even today been rid. For a long while it has been understood – and already Senart, in 1896, placed the distinction at the core of his interpretation – that it was necessary to separate out the *varṇa* from the *jāti*, but without, it seems, following this idea through to the end. It would, in fact, be prudent to cease to talk of castes and to use in future only the two terms *varṇa* and *jāti*. They designate two realities whose nature, function and logic are entirely different. The *varṇa* is a commonplace phenomenon of social stratification, whereas *jāti* is a morphological reality that is highly original. The two phenomena are linked to India by an historical accident. It is even possible, and probable, that the *jāti* was formed in imitation of the *varṇa* of the Brahmans. This does not preclude the possibility of having one without the other, for they have no particular structural affinity, as is perhaps attested by the case of the Toucouleurs, the perfect example of a society with *varṇa* ranks, without even the trace of *jāti* segmentation (Wane, 1969).

There are four *varṇa*: the Brahmans, the Kshatriya, Vaiśya and the Śūdra. There are thousands of *jāti*. Both *varṇa* and *jāti* have three basic characteristics. The first is closure. Recruitment is strictly hereditary, endogamy is rigidly applied, rigorous dietary taboos necessitate commensality, while customs and practices relating to food, clothing, ceremonial, culture and language and so on provide multiple criteria that allow the different *jāti* to distinguish themselves from one another. The Brahmans are specialists in the sacred; political authority and weapons are reserved for the Kshatriya; the Vaiśya are the producers – growers, breeders, artisans and merchants; the Śūdra are the servants of the three other *varṇa*. The *jāti* are much more narrowly specialized, especially in everything artisanal; many occupations in which the *jāti* specialize can by linked to religion and sacrifice – barbers, laundry workers, undertakers and so on (Hocart, 1972), but this does not mean that the *jāti* concerned carry on these occupations exclusively. Finally, *varṇa* and *jāti* are hierarchical, and the criterion for hierarchy relates to notions of pure and impure. The hierarchy of the *varṇa* is rigid, in the order in which they have been set out. On the contrary, that of the *jāti*, which has only a local reality, is unstable: over time, *jāti* move up and down the scale, although some Brahman *jāti* are almost always at the highest levels.

This is, in very general terms, the parallel that is almost always established between the two phenomena. It is a real comparison, but is lacking in the essential: namely what causes the people to live together? On this point, we can leave the *varṇa* on one side (to come back to them in the following point), for the *jāti* alone are a reality for people. It has even been possible to ask what proportion of the Indians have ever heard of the *varṇa* (Srinivas, 1966). The *jāti* display other characteristics that were a reality for the Indian world in former times. Firstly, a *jāti* has its own organization: almost always a chief, either of a hereditary lineage or elected *ad hoc*; a council of elders, the *pañcayat*, that brings together the most highly esteemed and is either permanent or *ad hoc*; an assembly of *jāti*, made up of all the men of an age to run their own affairs. Decisions are taken by majority vote; these organs have authority over everything relating to the customs and usages of the *jāti*; transgressions are punished by fines, purificatory penances, temporary or definitive exclusions. As for problems that may arise between *jāti*, especially disputes about their hierarchy, these have always lain in the domain of the political power, within the framework of the chieftainship and at the top level of the political grouping. Consequently the *jāti* are perfectly fluid. The regime is constantly being realigned, for every regrouping results in the formation of a *jāti* and every internal division ends in a break away. The typically segmentary mechanisms of fusion and fission are permanently at work, all the more so because up to the nineteenth century India still possessed many uninhabited areas, and because incessant internal wars and periodical foreign invasions provoked innumerable population movements. Moreover, the local hierarchy of the *jāti* was continually being modified, formerly principally because of political reasons, and in the nineteenth and twentieth centuries more for economic ones. Finally, the *jāti* are complementary to one another, through the so-called *jajmānī* system. This consists of a reciprocity of services and gifts within the framework of the village, which allows all the economic and religious functions to be performed without carrying on exchange in a market, whether by money or barter. It is a kind of system of reciprocal credits in the framework of the village, which serves as a clearing house.

In order to understand the *jāti* regime, perhaps the most important point is to locate its spatial framework. The general principle is as follows. At the village level there exist segments of *jāti* complementing one another so as to ensure economic and religious self-sufficiency. Each *jāti* extends over several villages, within the framework of the chieftain-ship. Powerful *jāti* can disperse their segments over several chieftainships within the framework of a super-chieftainship – the second political level. Only the *jāti* of the Brahmans goes beyond this framework and can be spread over one or even several kingdoms. But no *jāti* has any reality

at the imperial and continental level, even if there are Brahmans
everywhere, since everywhere they are indispensable as the exclusive
specialists in the sacred.

A morphology conceived of in this way possesses, as does the tribe, all
that it needs to survive in the face of everything. Fluidity allows it to
absorb every shock and assimilate every innovation. The organization of
the *jāti* guarantees the preservation of the rules governing its functioning.
Complementary at the village level, combined with the extension of the
jāti to several villages, ensures economic, cultural and demographic self-
sufficiency, independent of any political framework. The *jāti* regime is
thus a perfect solution to political instability. Finally, the Brahmans
ensure the cultural unity of the subcontinent, across a prodigious local
diversity, for the instability of political frameworks and the fluidity of the
jāti both determine and allow for the greatest possible cultural
heterogeneity.

With feudality, we do not abandon the segmentary morphology, but
encounter an organizational principle very different from the *jāti* regime.
We will dwell upon it less, for feudality is better known, having been
more closely studied. The parallel between Europe and Japan can be
taken to great lengths, on condition that the essential distinctions are
maintained. Feudality proper is an organizational principle resting upon
the personal bonds of allegiance that have developed between aristocrats.
An explicit oath of loyalty, both in Europe and Japan, links aristocrats
who are essentially free and equal, but some of whom possess greater
power than others. The seigneurie is an independent phenomenon
whereby centres of private power exercise public functions, particularly
as regards justice. Seigneuries are to be found in Europe as well as in
Japan, but, whilst feudality is peculiar to them, the phenomenon of the
seigneurie is much more widespread. It is to be met with every time that a
political authority grows so weak that it is no longer able to carry out its
political functions of ensuring security and prosperity: when the centre
grows weak the periphery grows strong on the vestige that remains. The
failure of empires, in Japan and Europe, led to the emergence of
seigneuries, as are to be found in Egypt and in China between the
dynasties. Feudality itself is in no way linked up with the seigneurie;
otherwise it would be found everywhere. The most plausible hypothesis
is that it utilizes afresh pre-imperial client practices, namely tribal ones.
In the Europe of the barbarians, as in the Japan of Yamato, one had to
deal with tribal aristocracies, which established client bonds and bonds
of loyalty, similar to those bonds between aristocrats, contrary to the
more general case, in which the bond was established between elements
of the social elites and members of the people – in the Roman fashion, for
example. Feudality may be the result of a morphological 'trial and error'

process – a response to the challenge of the dissolution of the polities and the accompanying growth of insecurity. As for the seigneuries, these would not be the result of trial and error, but a spontaneous and automatic consequence of the weakening of the centre.

Europe and Japan follow along their disturbingly parallel course by marking out large estates owned by the powerful – the local lords. Thanks to these estates these lords can be assured of the loyalty of their vassals by the granting of fiefs. Fiefs are a form of salary since they open the door to the confiscation of a proportion of the income from peasant labour. This aspect of affairs is particularly highlighted in Japan in the notions and realization of the *shōen* and the *shiki*. The *shōen* is the totality of lands withdrawn from imperial control and transformed into immune seigneuries. The *shiki* is a right of access to the produce of the land, shared out among workers, vassals and lords. The parallel between Japan and Europe only stops short at one point, which might have been important for the future. In Japan, the large estate never corresponded to the large-scale enterprise. The technical constraints of rice cultivation, a very great consumer of labour at certain crucial times in the cultivation cycle, dictated a kind of horticulture whose economic effectiveness is maximized in the *minifundium*. Independent of the form that property may take, the small family enterprise has always been the norm in Japan. Europe, on the contrary, experienced the large-scale exploitation of the Gallo-Roman *latifundium*, then of the Merovingian and Carolingian *villa*. Through a felicitous conjunction of various factors – the low productivity of serfs working on the lord's estate; vast projects of land clearance that required concessions advantageous to the labour force; the progressive transformation of the aristocracy into land rentiers – the large-scale enterprise broke down into a host of family enterprises. This situation was reached, at least in the Europe that counts historically, in the West, from the beginning of the fourteenth century. The conjunction was a happy one because, both in Europe and Japan, it safeguarded the chance that the small family undertaking might one day also benefit from the ownership of its land, and the countryside become covered with millions of small-scale enterprises run by as many entrepreneur households. This process of evolution was a decisive factor both for economic development and even more for the democratization of political regimes. These transfers of property to the benefit of the peasantry take place from the fourteenth century onwards in western Europe, continuing right up to the nineteenth century in central and eastern Europe, whilst in Japan the phenomenon will occur later, but more rapidly, since it essentially manifests itself during the eighteenth century (Smith, 1959).

Another decisive point is that neither feudality nor the seigneurie are, in the very long run, stable solutions. The seigneurie, by usurping or inheriting political functions, is transformed by this very fact into a quasi-polity. Consequently it is engaged in a permanent war that inevitably leads to the reconstitution of larger polities and to the disappearance of the seigneuries. From then onwards, feudality as a morphology has no longer any reason to exist since it was a response to the dissolution of the polities. But feudality had allowed the aristocracy to steer a course through a zone marked by extreme turbulence, to constitute itself as a group linked by powerful bonds of loyalty, to endow itself with a system of norms that developed within the framework of chivalry – in short, feudality endowed Europe and Japan with social elites that imparted special characteristics to their social stratification and above all also had repercussions on their political regimes.

Stratifications

The very fact of stratification is universal, occurring as soon as human societies pass beyond a certain threshold of technical and economic effectiveness (Baechler, 1985, part V, book III, section I). From tribal morphology upwards, there is to be found universally a division into three *categories*. At the top are the elites, who occupy the highest positions as regards power, prestige and wealth; because of this they are numerically in the minority. In the middle are to be found the people, deprived of power and prestige, but retaining that part of the wealth considered to be appropriate in the society under consideration; the people form the majority. Finally there are the dregs of society, gathering together those excluded from the social order, whose numbers may vary considerably. This tripartite distribution may be held to be almost a fact of nature. The various societies work upon this fact, both practically and ideologically, to transform these general categories into social groups that are experienced and thought of as such. It is a fact to be found in India, in Japan and in Europe. In all three cases it is easy to distinguish the existence of three basic categories. Since it is universal, it is impossible for it to have any connection with the emergence of modernity. Let us abandon that tack, in order to explore two other paths, perhaps more promising. The first might be outlined from the stratification that had been thought out, the second by the presence or absence of certain concrete social groups.

In all three cases we are dealing with societies with orders of rank, with the legal definition of stratification by a political authority and its justification by an ideology. It is not necessary to refer to the three Indo-European functions to explain the three orders of French society that emerged from feudalism. The clergy, the nobility and the third estate were, after the eleventh century, a fact that it was sufficient to conceptualize, and then to legalize. The hierarchy itself, in a Christian universe and a non-autocratic political context, could not fail to place the clergy at the top and, consequently, the nobility in second place. But Europe found it somewhat difficult to provide an ideological justification for this ranking. It could only be drawn from the Gospels, for every ideology drew its vocabulary from them. Yet one cannot find even the slightest glimmering of an argument in the Gospels that favoured the predominating social order. They fell back on banalities – the clergy who prays, the nobility who protects, in the service of the church and royalty, and the third estate who give support. As for the dregs of the population, in so far as they were excluded from society they could never constitute an order in it. Nevertheless it might be perceived as a quasi-order that grouped together those excluded. Europe did not bother itself with this subterfuge, and disdained its Jews, its vagabonds and, later, its gypsies, without designating them by any special technical term.

Japan, on the contrary, gave names to two quasi-orders of those excluded: the *eta* and the *hinin*. As in Europe at the end of the eighteenth century, the definition of orders in Japan takes over from feudality and corresponds to a restoration of the central authority. The Tokugawa, like the monarchs of Europe, contented themselves with institutionalizing the reality and defined a nobility of *samurai* and a people of *heimin*, comprising landworkers, artisans and merchants. The clergy did not have bestowed upon them the dignified eminence of their European counterparts; they are put in second place, without, it seems, constituting a clearly distinct order. Each of the two orders is subdivided into ranks or suborders, placed in a hierarchy not according to any sacred criterion, but, for the nobility, either as a function of their closeness to the *shōgun*, or, for the people, according to Confucian principles. Indeed the ideological justification for this society made up of orders, as, moreover, for the *shōgun* regime as a whole, was drawn directly from Confucianism. The warrior officials of the state are at the top, because they ensure order, without which nothing can exist. The peasants, at the very heart of the people, are esteemed of greater dignity than the artisans because they produce the food, whereas the latter only produce non-essential goods. The merchants are placed in the bottom position, because they move wealth around but do not create it.

The originality of India does not lie in the explicit definition of the four *varṇa*, or in the institutionalization of the dregs of society as the Untouchables, or in an ideological justification strictly religious in its inspiration. It lies in the fact that, in contrast to Europe and Japan, the orders of Indian society exist only in thought and do not correspond to any reality. More exactly, only the Brahmans exist, because they are to be found as much among the *varṇa* as the *jāti*. On the contrary, the Kshatriya disappeared for centuries, or, in the North, even for millennia, to come to life again in modern times in the north-west under the name of Rajputh, and, it would seem, have never been represented in the south. The *Vaiśya* are only to be found from the nineteenth century onwards. In fact only the *Śūdras* are present everywhere, like the Brahmans. But, unlike the latter, the closed nature and exclusiveness of the *jāti* and the fact that they are a meticulously hierarchized group means that the *jāti Śūdra* deprive the *varṇa Śūdra* of any real substance and remove from it any power to operate within the framework in which the *jāti* function: the village and the chieftainship.

The only Indian reality is the *jāti* – the *varṇa* is only a category or a concept that becomes manifest when the need is felt to think of Indian society as a whole. The thousands of *jāti* do not make up any coherent picture; coherence is only evident, for those concerned and for observers, at the local level. On the contrary, the *varṇa* exhibit a configuration that is simple, logical and, all in all, fairly commonplace. Yet who needs to think of society as a whole? First of all, the Brahmans, since they are the only ones who develop *jāti* on an almost continental scale. Next, travellers, British census administrators and ethnologists or sociologists. The latter had no alternative but to resort to the Brahmans in order to obtain that coherent vision they needed so as to perceive *the* Indian society through the real chaos of polities and the apparent chaos of the *jāti*. But from where did the Brahmans draw the *varṇa*? From two sources. At the outset, there was a social fact peculiar to Indo-Europeans, to be found explicitly in the Vedas, just as it may be read in Tacitus for the Germans, and in Caesar for the Celts. The Indo-Europeans have a warrior aristocracy, a pastoral–arable people and a clergy of sacrificers. These are not orders, because the groups are open and mobile. Even in the era of Buddha (Fick, 1920) the same situation exists, save that the Brahmans seem to have become a hereditary, almost closed group. To go beyond this, a political authority is necessary to institutionalize the reality. The testimony of Megasthenes indicates to us the epoch and the actors in this transition: the Maurya at the end of the fourth century BC. The failure of the empire almost immediately made the definition of the *varṇa* an unreal one. It continued to be thought out in the epics, and in the *Dharmaśāstras*. Social reality only retained the Brahmans, for the simple reason that from Vedic times onwards they were accepted as the exclusive specialists in worship, and, more exactly, as the actors indispensable for offering sacrifice, which is the keystone of Indian religions.

The mere fact that the Japanese and European orders are real and the

Indian ones are merely artefacts of thought would not have been of great consequence. The decisive clue for our problem must be sought in real groups. Three major differences exist between India and Japan and India and Europe. In the first place the nobility and the Samurai are aristocrats, whilst the Kshatriya are not. An aristocracy is defined on the one hand by the fact that it has the monopoly of power, wealth and prestige and, on the other hand, more decisively, by the fact that its social and economic roots are independent of the political authority. An aristocracy is rooted in peripheral segments or areas. Each aristocrat is surrounded by his own people, lives on the resources available from his lands and provides his own arms. He places himself in the service of a political authority of his own volition. His independence may be due to his origin or result from his being able successfully to distance himself from imperial authority. All these characteristics can apply to both European and Japanese elites. They are entirely lacking in Kshatriya. It is true that their Vedic predecessors are aristocrats of the first water. But, as pre-Maurya India was preparing for the emergence of the empire by the constitution of the northern kingdoms and the rivalries between them, the aristocracies were sliced apart and eliminated, to be replaced by 'service' nobilities, providing above all soldiers, but also public officials for the monarchs. All sources are at one on this point – the Jātaka, the Greeks, the epic stories, the *Dharmaśāstras*, court literature and travellers. There are no aristocrats in India, unless they are local, such as the Mahrattas, who represent a tribal revival. Imperialization, which failed to realize the constitution of a lasting polity, was socially successful, for every empire rests upon the physical elimination of the aristocracy or its transformation into a 'service' nobility. The consequence is crucial: for more than 2000 years India was deprived of those centres of autonomous decision-making constituted naturally by aristocrats. Civil society lacked the vital support necessary to oppose invasion by the political power.

The consequence was all the more serious because India did not possess another indispensable mainstay of civil society: a peasantry. India has its agricultural workers; it does not have its peasants. An agricultural worker cultivates the land and causes it to bear its harvest: India has such workers, as do all societies that have switched to food production. A peasant is an entrepreneur in miniature, who takes all the economic decisions regarding his own plot of land, even though it is not his property. A peasant cannot be reduced to one individual. He represents a household, for co-operating and the division of tasks between a man and a woman is necessary for the development to survive. From very early on, Europe is populated by millions of peasant entrepreneurs. By the fourteenth century the great transformation has taken place. In Japan the

54 *Jean Baechler*

peasant society is almost the founding society. On the contrary, in India
the unit of development is not the nuclear family: it is either the village
segment of a *jāti*, or an extended family, a *gotra*, which is the basic
exogamous cell of Indian society. The difference is expressed once more
by another contrast. Whereas the Japanese and European villages are
very strong realities, not only from the social and affective viewpoint, but
also politically, the Indian *grāma* is less one's native heath and a plot of
ground than a human grouping, whose consistency relies only upon the
complementarity of the *jāti* (Malamoud, 1976). Moreover, the Indian
village has no political reality of itself, even if there is something political
within it. The absence or presence of a peasantry is decisive:
economically, because development rests upon an efficient agriculture,
which itself rests upon the entrepreneurial spirit, the seeking after profit,
and the effective husbanding of those profits by those working the land;
politically, because democratization requires a people to be concentrated
in autonomous decision-making centres and also to be accustomed to
looking after their own affairs.

A third and last major difference lies in the presence in Japan and
Europe of towns, markets and merchants, and in their absence in India,
or rather in the different way they are defined. It is true that India did
possess towns, markets and merchants, but on the model typical of
empires. Towns in empires are only nerve centres of political authority,
the markets and the merchants are exclusively in the service of the class
enjoying power and leisure. On the contrary, in Europe and Japan the
towns have an existence of their own; they ensure economic functions,
even if, in addition, they also have a political function or even a political
origin. Moreover, the towns are not oases that are lost in an immensity of
villages; they are numerous and constitute among themselves a network
whose meshes are both closely knit and hierarchized. This assertion
holds good even more for Japan than for Europe. In both cases no village,
or very few of them, is located so far from the town that the town cannot
serve as an outlet for it. Countless local markets spring up, which, linked
to the fact that every increase in productivity directly benefits the peasant
entrepreneurs – soon also to be the land owners – are a constant driving
force in agricultural progress. In the same way provincial, national, and –
for Europe – trans-national markets are the driving force for progress in
the artisan trades, and then for industrial progress. These innumerable
markets, at the same time very variously defined but interconnected,
contrast most vividly with the situation in India. Within the framework of
the village there is no market at all, but a clearing house – moreover, an
unsymmetrical one because economically it works to the advantage of the
dominant *jāti*, the owners of the land, but not those who work it – for the
offer and exchange of goods and services. Between villages exchange is

virtually non-existent because the *jajmānī* system ensures the economic autarchy of each one of them. Finally, between villages and towns, the flow is one-way: the towns consume the products of the taxes levied on the villages by the political authority.

Aristocracy, peasantry and markets are the three major distinctive characteristics. In one way or another they are linked to the definition of polities and nature of morphologies. They depend above all on a still more decisive reality: political regimes. It is in this respect, it seems to me, that is rooted the most profound difference between India on the one hand and Japan and Europe on the other.

Political Regimes

A political regime is a specific way of regulating power relationships within a polity as such. In our terminology, the three cases depend upon the same genre – hierocracy – but Japan and Europe represent the aristocratic species, whereas India has developed the autocratic species. Being hierocracies, the three regimes conceive the titular holder of supreme political power as the deputy on earth of a transcendent principle, one who is entrusted with ensuring the link between the two kingdoms, and, in so doing, with drawing down upon their peoples every kind of blessing. Around this common nucleus each one has developed ideologies that have been refined to a greater or lesser degree, depending upon the cultural and religious context. Europe has retained the principle of the separation of throne and altar, combined with their harmonious co-operation so as to lead people to salvation. Japan has relied upon the Confucian conception and upon the idea of a harmony to be attained between the cosmos and society, through the mediation of the sovereign. India has concentrated its thinking upon the concept of *dharma*: by compliance with the duties of his office the king ensures a general state of order, which is the condition for all well-being.

The autocratic variety of the hierocracy is the regime that is peculiar to empires. It adds a decisive corollary to the general principle of legitimacy. Political power is theoretically rooted in transcendency, but in practice it is available to the one who represents it here below. All earthly power proceeds from him. In particular, all the organs necessary for the exercise of power are precarious emanations. The social elites are not independent of the political power, but are identified with the mechanism of power itself. This is why every imperial authority can have no respite until it has eliminated the aristocrats who have helped it to attain that power, in order to replace them by its own creatures, whose social existence depends solely upon it. The seizure of political power over society is not confined to being over its elites, but applies also to the people, at least in principle. The imperial ideal is to have at its disposal a people dispersed among a host of villages placed under the control of the central power, inhabited by subjects diligently working lands that have been appropriated and apportioned by the sovereign against the payment of land rents that reduce people to enjoying a minimum share. This renders them incapable of revolting to bring down that power, by virtue of the fact that they are so widely scattered. Finally, an imperial power claims the right to top up its revenues, of which it is always short, by the imposition of monopolies and the control of markets and exchanges. A controlled economy is its ideal.

At every level of the political structure India corresponds at all points to the logic of a hierocratic–autocratic regime. The structure has come into being by the Maurya era, as is testified by the observations of Megasthenes, handed down by his successors. Indeed the information gleaned by the Jātaka indicates that the movement towards autocratization had started, at least in northern India, before then. It is reasonably certain that Megasthenes and Kauṭilīya are not contemporaries (Stein, 1921, despite Kangle, 1963), and it is arguable that the Arthaśāstra dates from the first century BC or AD (Scharfe, 1968). The regime described or commended in it is very autocratic. The epics do not suggest a different picture, although the *Rāmāyaṇa* insists more upon the hierocratic dimension, whereas the *Mahābhārata* emphasizes rather the logic of autocracy. More anecdotal works, and therefore more revealing, such as the *Pañcatantra*, are on the same lines. From the time of the first Moslem invasions the testimonies are even more in agreement.

This weighty fact explains certain features of Indian political life through the ages. Constantly, and at all levels, the criterion of political legitimacy was the simple fact of being strong enough to hold power. It is only then that there is a preoccupation to add hierocratic justifications, if necessary by asking a Brahman to obtain for the conqueror a *Kshatriya* genealogy. This fact holds good at the level of the empire, the kingdom, the super-chieftainship and the chieftainship. It is clearly related, in a reciprocal influence, to the inconsistency of polities. A second feature is the complete absence of any aristocracy or social elite independent of the political authority. This is the deepest cause of the whole political situation and, at the same time, its effect – one that is continually being renewed. A third feature is at least just as important: it concerns the villages. The hundreds of thousands of Indian villages are *not* so many little republics, in which people are initiated into political life and democratic practices. It has already been pointed out that the *grāma* village has no existence as such; it is only the result of the complementarity between the segments of the *jāti* and the projection 'on the ground' of this social origin. It is reflected in the absence of a village centre, by the division into districts, with the prominent *jāti* in the middle and the Untouchables on the outskirts, and by the absence of a coherent overall plan. From the time of the Maurya, the village chief is appointed by the central power or by a lower level of the political organization. This direct control of the village by the political power was an ideal that was only realized during periods of vigorous political activity. In more recent and better documented periods, the leadership of the village is ensured purely and simply by the *jāti* that was locally predominant. Its chief serves as the village chief, and its *pañcayat* as the village council. In this way the self-sufficiency of the *jāti* regime is ensured. Within the framework of the chieftainship and the village the regime can satisfy all needs independent of any political power, save in one respect: the conflicts about precedence among the *jāti* can at any moment degenerate into bloody struggles – which they did not fail to do and continue to do even today – giving the political power the opportunity to intervene. A final feature is a permanent lethargy as regards the economic activity of exchange. Initiatives are held in check, before the creation of the imperial regime, by the regime of corporations – *śreni* – and after imperialization, either through public monopolies when the authority is strong enough to impose them, or by the occupational specialization of the *jāti*, which combines the disadvantages of the corporation with those of monopoly. It should be added that fortunes in fixed and moveable assets undergo a fate that is normal under an autocratic regime: they are sudden and ephemeral, subjected to permanent insecurity because of the risk of political confiscation [see, for example, the testimony of Dubois (1906) for the first quarter of the nineteenth century].

Japan and Europe portray opposing pictures in every respect. The hierocratic dimension of the regime grows stronger, the autocratic one grows weaker. Logic was pushed to its limit in Japan, where the Temmu is, from Heian onwards, restricted to a symbolic religious role. The position is so bereft of any power, and, if appearances are to be believed, such an uncomfortable one, that the emperors got in the habit of abdicating very early, in order to shut themselves off and in fact become the active heads of their household. From then onwards, as in Europe, the emperor is no more than 'the first gentleman in his kingdom'. The radical break between hierocracy and the exercise of political power permitted, on the one hand, the perpetuation of the dynasty, by removing from it any danger of usurpation, and, on the other hand, imposed upon the political power an auxiliary aid. This was the Shōgunate, which is the indispensable complement to the Temmu, of which it presents itself as the delegate entrusted with day-to-day affairs on earth. Since the post was divested of any sacred dimension, it can be allocated to the one strongest through force of arms. In Europe, monarchs preserved both the aura of hierocracy and the effective exercise of power. As regards that aura, one remarkable feature – and the decisive factor in the reconstitution of polities after the dispersal wrought by feudality – is the rareness with which usurpations and murders of kings occur. Three only can be distinguished during the feudal period: in England, the murder of Edward the Martyr in a palace revolution that benefited his brother; in France, that of Robert I, a usurper, by a supporter of the legitimate heir; in Italy, that of Berenger I. Even more remarkable is the infrequency with which royal functions are conferred on those holding local power. They include only two: Rudolf, who in 888 had himself anointed at Toul as king of the lands lying between the west and east; and Louis the Blind, anointed king at Valence in 890 (Bloch, 19: 146–9)   The contrast with the Indian scene is striking.

The contrast is even more striking as regards the second point. The backbone of Japanese and European societies is provided by aristocracies strong enough to contain either the royal power or that of the Shōgunate. Although the *shōgun* occupy their eminent position as a result of fierce struggles with their rivals, their power is in no way autocratic. In fact the position only exists because it allows a balance to be maintained between aristocrats. Proof of this is the unwavering policy of conquerors not to eliminate those they conquered, but to incorporate them among their vassals, requiring from them an oath of loyalty. The regime reaches the height of perfection with the Tokugawa, where the *shōgun* receives the personal homage of each *daimyo*, maintaining between them all an equilibrium that guarantees public order, whilst handing over to each *daimyo* the administration of his province, through his own *samurai* vassals who have been converted into public officials. In Europe the royal power, resting upon the aristocracy and limited by it, provides the very definition of an *ancien régime*. Whether it be in its English parliamentary constitutional form, or the French absolutist form, or even the form of enlightened despotism in central and southern Europe, the principle always remains the same. The aristocracy preserves its roots independent of the royal power, it makes itself available for the king's service without submitting to it, the king governs with his nobility, king and nobility come into conflict if one side contravenes the rules of the game. In Japan, as in Europe, centuries of wars and quarrels have led to the point where a clear distinction is drawn between the public domain, which is managed by the political power, and the private domain, which is left to people's own initiative. What is specific to the Japanese is merely the blurring of the distinction at the central level, which is still plunged into feudal confusion, whilst imposing it clearly within each province. What has been termed the administrative monarchy of Louis XIV is not to be found at Edo, but in every capital of every province.

The power and vigour of the private domain is particularly given expression in the villages. These are, both in Europe and Japan, political communities that are self-governed by the peasants themselves. The political definition of the village is the outcome of a complicated history, relating to the lord, the parish and taxation. The result is clear-cut. Each village is a small oligarchical republic, managed by a council in which the largest landowners predominate, in accordance with a logic that is peculiar to the 'city' (Baechler, 1985: part III, book III, chapter II). In Japan the village is a very ancient reality. The term *mura*, to designate it, appears in 774, but the fact of it very much pre-dates Nara. The reforms imposed at this time rest upon a basic unity, the *ko*, or an extended family, or, in central Japan, on several nuclear families, whether linked by kinship or not – on the average, twenty-five persons in two or three nuclear families, led by a chieftain responsible for the good behaviour of everybody, and for the payment of taxes. The *mura* groups together up to fifty *ko* and is placed under the leadership of a *ko* chieftain who is responsible for the census registers, the allocation of the paddy fields, the payment of the village taxes, and law and order. From the fourteenth century onwards this organization undergoes a profound transformation, which triumphs by the end of the sixteenth century. The village becomes a political reality, self-administered by the *myō* chieftains, consisting of extended families that are themselves self-governed. It was sufficient, at the turn of the eighteenth century, for the *myō* to break down into its constituent parts, for the nuclear family to become the basic cell of the village. As in Europe, the government of the village will from then on be dominated by a kind of peasant aristocracy, the more fortunate of whom will be able to slide out of their peasant status.

The two regimes, by containing the political power and insisting upon the distinction between the public and the private domains, set free economic initiative and gave definition to the markets. It can be maintained that Japan preceded Europe. The unification of the Japanese market was fully completed by the seventeenth century, when the Tokugawa had abolished all those obstacles that were still hampering the European markets in the eighteenth and even the nineteenth century. From the end of the sixteenth century Nabunaga dismisses the guilds and frees trade. He likewise confiscates entailed property that had been immobilized by religious orders for centuries, reinserting it, at least indirectly, into the economic circuit. In fact, the Japanese economic take-off predates the Tokugawa by a long time: it begins with Kamakura in the thirteenth and fourteenth centuries. The question therefore arises:

was Japan on the road to industrial transformation? We shall never be
able to answer that question. In this respect Europe benefited from a
decisive advantage. Whereas Japan, by reason of its political unity and its
insularity, was only a small market, Europe was made up of a market of
markets, in which rivalry and competition between polities whipped up
energy and placed them beyond political seizure: an authority that was
unreasonable in economic matters did not stifle them; it merely favoured
the prosperity of its rivals.

Conclusion

The problem we posed is not yet resolved, but it is perhaps posed in
more precise terms. In seeking to explain European economic development from the ninteenth century onwards by considering it either as an
aberration or as a turning point in history, the best way to start is by
identifying the most general conditions of possibility of the phenomenon.
These can be reduced to three: the definition of property rights, which
guarantee to the various factors returns proportional to their contribution
to the production of wealth; regulated markets that are as fluid as
possible, in which transactions lead to the optimal allocation of
resources; entrepreneurs who, on the look-out for any opportunity for
profit, are constantly looking for new combinations of factors in order to
replenish supply. These conditions of economic progress in turn rest
upon a more general condition of possibility: a political regime whose
logic is democratic. In a third stage, sketched out here, it is necessary to
show how the historical conditions of possibility for this specific regime
have in their turn been brought together. One could and should carry the
matter further. We have, for example, assigned a central historical role in
India to the failure of imperialization and the lasting inconsistency of
polities. One would need to attempt to explain why the failure of the
Maurya was so definitive. In the same way, if the *jāti* regime is effectively
a morphological response to the failure of empire and to the impossibility
of returning to a tribal morphology, it would be appropriate to show why
the actors in that morphology found this solution rather than another.
Europe and Japan have not yielded up all their secrets either, even if the
abundance of datable documents has largely allowed the ground to be
cleared.

The thesis defended and the facts set out have, it seems, allowed us to
contrast sufficiently India on the one hand and Japan and Europe on the
other, for at least one condition for the explanation to be fulfilled: namely
the parallelism with Japan and Europe is strong enough to make
plausible these two quasi-simultaneous cases of modernization, and the

divergence of these two cases from the Indian case is marked enough to make the delay in Indian modernization comprehensible. At no time have we evoked ideological factors, taking this term in the very wide sense of representations shared by a social group. Indeed, I believe that the attempts of Max Weber were admirable but vain, and that religion has only insignificant points of connection, distant or indirect, with economic modernization. If there were still need to do so, our three cases would demonstrate the proof of this. In spite of the intermediate concept of 'inter-worldly asceticism', one can be convinced only with difficulty that the Christian doctrine, whether as in Holy Scripture, in the Church Fathers or in the teachings of the churches in medieval or modern times, harbours the slightest encouragement to capitalist activities. In the same way one can hardly seen how such activities would be stimulated by Shintoism, Buddhism or Confucianism in a society which explicitly places merchants in the penultimate rank in society, immediately before the pariahs – the *burakumin* or *eta* – and the beggars – the *hinin*. Brahmanism is the sole ethical and religious doctrine from which the defence and glorification of the spirit of capitalism can be quite naturally deduced. It is sufficient to combine together the stages of life – the *āśrama* – and the aims of man – the *puruṣārtha* – to justify the City of London and the Ruhr Basin. These two concepts are at the very heart of Hindu civilization, immediately after that of sacrifice, which is even more essential to it. There are four 'stages of life': student (*brahmācarin*), head of the household (*gṛhastha*), the forest hermit (*vānaprastha*) and the 'renouncer' (*sannyāsin*). There are also four 'aims of man': desire (*kāma*), interest (*artha*), order (*dharma*) and deliverance (*mokṣa*). Correspondences are established spontaneously between the two classifications, whose 'natural' aspect, in conformity with the human nature and condition, might be stressed. The 'renouncer' aims at deliverance; the hermit, deliverance and order; the head of the household, order, interest and desire; the Brahman scholar, order. The *puruṣārtha* and the *varṇa* can also be combined with this result: the Brahmans have affinities in their condition with deliverance and the enunciated order; the Kshatriya, with the protected order, political interest and desire; the *Vaiśya*, with economic interest (Malamoud, 1982). Since historically the Kshatriya and the *Vaiśya* have almost disappeared from the social scene to the benefit of the *Śudra*, it is very easy to extract from that doctrine a 'capitalist ideology', which would impose an *obligation* upon the *Śudra* head of the household to devote himself to the chrematistic. Contrary to the Christian and the Buddhist who, as such, can have a bad conscience in regard to their capitalist state, the Brahman capitalist would be very much at ease with himself, on condition that he prepared for himself, shortly after the birth of his first grandson and the appearance of his first white hairs, a fitting retreat for spiritual 'adventures'. If India did not invent capitalism and modernity, it was not through a lack of the appropriate doctrine. But once modernity and capitalism had been imported from Europe, certain social actors did not fail to make the comparisons outlined above.

References

Translator's note. The references given here favour India exclusively, as the essay derives from a study centring on the societies of pre-modern India. For this edition, wherever possible, the author's French sources have been replaced with the most easily available English-language edition.

Sources

Al Biruni 1910: *Al Hindi*, trans E. Sachau as *Alberuni's India*, 2nd edn, London.
Arrian 1958: *Indica*. In *The Life of Alexander the Great*, trans. A. de Sélincourt, Harmondsworth, Middx.
Fa-Hsien 1956: *The Travels of Fa-hsien*, trans H. A. Giles, 2nd edn, London.
Herodotus 1927: *Historiae*, 3rd edn, Oxford.
Ibn Battúta 1958: *The Travels of Ibn Battuta, A.D. 1325–1354*, trans. H. A. R. Gibb, Cambridge.
The Institute of Visnu 1884: trans. J. Jolly, vol. 7.
Kautilīya 1960–5, *Arthaśāstra*, trans R. P. Kangle, Bombay.
Mahābhārata 1973–8: trans. J. A. B. van Buitenen, vols I–III, Chicago.
Mānavadharmaśāstra n.d.: trans. A. Loiseleur; Deslongchamps, Paris.
Marco Polo 1958: *The Travels of Marco Polo*, trans R. Latham, Harmondsworth, Middx.
Megasthenes 1848: *Fragmenta Historicorum Graecorum*, ed. Ch. Müller, vol. II, Paris.
The Minor Law Books: trans. J. Jolly, vol. 33.
Pañchatantra 1964: trans. A. W. Ryder, Chicago.
Pliny the Elder 1938: *Natural History (IV, 18–26)*, ed. H. Rackham, London.
Ptolemy 1932: *Geography of Claudius Ptolemy (VII, 1–4)*, ed. E. L. Stevenson, New York.
Quintus Curcius 1976: *Histoire d'Alexandre*, ed. H. Bardon, 3rd edn, Paris.
Ramayana (of Valmiki) 1952: trans. H. P. Shastri et al., London.
Strabo 1917–32: *Geographica*, trans. H. L. Jones, 8 vols, London.
Xuan Zang 1857–8: *Mémoire sur les contrées occidentales*, trans. St. Julien, reprinted in *L'Inde du Bouddha, vue par des pélerins chinois sous la dynastie Tang (VIIe siècle)*, 1968, Paris.

Books and Articles

Allchin, B. and Allchin, R., 1982: *The Rise of Civilization in India and Pakistan*, Cambridge.

Arnesen, P. J. 1979: *The Medieval Japanese 'daimyo'*, New Haven.

Asakawa, K. 1929: *The Documents of Iriki*, New Haven.

Auboyer, J. 1975: *Daily Life in Ancient India, From Approximately 200 BC to AD 700*, London.

Baechler, J. 1985: *Démocraties*, Paris.

Bailey, F. G. 1963: Closed social stratification in India. *Archives Européennes de Sociologie*, IV, 107–24.

Banks, M. 1960: Caste in Jaffna. In E. R. Leach (ed.), *Aspects of Caste in South India, Ceylon and North-West Pakistan*, Cambridge, pp. 61–77.

Bergaigne, A. 1963: *La religion vedique*, 4 vols (1st edn, 1878–83), Paris.

Béteille, A. 1962: Closed and open social stratification in India. *Archives Européennes de Sociologie*, VII, 224–46.

  1964: A note on the referents of caste. *Archives Europeennes de Sociologie*, V, 130–4.

Biardeau, M. 1981: *L'Hindouisme, Anthropologie d'une civilisation*, Paris.

Biardeau, and M. Malamoud, C. 1976: *Le sacrifice dans l'Inde ancienne*, Paris.

Bloch, M. 1962: *Feudal Society*, 2 vols, London.

Bouglé, C. 1971: *Essays oin the Caste System*, Cambridge.

Boutruche, R. 1968, 1970: *Seigneurie et féodalité*, vol. I, *Le premier âge des liens d'homme à homme*; vol. II, *L'apogée (XIe–XIIIe siècles)*, Paris.

Buss, A. 1978: *Société, politique, individu. Les formes élémentaires de la vie sociale en Inde ancienne*, Amsterdam.

The Cambridge History of India 1957–8: vols I, III–VI, Delhi.

Cohn, B. S. 1962: Political systems in eighteenth century India. The Banaras Region. *Journal of the American Oriental Society*, 82, 312–20.

Deloche, J. 1980: *La circulation en Inde, avant la révolution des transports*, vol. I, *La voie de terre*; vol. II, *La voie d'eau*, Paris.

Drekmeier, C. 1962: *Kingship and Community in Early India*, Stanford.

Dubois, J. A. 1906: *Hindu Manners, Customs and Ceremonies*, 3rd edn, Oxford.

Duby, G. 1968: *Rural Economy and Country Life in the Medieval West*, London.

  1974: *The Early Growth of the European Economy: Warriors and Peasants from the Seventh to the Twelfth Centuries*, London.

  1970: *The Three Orders: Feudal Society Imagined*, Chicago.

Dumont, L. 1972: *Homo hierarchicus*, London.

Duus, P. 1976: *Feudalism in Japan*, New York.

Embree, A. T. and Wilhelm, F. 1967: *Indien*, Fischer Weltgeschichte, vol. 17, Frankfort.

Fairservis, W. A. 1974: *The Roots of Ancient India*, Chicago.

  1979: The Harappan civilization: new evidence and more theory. In G. L. Possehl, *Ancient Cities of the Indus*, Durham, NC, pp. 49–65.

  1979: The origin, character and decline of an early civilization. In Possehl, *Ancient Cities*, pp. 68–89.

  1983: L'écriture de la civilisation de la vallée de l'Indus. *Pour la Science*, 67, 14–25.

Fick, R. 1920: *The Social Organisation in North-East India in Buddha's Time*, Calcutta.

Foy, W. 1895: *Die königliche Gewalt nach den altindischen Rechtsbüchern*, Leipzig.

Fussman, G. 1982: Pouvoir central et régions dans l'Inde ancienne: le problème de l'empire Maurya. *Annales ESC*, 37, 621–47.

Ganshof, F. L. 1964: *Feudalism*, London.

Gonthier, A. 1936: Le régime féodal au Japon. In *Société Jean Bodin*, Recueil I, *Les liens de la vassalité et les immunités*, Brussels.

— 1937: Le servage dans l'Empire du Japon. In *Société Jean Bodin*, Recueil II, *Le servage*, Brussels, pp. 315–27.

— 1938: Le 'Shô' japonais. In: *Société Jean Bodin*, Recueil III, *La tenure*, Brussels, pp. 303–13.

— 1949: L'organisation générale du 'Shô' japonais. In *Société Jean Bodin*, Recueil IV, *Le Domaine*, Brussels, pp. 25–34.

Gough, E. K. 1960: Caste in a Tanjore village. In Leach, *Aspects of Caste*, pp. 11–60.

Gourou, P. 1957: *L'Asie*, 2nd edn, Paris.

Greenwold, S. M. 1975: Kingship and caste. *Archives Européennes de Sociologie*, XVI, 49–75.

Hall, J. W. 1966: *Government and Local Power in Japan, 500 to 1700*, Princeton.

— 1968: *Das japanische Königreich*, Fischer Weltgeschichte, vol. 20, Frankfort.

Heers, J. 1974: *Le clan familial au Moyen Age*, Paris.

Hillebrandt, A. 1923: *Altindische Politik*, Jena.

Hocart, A. M. 1972: *Caste: A Comparative Study*, London.

Hubert, H. and Mauss, M. 1964: *Sacrifice: Its Nature and Function* (1st edn, 1899), London.

Hutton, J. H. 1946: *Caste in India, its Nature, Function and Origins*, Cambridge.

Jolly, J. 1896: Die Entstehung des Kastenwesens. *Zeitschrift der Morgenländischen Gesellschaft*, 50, 507–18.

— 1928: *Hindu Law and Custom*, Delhi.

Juon des Longrais, F. 1958: *L'Est et l'Ouest. Institutions du Japon et de l'Occident comparées*, Tokyo and Paris.

Kane, P. V. 1930–62: *History of Dharmaśāstra*, vols I–V, Poona.

Kosambi, D. K. 1965: *The Culture and Civilisation of Ancient Judia in Historical Outline*, London.

Lannoy, R. 1971: *The Speaking Tree. A Study of Indian Culture and Society*, Oxford.

Leach, E. R. (ed.) 1960: *Aspects of Caste in South India, Ceylon and North-West Pakistan*, Cambridge.

— 1960: What should we mean by Caste? In Leach, *Aspects of Caste*, pp. 1–10.

Levi, S. 1966: *La doctrine du sacrifice dans les Brāhmanas* (1st edn, 1898), Paris.

Lewis, A. 1974: *Knights and Samurai. Feudalism in Northern France and Japan*, London.

Lingat, R. 1967: *Les sources du droit dans le système traditionnel de l'Inde*, Paris and The Hague.

Losch, H. 1959: *Rājadharma, Eisetzung und Aufgabenkreis des Königs im Lichte der Purana*, Bonn.

Macdonell, A. A. 1914: The early history of caste. *The American Historical Review*, 19, 230–44.

Malamoud, C. 1976: Village et forêt dans l'ideólogie de l'Inde Brahmanique. *Archives Européennes de Sociologie*, XVII, 3–20.

1982: Sémantique et rhétorique dans la hiérarchie hindoue des 'buts de l'homme'. *Archives Européennes de Sociologie*, XXIII, 215–38.

Masson-Oursel, P., de Willman-Grabowska, H. and Stern, P. 1933: *L'Inde antique et la civilisation indienne*, Paris.

Miller, E. J. 1954: Caste and territory in Malabar. *American Anthropologist*, 56, 410–20.

Mughal, M. R. 1979: The present state of research on the Indus Valley civilization. In: Possehl, *Ancient Cities*, pp. 90–8.

Muir, J. 1872: *Original Sanskrit Texts on the Origins and History of the People of India, their Religion and their Institutions*, vol. I, London and Edinburgh.

Oldenberg, H. 1897: Zur Geschichte des indischen Kastenwesens. *Zeitschrift der morgenländischen Gesellschaft*, 51, 267–90.

Papinot, E. 1984: *Historical and Geographical Dictionary of Japan* (1st English edn, 1910), Rutland, Vt.

Possehl, G. L. (ed.) 1979: *Ancient Cities of the Indus*, Durham, N.C.

Rau, W. 1957: *Staat und Gesellschaft im alten Indien*, Wiesbaden.

Renou, L. 1959: *The Civilization in Ancient India*, Paris, Calcutta.

1978: *L'Inde fondamentale*, Paris.

Renou, L., and Filliozat, J. 1947, 1953: *L'Inde classique. Manuel des études indiennes*, vol. I, Paris, vol. II, Hanoi.

Richards, J. F. 1975: *Mughal Administration in Golconda*, Oxford.

Sansom, G. 1958–63: *A History of Japan*, 3 vols, Stanford.

Scharfe, H. 1968: *Untersuchungen zur Staatslehre des Kautalya*, Wiesbaden.

Schlerath, B. 1960: *Das Königtum im Rig- und Atharvaveda*, Wiesbaden.

Senart, E. 1930: *Caste in India: The Facts and the System*, London.

Smith, T. C. 1959: *The Agrarian Origins of Modern Japan*, Stanford.

Srinivas, M. N. 1966: *Social Change in Modern India*, Berkeley.

Stein, O. 1921: *Megasthenes and Kautilīya*, Vienna.

Vergati Stahl, A. 1975: M. Greenwold et les Néwars. Doit-on vraiment recourir à deux modèles du système des castes au Népal? *Archives Européennes de Sociologie*, XVI, 310–16.

Wane, Y. 1969: *Les Toucouleurs du Fouta Tooro (Senegal). Stratification sociale et structure familiale*, Dakar.

Weber, M. 1968: *The Religion of India* (1st end, 1920), New York.

Werner, K. F. 1984: Adel (Fränkisches Reich, Imperium Frankreich). *Vom Frankreich zur Entfaltung Deutschlands und Frankreichs*, Sigmaringen, pp. 12–21.

1985: Du nouveau sur un vieux thème. Les origines de la 'noblesse' et de la 'chevalerie', *Comptes-Rendus de l'Academie des Inscriptions et Belles Lettres*, janvier–mars, 186–200.

Zimmer, H. 1879: *Altindisches Leben*, Berlin.

4

The Uniqueness of the East

Chris Wickham

Harbans Mukhia, in his stimulating article, 'Was there feudalism in Indian history?' (1981) rejects the use of the Marxist concept of feudalism outside restricted areas of the world, principally Europe. He is not the first to do this; another recent discussion, Perry Anderson's at the end of his *Lineages of the Absolutist State* (1974), does so equally forcefully, if on different grounds. This essay, a critical response to such a limitation of feudalism, draws primarily on my experiences in attempting to reformulate the problem of the fall of the Roman empire in the west in Marxist terms. Here I propose to discuss the contrast between the Roman empire and its failure on one hand (see Wickham, 1984), and the remarkable continuity of some of the Asian empires on the other, concentrating on those of China and of the Islamic world (Arab, Persian, and Turkish). I write as a Western medievalist, without any pretensions to expertise in the areas or the languages: I have, that is to say, followed Anderson's example in moving into everyone else's field. It would in fact be churlish not to admit my debt to Anderson at the start, though I will disagree with him; I started with his analysis – and with his bibliography – even if I have finished elsewhere.

There are two typical ways of seeing Asia in current Marxist historiography. The first is to take the modes of production from Marx's published and unpublished writings and try to fit the peculiar patterns of Asian history to them: the feudal mode of production, the Asiatic mode, even the slave mode sometimes, with particularly unhappy results. This

This chapter first appeared in *Journal of Peasant Studies*, vol. 12, nos. 2 and 3, pp. 166–96, © Frank Cass & Co. Ltd. 1985. Reprinted by permission of Frank Cass & Co. Ltd.

method has led to the straitjacketing of Asian historical development and sometimes to serious misunderstandings of whole socio-economic processes. The second method is to abandon Marx's systems altogether and to formulate new modes or categories of analysis that are, in effect, nothing more than claims in traditional historical fashion for the historical uniqueness of specific areas: 'I study Byzantium, or some part of Africa, or India, or the Mediterranean; it is empirically different from the medieval West or the Roman Empire; therefore I can establish a new mode' – the Byzantine, or African, or Indian mode. Irfan Habib's 'Indian medieval economy' and Gunther Lewin's refusal to categorize the medieval Chinese economic system at all are other variants of this, put into different terminology (Habib, 1978: 298; Lewin, 1973: 260–2, an appendix in English). Harbans Mukhia and Perry Anderson are also very firmly in this second group. It seems to me that, whereas the first method is overschematic, the second is defeatist. Often defeatist, too, is a third method, the habit of some historians to say, in effect, that there must be some undefined sort of mixture of modes inside the social formations of different places in Asia, that can explain the Asian divergences from European 'norms'. This often leads once again to a refusal to categorize at all: Maxime Rodinson's *Islam and Capitalism*, though providing a succinct critique of a variety of analyses of medieval Islam, is an example of this tendency. Modes of production are ideal constructs; social formations are real societies in all their complexity, and thus in practice virtually irreducible to formal categories. This argument is little more than an excuse for the absence of analysis. But the method none the less seems to me to be the most useful to pursue. There have been close on no societies in human history, after the development of classes, with a single mode of production in them. What matters is to find out *how* different modes articulate together, a procedure that has generally been neglected, not least by the philosophers who have set out the complicated patterns in which mythic modes might behave.[1]

Why do we try to categorize world history in Marxist terms at all? Leaving aside the devotional elements in such categorizations – an element that is, as is well known, still strong – the only answer can be Marx's own: that we understand the world better by so doing, so that we can change it. Such categorizations must set out and make comprehensible the more or less latent socio-economic processes that underly the social formations, social systems, societies, which we study and whose

1 Rodinson (1974: 58–68). Some Soviet scholars tend to nod towards such formulations, too; e.g. a number of comments in *Soviet Studies in History* (1966). These are now given context, and indeed endorsed, by Dunn (1982: see esp. 81–4, 123–4). The problem of articulation is confronted by relatively few people; good (contrasted) instances are Islamoğlu and Keyder (1977), and Hilton (1979).

ruling classes (usually) have produced the surviving material at our disposal. Marx's great achievement was to lay bare the economic logic underlying capitalism, while making it clear that this logic was specific *to* the capitalist mode of production, rather than a timeless historical given. Marx's own musings on pre-capitalist systems were virtually all side-effects produced by this insight. But while this has given all of us our clues, it also, for pre-capitalist historians, produces a problem: what sorts of economic logic did pre-capitalist modes actually possess?

Marx's list of pre-capitalist modes of production varies through his – and Engels's – lifetimes, and it is absurd to assume *a priori* that it has to have been complete, or even properly thought out. But economic systems with their own procedures and logics of development cannot be unlimited. It is quite notable how few attempts there have been since Marx to invent new modes of production outside the individual contexts that historians have found themselves studying; and how such modes work, what their specificity is, is seldom explained. There are, of course, the non-exploitative modes, where combinations and recombinations seem to be endless (nomadic or semi-nomadic/transhumant or settled exploitation of resources; communal or collective or private ownership; clan/kin-group or village or household cooperation; and so on), and these elements indeed also underlie exploitative modes in a complex array that, in the absence of serious study, sometimes at first sight seems random. But what distinguishes exploitative modes is that their social relations of production contain, and are largely defined by, specific systems of the appropriation of the surplus; and there are certainly not a limitless number of these. Methods of surplus-appropriation in practice seem to be restricted to a few basic types – slavery, rent-taking (either 'feudal', that is backed up by coercion, or determined by market forces), tribute and taxation, wage-labour, the manipulation of the petty commodity market. There may be others, but there are not a lot of others. And it is in the difference between these elements, in my view, that the differences between modes of production lie.[2]

Barry Hindess and Paul Hirst have pursued some of this line of argument – though they would certainly not agree with my formulation of

2 Varying economic logics; see, for example, the substantivist analyses in Sahlins (1974), Godelier (1972: esp. 303–18), or the more mainstream discussion in Kula (1976). Non-exploitative modes: no fully coherent categorizations exist, as far as I know, despite much discussion of some aspects. (Nomadism, note, is not necessarily non-exploitative: see n. 5.) For some useful general comments on defining modes, see E. J. Hobsbawm's introduction to Marx (1964). I stress social relations of production, as against, for example, Cohen (1978: 134–74); productive forces can be rather more various. But there is of course a mutual conditioning and interrelation between them. For a lapidary statement of the basic position I am taking up, see Marx (1971: 791–2).

it – in their acute (if somewhat criticized) book, *Pre-Capitalist Modes of Production*. They laid down some strict criteria about what constituted a mode of production; over-strict, it is true, particularly in their insistence on a one-to-one correspondence of given sets of productive forces and relations of production (1975: 183), and sometimes contradicted by their own practice, but useful as a critique of many more sloppy formulations.[3] Their demonstration that the core of the feudal mode of production lies less in the political–juridical aspects of serfdom than in the rent extraction relationships intrinsic to all pre-capitalist landlordship is particularly important for us here. Such a relationship is defined and backed up by non-economic coercive force, of course, but it is not dependent on peasant unfreedom, for tenants can perfectly easily be legally free; it is their rent-paying (or labour-service) that defines their economic world as feudal, not their political subjection.

This definition of feudalism is certainly one that would be opposed by Mukhia. He sees feudalism as almost wholly specific to Europe, because he defines it as constituted above all by labour-service. Such a characterization is too restrictive, however. Apart from the fact that very little of medieval Europe would be feudal if it were so, it presupposes that labour-service constituted a landlordly control over the work-process different in *type* from that involved in the specification, say, of precise types of produce required as rent in kind. In fact, landlords did not often regard their demesnes as the places *par excellence* where they could closely direct the work-process of subjected labourers; peasants performed their labour-services according to the same locally determined procedures that they used in cultivating their own land. (Attempted control by landlords tended to be at the level of trying to dominate the process of determining such procedures; see pp. 92 ff.) There is a lot of interplay in Western history between different forms of rent – labour, kind, money; there is nothing to show that these were different economic systems. But the *set* of relations between landlord and tenant gives an analytical coherence to feudalism as an independent mode, and it is Hindess and Hirst's definition that I will use in what follows.[4]

3 Hindess and Hirst (1975). Useful critiques are in Carandini (1979a: 354–75), Cook (1976–7), Asad and Wolpe (1976). Their theory of knowledge is particularly unacceptable to historians; it is almost comforting to reflect how irritated they must be at the uses I and others put their models to.
4 Hindess and Hirst (1975: 221–55) (it is worth noting that they discuss labour rent extensively, but explicitly exclude that it *defines* the feudal mode – pp. 254–5); Mukhia (1981: 273–80). Mukhia has been criticized for his definitions and has defended them in *Compte rendu des séances de la société d'étude du féodalisme* (1979–80: 59). Capitalist rent is of course different, for it is market-determined; more and more of the peasantry of the world are coming into this sector. See Marx (1971: 614–39, 782–813) for the classic account.

It seems to me that feudalism was a world system. That is, not in the sense that it had to be because of some extra-historical teleology; but because *empirically* there have been few if any class societies that have not experienced some form of landowning and coercive rent-taking. This experience unifies Capetian France and *ancien régime* France and Russia and Sung China and Qajar Iran and the late Roman Empire and modern Guatemala. Anyone who looks at analyses of the experience of tenants in different places and times in world history must recognize the similarities – not just existential ones, but in the logics of the economic system of rent-taking compared. Sung China is *not* unfamiliar, unrecognizable, to Western economic historians; not in this respect, at least.

The standard counterargument is the clear and irrefutable statement that in all other respects these latter societies are rather unlike Capetian France; so their modes of production cannot be the same, that is, cannot be feudal. Anderson (1974: 401–31) has made the point at some length, and perhaps in the clearest manner; he is paralleled by many others, particularly by historians of the individual societies concerned. Sometimes the argument is beside the point, for the definition of feudalism is simply taken as being the existence of fiefs, vassals and military service based on contract; this is not and never has been a Marxist definition, and arguments of this kind are based on a simple misunderstanding. Anderson is more sophisticated; he certainly recognizes that a 'minimal' definition of feudalism, such as the one I have outlined above, could indeed cover wideish tracts of world history. What worries him, however, is only in part the inexactness of analysis he says results; it is that the unique Western development towards capitalism becomes inexplicable. He resolves the problem by *defining* a mode of production in terms of its superstructure – for feudalism, therefore, the political–military systems of vassalage and the rest. Paul Hirst (1975: 462 – feudalism as fiefs etc., see especially the discussion on 'Islamic feudalism') has effectively analysed the sleight of hand through which Anderson does this; in his words, 'This means that there can be as many modes of production as there are distinct legal–political constitutions and forms of extra-economic sanction which follow from them.' Anderson is here abandoning Marxism – indeed, abandoning systematic economic analysis (I'll leave it to the reader to decide which is worse).

But the problem need never have arisen. All these writers know and state that a single mode of production almost never defines a whole society (that is social formation). All of them as regularly forget it in their actual analyses, whether Hindess and Hirst on the Roman Empire or Anderson on China (contrast Anderson's skilful discussion of the relationship between modes in Russia, though). If feudalism is not necessarily the dominant mode everywhere that it is present, then the notable differences, especially in political system, between the vast range of societies where feudalism can be found, are more easily explained. Anderson's problem of the West's uniqueness (or primacy) is a lot less difficult to solve if his world is reformulated: the medieval and post-medieval West was one of the few societies where feudalism has *dominated*. Not that I am going to discuss, still less explain, the problem of the origin of capitalism here. Instead, as a realistic alternative to the task of characterizing all world history in 10,000 words, I shall restrict myself to a relatively narrow question: the relationship between two modes of production, characterized respectively by rent-taking and tax-raising, in a number of pre-capitalist state societies stretching west–east from Rome to China. I shall discuss the relationship between these two modes at two levels, that of the economy itself and that of politics and the state; I will thus for the most part exclude the problem of ideology. My other exclusion will be any discussion of other modes and their role in these societies, even the capitalist mode (potentially nascent in most of the societies I shall discuss) despite its evident importance for the classic problem of their 'blocked development'; indeed, I shall not dwell on problems of distribution at all. Often more significant an omission, however, will be the array of more primitive modes that these societies also contained, and which have often been of considerable relevance to their historical development (particularly what has sometimes been called the 'nomadic' mode; nomads conquered every Asian state I shall discuss at least once, and often several times; nomadism, in both exploitative and non-exploitative forms, is still an economic and social system of some importance and political weight in, for example, Iran).[5] Rent and tax have, however, been until the present century the major forms of surplus extraction everywhere in the states of Asia, and the relationship between the two is historically and analytically crucial; here must be the place to start.

Coercive rent-taking is the feudal mode of production; it represents the exploitative relationship between tenant and landlord, and it has been extensively discussed by generations of experts.[6] What is tax? What it is not is the traditionally defined Asiatic mode of production. There is no space to repeat the varying criticisms levelled against this category of

5 See the journal *Iranian Studies* for some current discussions; empirically, Lambton (1969: 140–4, 157–64, 283–94) is the starting point, together with a substantial anthropological literature. Asad (1979) attacks the concept of the nomadic mode as an independent category, pretty effectively. Nomads as conquerors – see conspectus and references in Crone (1980: 18–26, 215–23), and the warnings against over-enthusiastic use of Ibn Khaldun in Asad (1980: 456ff.).
6 Its economic logic is most clearly explicit in Kula (1976), though parts of this study are only specific to Polish feudalism; a brisk characterization can be found in Bois (1976: 351–6).

analysis and its less or (recently) more sophisticated advocates; it is sufficient here to state that one or other or both of autarkic village communes, and a tax-raising state owning all landed property and carrying out large-scale necessary public works, are actually rather rare. Indeed, the absolute predominance of state landed property, as we shall see, is a feature of societies so developed that village autarky and communality are effectively excluded, and the absence of classes, another traditional feature, is nonsensical. State irrigation, state landed property, and a tax–rent equivalence are present in different places at different times, but are rarely together. The Asiatic mode as it has always been formulated cannot be regarded as having any analytical validity.[7]

The real problem about the Asiatic mode is that it is too politically and legally specific. Like the private-justice-and-serfdom-and-labour-service version of the feudal mode, it has too many institutions arbitrarily attached to it for it to be of much help as an economic category. But the simpler relationship represented by a state bureaucracy taxing a peasantry is another matter. Samir Amin (1976: 13–58; cf. 1974) uses an alternative term, the 'tributary mode of production', and this gives him *carte blanche* to reformulate its elements without going eternally back to what Marx thought of Bernier and Kovalevsky; I will follow his example. (It will give me, too, *carte blanche* to depart where necessary from Amin.) A 'state class' based on a public institution, with political rights to extract surplus from a peasantry that it does not tenurially control, is certainly common enough in Asia, and not only in Asia. Since the Asiatic mode lost credibility, this pattern has often simply been regarded as a state version of feudalism, particularly by Soviet historians; but it is important to recognize that it normally *co-exists* with more typical feudal relations, those of landowners taking rent from tenants, and that taxation is always in an explicitly antagonistic relationship to such rent-taking – landowners do not want to pay taxes any more than peasants do. Tax and rent are thus frequently perceived as in opposition. That they are also opposed in their economic logics, as different modes must necessarily be, is less obvious; I will return to the question at the end (below, pp. 88–94) and try to set out how such an opposition works. In the intervening section I will take the tax versus rent antagonism for granted, and show how it is useful in explaining some specific societies and their

---

7 The vast historiography is best analysed in Sofri (1973) and Bailey and Llobera (1981); Dunn (1982) analyses and explicates the Soviet discussions. Attacks: Anderson (1974: 484–95, 548–9); Hindess and Hirst (1975: 178–206); and many empirical criticisms. One useful note (for the 'village autarky' aspect) is Owen (1975: 109–10) (cf. also Anderson, 1974: 489–90). The only general discussion of taxation I know (Ardant, 1965) is of curiously little use for its length – 1200 pages.

developments; this will give me a firmer heuristic position from which to discuss some of the problems that are left.

I started with an attempt to explain the fall of the Roman empire in the west, a full discussion of which I have published elsewhere. I posited the relationship between tax and rent there as being one between 'ancient' and feudal modes, the ancient mode in its class form being seen as a city-based subtype of the tributary mode. The ancient mode predominated over feudalism in the good days of the late Roman empire, through the fact that tax at times actually took more from peasants than rent, and (more important) through the dominance that the hierarchies of state office, and state financial handouts, had over the social relationships of the landed aristocracy, and even the relations between the latter and the peasantry. But the two modes were structurally antagonistic, even though the aristocracy participated in (and took the benefits from) both: in an underdeveloped economy, there is not much to do with wealth except put it into land, and land carried tax liability. As the aristocracy increased their landholdings, the state was less a benefit to them, and more and more a burden. When the state was threatened by Germanic invasion and settlement, the aristocracy and peasantry were unprepared to pay increasing taxes in return for less and less defence; the state simply broke up. The Germans found no tax-raising infrastructure left that was sufficient to allow them to maintain the major Roman expense, the standing army. The German armies settled on the land, becoming aristocracies and peasantries in their turn; although taxation took a century and more to disappear entirely, feudal relations dominated in western Europe henceforth.[8]

The key feature – one could indeed say peculiarity or particularity – of this account is the ultimate *failure* of the Roman state in the west when opposed directly to the landed aristocracy. It seems obvious to westernists: the civic aristocracies were closer to the land than the state was; they were locally powerful enough to sabotage tax-collecting by the state's functionaries – who were usually other aristocrats, in fact, in collusion; they extended their *de facto* protection against taxation to any free peasants prepared to become their tenants, and so on. The state was starved of funds and collapsed; perhaps the economy was too undeveloped to allow for large powerful states. But this did not happen even in the eastern empire (soon to become Byzantium), not to speak of Iran, China, and the innumerable Arab successor-states in the Middle East.

8 See Wickham (1984). I exclude the slave mode, which had almost totally vanished by the late Empire; I doubt it ever existed in the Old World as a mode outside the ancient Mediterranean.

Individual states had their bad times, or were replaced by others, but the state *itself* did not go away. Why not?

Let us start with China. One of the most striking features of Chinese history is by no means its uniqueness; it is, rather, its almost exact homology, often phrase for phrase in the books, with much of the development I have just outlined for late Rome. The difference is, of course, that the Chinese state did not collapse; to be more precise, it eclipsed, sometimes temporarily broke up, and then reformed, several times in the two millennia or so since unification in 211 BC. The 'dynastic cycle' occurred under the Ch'in and Han (221BC–AD 220), Sui and T'ang (581–907), Sung (960–1127/1279), Ming (1368–1644), and Ch'ing (1644–1911).[9] The recurrent nature of this cycle has always formed the basis for the false image of static Chinese history, which in reality, anyway until the Ming, showed a steady development in the political and ideological coherence of state structures, as well as in agricultural expansion and commerce (especially under the Sung and early Ming). But our concern here is the relationship between the aristocracy and the state, in so far as it can be sketched out in its full complexity from documentation that almost exclusively, until at least the Sung, comes from the state itself.

Recently, a considerable body of high quality socio-economic historiography on China has appeared in western languages, above all in English, and this makes our task a lot easier, if a little difficult to summarize in a few pages. One development during the whole of Chinese history that is now increasingly clear is the slow political absorption of the landed aristocracy in the state, which carries on across dynastic boundaries and times of trouble, independent of the expansion and contraction of aristocratic landowning in general. The aristocracy were older than the unified state, and the Han recognized the independent powers at least of the greatest aristocratic clans of the north. Such independence was certainly in part an ideological feature, in that such aristocrats did not depend on state office-holding for their self-definition; but we have reference to the effective political control they had locally, as well. The T'ang still recognized this ideological autonomy, in the aristocracies of both the north (the Yellow River) and the south (the Yangtse valley), but on the other hand they succeeded in recruiting the old northern aristocracies to the Imperial court as officials; so much so, that the great families of aristocrats actually died out when the T'ang

9 I shall not go back further than unification. The Yüan (Mongol) period (1263–1368) is a special case. I use the traditional Wade-Giles transliteration, as does all the English language historiography; the French and Germans have sensibly adopted the more accurate pin-yin transcription used now by the Chinese. A good brief traditionalist discussion of cycles can be found in Wu (1952).

fell after the 870s, and before the Sung recentralized China in the 960s–70s.[10] Under the T'ang, smaller local aristocracies all over China began to be systematically involved in state service (and thus the state financial patronage network), through the pseudo-meritocratic examination system; under the Sung, these became the whole ruling aristocracy, the 'bureaucrat-gentry' stratum, a vast (if fairly thinly spread) field of small to medium landowners, ready for state patronage, and in general dependent on state recognition as officials for the establishment of their places in local aristocratic hierarchies.

This pattern persisted and perfected itself. As late as the Ch'ing, when the western world was already closing in on China, its force can be seen in Chang Chung-li's calculations that the nineteenth-century gentry globally got nearly half its income from official pay and services, and only a third from land (the rest was from commerce). Here, the gentry look like a real state class, financially dependent on tax-raising, rather than an aristocracy. But these figures are only valid for the officials themselves, and not, for example, for their non-degree-holding kin. It would, indeed, be wrong to see the gentry of any period between Sung and Ch'ing as defined exclusively by their office, either in economic or political terms. Office-holders – even, or especially, those few who had risen from the peasantry – typically and consistently used their wealth, as in the Roman Empire, to buy land. The Sung period, the first period where the state really controlled the ideology and social hierarchies of the aristocracy, was also the great age of the establishment of large estates, mostly by officials using their new wealth while they had it and before they were replaced by other officials. A recent study of T'ung-Ch'eng county, part of the lower Yangtse plain, under the Ming and Ch'ing shows how such official families came to have real local power as a result of their landowning (and, of course, of the patronage possibilities of office), which persisted whether the family-members were in office or not. Even when subsumed into the state, these office-holding aristocracies valued local control that was essentially based on the feudal relationships functional to landowning. Indeed, when aristocracies became linked too tightly to the state, as were the old northern families of the T'ang, they could founder when the state did, as they had *lost* such a feudal base. Aristocracies in China, then, never ceased to be feudal, no matter how firmly attached they were to the state class and its vast cultural/

10 For this survey, I have focused on the T'ang historiography, based firmly on three generations of great Japanese historians, whose work is inaccessible to me; see, for a basic guide, *The Cambridge History of China* (*CHC*) (1979, vol. 3), the political history of the Sui and T'ang (vol. 4 will be on other aspects of the period). For the aristocracy, see Twitchett's introduction to *CHC* (8–31); Twitchett (1962, 1966, 1973); Ebrey (1978), and the older general economic survey in Maspéro (1959).

ideological apparatus (Confucianism, the literary ethic of 'mandarinism' and so on); or, if they did, they fell.[11]

Over time, again regardless of the dynastic cycle, the state became more powerful. The early (seventh-century) T'ang state was relatively small scale, based on landed peasant armies and with light taxation. This must indeed partly explain why the T'ang emperors (with some notable exceptions) recognized that the old aristocracy were necessary to the state even on the aristocracy's own terms; the T'ang did not have the strength to usurp, or even overawe, them. But – largely as the nomad threat to China built up, not for the first time – armies became salaried, and taxation rose. The bureaucracy, in other words the patronage-network that was beginning to incorporate the local aristocracies into the state, was also expanding fast; taxation rose further. This then ran into the classic pattern of the dynastic cycle: raised taxes resulted in networks of clientage, protection, tax-evasion, the weakening of the state. But the trend was slowly upward; the Sung re-establishment presupposed taxes that, though perhaps lower than in the late T'ang, were certainly higher (and better collected) than in the early T'ang; the late T'ang, Sung and Ming also benefited from systematic large-scale taxes on trade and minerals extraction. On the other hand, the scale of taxation can be exaggerated. By Western standards, formal taxes were never high: under the Ming, seldom over 10 per cent of crop even in the fertile Yangtse, where landlords could take 50 per cent of the crop as rent (though tax came out of this). The state had financial drawing-power because it took taxes from so vast an area, not because it took a lot of tax. And locally, even at the height of dynastic power, its officials had in practice to negotiate with powerful interests; government could not always be uncompromisingly coercive ('despotic'), even if potentially backed up by force.[12]

11 On Sung change and the fall of the old aristocracy see: Ebrey (1978: 87–119) (for the Po-ling Ts'ui); Johnson (1977: 50–102) (for the Chao-chün Li); both of these authors stress ideological changes more than I would. Post-Sung: Eberhard (1977: 205–16), for introduction; and especially Beattie (1979) on T'ung-Ch'eng, against Chang (1962).

12 The basic T'ang taxation book is Twitchett (1970). For the skeleton early T'ang state, ibid. [11, 104–6, 229–30]; *CHC* (12ff., 203–10) – though (134–8) the Sui in the preceding decades were organized enough to complete the Grand Canal with corvée labour. Note, too, that the Han and their pre-unification predecessors regarded 10 per cent as a minimum, and 20 per cent was common; the formal rate of exploitation and the power of the state did not necessarily go hand in hand. See Hsu (1965: 108–13), with caution. On low formal taxation under the Ming, see: Beattie (1979: 56–87, cf. 135–7) and Huang (1974: esp. 182–8). Officials frequently extorted rather higher rates, however. Taxation may even have got lower: see Perkins (1969: 175–8). On government by negotiation, see, for example, Beattie (1979: 67–80); for the T'ang, Twitchett (1976: 93ff.); for the small personnel of Sung bureaucracy and the resultant reliance on local elites to keep order, see McKnight (1971: esp. 3–10, 183–5).

China is a big country, with a lot of mountain land obstructing communications. Even though it should be recognized that my descriptions relate very largely to the two interlocking basins of the Yellow River and Yangtse, linked after 600 by a canal system, the size of the area is still vast, and difficulties of control were enormous right into the present century. This is clearly seen in the early centuries of central government, with long (if lessening) periods of breakdown in the face of foreign invasion and internal disorder, particularly in 220–589 and *c*.880–979. But even these years were ones of more or less effective *regional* states, not of the total breakdown of the state itself and the tax system. The collapse of the tributary mode, so visible, almost inevitable, in Rome, did not occur.[13]

The chief reason for this must have been the existence, in particular over much of the North China Plain, of a free land-holding peasantry. In the north, even in the Ch'ing period, there was relatively little landlordship; the stronghold of estates has always been the more fertile Yangtse valley. Though there were certainly strong aristocratic families in the north at least until the T'ang, the trend of scholarship is to stress the dominance of a free peasantry in the Yellow River valley throughout historical times. The northern plain was perhaps too poor to attract the concentration of estates of the Yangtse delta. But, as a result, it has always offered an easier locus for state exploitation; there are fewer landlords to undermine the tributary mode. The state, even at its weakest, even when fragmented into warring provinces as after the Han and after the T'ang, was always able to tax.[14]

The dynastic cycles, when they are looked at more closely, thus take on a slightly different form: not the rise and fall of strong government, but the expansion and contraction of the scale of *centralized* government. The political core of the Chinese state was always in the poorer and more 'egalitarian' north; the post-Han and post-T'ang periods see the shrunken 'legitimate' state surviving there, and one might almost say experimenting with new forms of state organization that might act as a springboard for the reconquest of the richer and more feudal south. The Toba Turks of the fourth- to sixth-century north began to generalize the so-called *chün-t'ien* or equal-field system, the state-sponsored land

13 The problematic is best expressed in Elvin (1973: 17–110). Cf. also Perkins (1969: 169–82).
14 For figures for the last century or so see Perkins (1969: 85–110), and Chang (1962: 144–5). I overgeneralize in my counterposition of 'north' and 'south' – there were many exceptions. On estates in the Yangtse, see: Lewin (1973: 66–150), Elvin (1973: 69–83), Beattie (1979: *passim*). On the state always being able to tax, see: *CHC* (514–22) (C. A. Peterson on provincial government *c*.750–880); Wang (1963); and the fairly awful Schafer (1954), on tenth-century Fukien. The latter two *show* state and provincial taxation, rather than analysing how it survived.

redistribution that underlay the landed armies of the early T'ang; the Five Dynasties (907–60) reshaped the sclerotic late T'ang bureaucracy and recentralized the provincial armies of the north, to serve as the basis for Sung reunification. When the emperors reconquered the south, on each occasion they discovered that the south had developed economically in its independence, which they were then able to exploit; the Sung takeover and exploitation of southern development clinched central government power for nearly a millennium.[15]

So: which mode was dominant? Some historians have tended to stress the lightness and weakness of central government, and attribute the failure of China to break up in a feudal manner entirely to the force of Confucian ideology among the upper classes. But, although it may seem that central government was by no means financially onerous in world terms (even if the poor of the north would have found even 10 per cent of crop excessive), individual private ownership was never, in any period, able to destroy its structure. Landlords, however extortionate, only ever controlled a minority of China's peasants, concentrated in the centre-south, and they too were in world terms quite notably small-scale owners. There were few aristocrats (after 880 perhaps) large enough to envisage a firm feudal alternative to the public tax-raising of the tributary state – although they were certainly always happy to evade or expropriate it on a small scale where they could. Even when central government broke down, often in the face of generalized peasant revolts, aimed at state and landlords alike (the 880s, the 1350s, the 1630s),[16] government and taxation still survived in the north. One might expect the breakdown of the tributary mode in front of the feudal mode to be found, if anywhere, in the independent tenth-century kingdoms of the Yangtse delta, where feudal power was strongest; it would be interesting to have a study of the states of Wu and Nan T'ang, for example. But otherwise, the tributary mode remained dominant – ideologically, certainly; economically, probably (indeed, total tax perhaps surpassed total rent in all periods); politically, without doubt, for the landlord class was always too divided, and over the centuries became even more so, as average aristocratic holdings tended gradually to diminish in size. The state could thus always give aristocrats more than they could get on their own.

15 On Toba (Northern Wei) and other dynasties, see: Ebrey (1978: 17–20, 24–9), Elvin (1973: 34–61). On Five Dynasties, see: Wang (1963: *passim*), Twitchett (1973: 79), Eberhard (1977: 195–204), building on his idiosyncratic *Conquerors and Rulers* (1952).
16 *CHC* (R. M. Somers) is unhelpful on the 870s–80s risings (for example, p. 723): they aren't 'peasant rebels', but 'bandits' (cf. Eberhard, 1952: 54–64). It would be a bit much to expect twentieth-century social consciousness in the ninth century, though (cf. Hobsbawm, 1972). They terrorized everyone, perhaps, but they certainly killed many landlords. This is one of the points at which the absence of Chinese historians in *CHC* becomes particularly obvious.

The tributary mode dominated the social relations of production: the peasantry were always nominally free tax-payers, and the aristocracy and gentry accepted the ground-rules of the hierarchies of the state. But the feudal mode was always there, ready when appropriate to undermine it.[17]

This underlying framework to Chinese historical development shows the pattern I want to explore very clearly. The dominance of the tributary mode over the feudal mode characterizes, in my view, the relation between state and landowners/peasants in most traditional state societies. Let us pursue it in the case of our second example, the Arab empire and its successors in the medieval period. I shall in fact focus less on the period of the Arab empire proper (636–945) than on its Iranian and Turkish heirs in the tenth to twelfth centuries, for the latter period is a relatively low point for state power in general, and is quite well documented and studied; there are some good test cases for the problem of state survival. I shall concentrate on the kingdoms of the Buyids (945–1055) in western Iran and Iraq, the Ghaznavids (994–1040) in north-eastern Iran (Khurasan), and the Saljuqs (1037–1157), rulers of the whole Middle East, and survivors after the mid-twelfth century in several areas of western Iran and Turkey until their final supersession in the thirteenth century by the Mongol Ilkhans.[18] These states, different enough in detail, had one socio-political feature in common that is of relevance here: unlike in the Roman and Chinese empires, where a roughly homogeneous aristocratic class participated in the profits of both state and landownership, in most of these 'Islamic' states a state class clearly stood in opposition to an aristocratic class of local landowners. There was certainly overlap, but the two were socially and often ethnically distinguishable, and frequently antagonistic in ideology, as well as in their economic base.

The origins of this counter-position are easy enough to explain: they are the product of conquest, first by Arabs, then by various waves of Turks, and eventually Mongols. Each new regime had a new armed backing which represented the military power of that state for the century or so of its rule over some part of the Arab empire. It is always, then, the army that is most clearly distinguishable from the local civil aristocracy. Central government in its civil sense, by contrast, the bureaucracy that ran the states and their taxation, was more continuous. Though this too was seen in opposition to local power, there was here rather more overlap in personnel; civil bureaucrats had to come from somewhere. Thus

17 Vietnam fits into this pattern, too, following Le Tranh Khoi (1972).
18 Dates are approximate. I shall in what follows stick to Arabic spellings and terminology, for greater consistency, rather than their Persian/Turkish/Mongol variants, except when it would be ridiculous. All diacritical marks have been eliminated.)

Nizam al-Mulk (Aubin, 1966: 325), the great vizir of the Saljuqs
(1063–92), and the greatest lay theorist of government of his century,
was of a local landowner (*dihqan*) family from Baihaq in Khurasan, rising
through Khurasani civic office to central (and almost absolute) power.
Such roots are normal. But the military elites were not so rooted, or not
so often, and it is this fact that gives the period its flavour (see, for
example, Crone, 1980; esp. 82–9; Shaban, 1976).

The Arabs conquered parts of the east Roman (Byzantine) empire and
the whole of the Persian (Sassanian) empire, both states with a long
tradition of tax versus rent, and of military and civil officials who were
themselves landowners. The Byzantine empire had been institutionally
decentralized in the Roman sense (see pp. 95 f), but the Arabs changed
that; like the Sassanians (and like the Byzantines themselves from now
on), their empire was administered and taxed centrally, from the capital.
Exactly how the Sassanian state worked socio-economically is very
obscure; it seems that tax was collected by the lowest stratum of the
aristocracy, the *dihqans*, who ranged in wealth from rich peasants to
substantial local landowners. Presumably they had the force to collect tax
from the free peasantry, still a considerable group, but not from the *de
facto* exempt greater nobility, who could be very large owners indeed
(with dependent tenants, both slave and free). The Arabs settled their
ethnic armies, with some tensions, but left the *dihqans* alone. Indeed,
they still used them as tax-collectors, especially in Khurasan, although
the organization of taxation was eventually bureaucratized. There were
considerable local differences in the extent to which the Arabs left the
social structure alone, particularly as regards the position of the upper
nobility (in noble-dominated Iran, almost totally; by contrast, the equally
rich aristocracy in Egypt soon vanished, its lands falling to the state). But
the major changes were in central government and the army; traditional
private landowning remained the basis of *local* power into the tenth to
eleventh centuries, and beyond. The Arab rulers maintained substantial
state lands, too, though these fluctuated in size, as some were handed out
in small blocs in effectively full ownership, *qati'a*, mostly to ethnic Arabs
(a feature of the early period), and as others were seized back at times of
dynastic change.[19]

Few large, centrally run, pre-capitalist states have been able to do

19 On taxation, see: Løkkegaard (1950: 168–72) for survival of *dihqans*. *Dihqans*, etc.,
under the Sassanians: Christensen (1944: 111–13), Pigulevskaja (1963: 133–58),
Lambton in *Encyclopaedia of Islam* (*EI²*) [1960–], *s.v.* Complexity of Arab conquest
Dennett (1950), Shaban (1970: 5, 19–21, 91–2, 96–7, 129–30), cf. Asad (1980: 464–7).
Qati'a: Cahen (1953: 26–8). Landowning patterns after the conquest: Cahen (1954),
Lambton (1947–8), a reference I owe to Martin Hinds. Kennedy (1981), which I only
read at a late stage of preparing this article, is the most sophisticated discussion of the real
complexities of pre-tenth-century state power I have seen.

without tax-farming, and that of the Arabs was certainly no exception. Tax-farming, however, is dangerous to central government, as it can too easily be turned into private power. So it was with the Arabs. And increasingly, from the ninth century on, the concept of tax-farming was extended to the army. In the tenth century the Buyids began to adopt the procedure of granting their soldiers *iqta'*, the right to exact tax from particular areas, instead of part or all of their pay. This was generalized under the Saljuqs, and became the predominant governing principle for the remuneration of the army in the whole Islamic world for many centuries. Much has been written about the *iqta'*. There is a long argument about whether it is 'feudal' or not, for example, in the sense of western military feudalism (answer: yes, sometimes, but it depends on time and place).[20] Claude Cahen, who dominates the historiography, discussed at some length its classic development; he pointed out the easy procedures by which a *muqta'* (*iqta'*-holder) could usurp all the powers of the state, privatize them, and turn the tax payable from estates to him as *muqta'* into rent paid to him as landlord, especially as *iqta'* became hereditary in the twelfth century or so. Indeed, in a classic western-style development, a *muqta'* was able to extend his non-taxpaying privileges by persuasion or coercion to his neighbours, in exchange for their land. Cahen tends to assume in his discussions that all taxpayers are peasants, even though we know that there were many private landlords who could presumably have resisted the privatization of *muqta'* powers more effectively. Nevertheless, the development (or its potentialities) is clear: the tributary state was tending towards feudalism, this time meant in Marxist terms.

States, of course, resisted. They often redistributed *iqta'* and made sure for as long as possible that they were not hereditary; they kept the bureaucracy of tax-assessment in their own hands. *Muqta'* did not reside on their estates, so this, at least, decreased the immediacy of their possession. Nevertheless, the failure of states lay in their growing incapacity to maintain such controls. Hereditary *iqta'*, as in twelfth-century Syria or the fourteenth-century Ilkhanate, is a sure sign that the state is weak.[21] If we read the laments of central government bureaucrats in such periods, we might marvel that the state ever survived at all. Tax no longer comes into the exchequer; central authority over far-off provinces is growing weak. Tax is turning into rent; private and local

20 Cahen (1953) is still the touchstone after thirty years. See also *idem* in *EI*², s.v.; Lambton (1969: 31–76 and *passim*; 1967); Poliak (1936), among many general surveys. I will use *iqta'* as both singular and plural, and likewise other words in Arabic.
21 Egypt is the exception: here, the Ayyubid and Mamluk state from the late twelfth century onward maintained *iqta'* as entirely fiscal (Cahen, 1953: 45–8; Rabie, 1972). Egypt is easily controlled politically, being all flat; state landowning was high.

lordship is replacing public power. There are even hierarchies of *muqta'*, linked by private bonds of loyalty. We can see the same process, indeed, in the late (thirteenth- to fifteenth-century) Byzantine empire, where it is in fact better documented. There, it is arguable that the state was falling to feudal patterns by the time of the Ottoman conquest. But the Islamic states did not. Possession of *iqta'* never became ideologically separated from a recognition of the tax system; it never became *simply* landholding. Partly, this is because the scale of *iqta'* concessions has sometimes been exaggerated; rulers kept a sizeable proportion of tax-raising in their own hands and those of their more dependent civilian tax-farmers.[22] But it is also because Middle Eastern society was more locally complex and diverse than central government documents admit.

Recently, there have been some good studies of local elites in the cities of northern Iran and Khurasan in the tenth to eleventh centuries, particularly Nishapur, based on local urban and lineage histories. The city focus of these histories is not misleading, for the areas were very urbanocentric: all important landowners, and many less important ones, lived in cities. (The religious focus of the histories is more misleading, but cannot be helped.) From these, it is clear how decentralized social life in a wide-spaced and thinly populated society such as Iran actually was. Urban patrician elites (*a'yan*) genuinely controlled Nishapur, Bayhaq, Qazvin. Though not formally self-governing, they were at least legally autonomous in the sense that there was no appeal from the local judge, the *qadi*, who was almost always chosen by and/or from the local elite. There is dispute as to how organized local government was (the urban headman or *ra'is* is a particularly shadowy figure, though of crucial importance to the city and its relation to the state, and again almost always from the *a'yan*), but it is clear that local power was sufficiently coherent to be worth fighting for – local factionalism was rife in all these cities. And the state, even in the figures of the strongest rulers like Mahmud of Ghazni or Nizam al-Mulk, had to respect the cities and their factions – heavy intervention led to disloyalty. These elites were based very largely on landowning; although religion and commercial wealth were also status indicators and indeed ladders up into the patriciate, landowning was the base that every *a'yan* family had, or obtained as soon as possible. Landowning and local power were inseparable; every major

22 Cahen (1953: 50–1). There were taxes on commerce too, that the state held on to better. *Muqta'* elites in fact constantly were replaced, as states recovered their power or were overthrown by new ones (cf. n. 25). This is not because *iqta'* were legally precarious, though they were – so were European fiefs, after all – but because states could obtain (i.e. pay for) sufficient armed strength to do so. It is an expression of state power, not its cause. It should anyway be remembered that the turnover in individual aristocratic *families* in western Europe was almost as great, without threatening global feudal dominance.

local owner was in a position to be an important figure in one of the factions of the urban arena. Economic and social power in these cities was thus ultimately feudal, despite a considerable commercial (and ideological) element. But it was all civilian. The *iqta'* developments described above do not visibly enter into it at all.[23]

In part, this division must be because there are as yet no systematic analyses of the political interrelation between the central power-structure and the local elites. It is as if they belonged to two separate worlds. They cannot have done, of course; the central elites cannot have been quite as deracinated as they sometimes seem. But we do none the less have two separate tendencies to feudalism in the one society, one the decentralization and privatization of central government tax-raising, and the other the continuing independence of private civilian landowning. They were distinct, and in structural rivalry. The state actually benefited, as 'honest broker' between factions.[24] This on its own cannot explain the state's survival, of course; it is too contingent an explanation. As I have said, a major element in the political survival of states has to have been their continuing control over at least some of the tax wealth of their localities. The local angle on the Iranian political system does, however, show that the picture of total dominance by *muqta'* is incomplete, for local differences, and local elites, are left out of account. And, on the other hand, the break between land and central government (military) power in the successor states meant that land on its own did not bring automatic rights to direct rule. There was less incentive to reject the opportunities and responsibilities of civil or military office and go it alone as a landowner: power was still defined in central government terms, and office (or more *iqta'*) was still in the gift of the state. Local power was in the hands of the urban elites, but few of them attempted independence – they had no armies. The only solution for the disloyal was to re-invent central government locally (a development aided when, as became common, whole provinces and their administration were handed out in

---

23 Aubin (1966); Bosworth (1973: 163–200) (the Ghaznavids did not use *iqta'*), Bulliet (1972) – cf. review by Mottahadeh (1975); Mottahadeh on Qazvin and Bulliet on Nishapur in Richards (1973: 33–45, 71–91); Bulliet (1978), the neatest survey, Cf. also Kennedy (1981) for an earlier period. Note that in the late Mamluk state, where local landowning was in the hands of *muqta'*, the state's men (and under considerable central control), cities were far less independent, and heavily subject to local state (emir) patronage (Lapidus, 1967).

24 Mottahadeh (1980) is the only systematic analyst of Buyid state *vis-à-vis* civil society, almost entirely from the standpoint of ideology. He claims that people needed the state (175–90), against, for example, the implications of some of Bulliet's work. He also stresses the informality of many of the structures of local power (123–74); but I suspect he may be too influenced by Lapidus's work, which is dealing with a rather different socio-political power structure (see n. 23). Later parallels for the state as broker: see Abrahamian (1974).

iqta' to governors). Central government breakdown in Iran and its neighbours, as in China, thus meant the establishment of regional states on the Baghdad model, not the end of the state (and its tributary underpinning) itself.[25]

Tax rates varied greatly. In ninth-century Iraq, Adams calculates that one-quarter to one-third of gross grain crop went in tax, a considerable figure; in the thirteenth century, tenants still paid this, and another third to their landlords. In neighbouring Khuzistan in the latter period, though, tax was apparently only at 10 per cent and rent up to 50 per cent. We cannot produce global figures for each, for, quite apart from the chance nature of the survival of these rates, we cannot even guess at how much land was held by landlords at any period; we can thus draw no general conclusion about the relationship.[26] This is unfortunate, for the global extent of aristocratic landowning and the general relation between rent and taxation is of obvious importance for the power of the state, as the contrasting experience of Rome and China shows. In Iran, we must accept that this quantitative aspect of the analysis is closed to us. But the key qualitative aspect for state survival is the state's continuing control over the terms of the relationship between aristocrat and peasant; this, as we have seen, can be studied, and it is arguably more important.

Whether peasants themselves ever saw tax and rent as separable, especially as it was the responsibility of the landowner to divide them and pass the tax on, is in doubt; the implications of this I shall return to below. But on one type of land, peasant perception would have been correct: on state land there cannot have been any structural difference between tax and rent at all. And in one area of the Middle East, Saljuq and Ottoman Turkey, this becomes a crucial fact, for there, unlike anywhere else, almost all the land belonged directly to the state. How the state came to take over all the land is not fully clear, but it certainly lay in the chance circumstances of conquest, and is thus not relevant here as a problem. (See Turan, 1948; Cahen, 1954–5; 1968: 173–89; Beldiceanu-Steinherr, 1976.) It is a theoretical possibility, of course, in any state

25 Continual conquests from the steppe and the deserts, though contingent, did help periodically to re-establish the state in the Middle East, especially Iran, and to undermine independent landowning. The deserts *were* close, after all (as they were not in western Europe). An extreme is Ibn Khaldun, in fourteenth-century North Africa, who states flatly that landowning is *worthless* without state protection (1958, vol. 2: 283–6 = Bk.IV §§ 15–16). But North Africa is particularly exposed to nomad pressures – Ibn Khaldun's whole theory of history is based on this fact.

26 Adams (1965: 101–2); Petrushevsky (1968: 525–6). This latter is the basic analysis of the peasantry, a marvellous article, shortened from his book in Russian (1960); cf. also F. Nomani (1976; 1977). Peasants were tied, but free; no other 'feudal' controls were put on them – there were no demesne labour services; all corvées were for the state. There were no general statistics in Iran as late as the twentieth century (Lambton, 1969: 266).

society. Indeed, many societies regard all land as nominally owned by God (= the community, = the state), as the Arab legists did, as the Saljuqs did even outside Turkey, and as indeed Zoroastrian and Confucian ideology enjoined. Under normal circumstances, however, this has no meaning, for private landowning persists without interruption. It certainly does not mean that such societies are 'Asiatic', as is often said; William the Conqueror claimed no less full ultimate ownership, and indeed exercised his eminent rights rather more seriously, without being any less the emblematic feudal monarch, in all senses. But the Saljuqs in Turkey, and, still more, the Ottomans, went beyond this: they did not merely have eminent rights; they owned. This difference does not turn on legal prerogatives; it turns on *power*.[27] In Turkey, the state had the political strength to maintain its rights to all land as the state *and* as the immediate landowner, real and uncontested for centuries. In its doing so, all relationships that can be called feudal in Marxist terms withered; it is in many ways legitimate to see post-eleventh-century Turkey as the purest tributary society. I shall end my descriptive section with a discussion of how this seems to have worked.

The Ottoman state owned more or less all the land of Anatolia and the Balkans: at its height, in 1528, some 87 per cent (of Anatolia only?), on Inalcik's figures.[28] Ottoman peasants paid no rent; only tax to the state. But the fifteenth- to sixteenth-century state assigned over half of this back, in *timars*, to their *sipahi* cavalry, called in the fiscal context *timariots*. Whether the *timar* was a direct descendent of the *iqta'*, or of the *prónoia*, the parallel Byzantine institution, is not important; the function of the *timar* was the same as both (names proliferate after *c*.1500: the Mongol–Iranian *tuyul* and the Mughal *jagir* are the same institution). *Sipahis* lived on the land, however, on their *timars*. *Timars* were not hereditary, and could be transferred; such transferrals became less and

27 *Contra* Anderson (1974: 424–6, 497–9, 522), for whom the tight legal forms of Roman property law are a real cause of capitalist development, against feudal, Islamic, Chinese vagueness. The Ottomans would sin here, more than anyone else (cf. ibid.: 387–8) – and, indeed, western representatives in the nineteenth century worked hard to introduce private property into the Turkish empire. But the expropriation of rivals, and its converse, security of property, depend less on legal rights than on power – ask any Russian landowner after 1917. Limits to the powers of rulers do exist, but they are seldom delineated by the legal system. Cf. also n. 31.
28 Inalcik (1973: 110). The rest was mostly *waqf*, charitable estates incorporated by Islamic law for religious purposes, though in practice often acting as lineage foci for the aristocratic families that controlled them (like Chinese lineage charities and western proprietary monasteries). This, at least, was feudal; but *waqf* remained a minority element in Ottoman landholding, even after their eighteenth-century expansion. They were relatively numerous in the Balkans, and were something of a basis for the survival of ethnic landowners (Zakythinos, 1976: 38–42, 110–14; Demetriades, 1981; these references I owe to A. A. M. Bryer). However see Anderson's warning footnote (1974: 386).

less common, however, especially after 1550 or so. The fact that the
sipahis lived locally and took crops directly produced an unusually close
link between them and their tied (but 'free') peasants, reinforced by the
wide powers delegated to *timariots*: local justice and policing, the right to
exact private corvée service, control over land and produce sales. *Timars*
were, however, never entirely privatized, or even immune from central
government; the state always kept up its fiscal registers.

The Ottomans doubtless realized the feudalizing dangers of the *timar*
system, and, when military technology changed, making the *sipahi* system
less useful, they moved away from it. After the late sixteenth century,
therefore, the Ottomans began to use a salaried army; *sipahis* declined in
importance (not without the occasional revolt, with peasant support, in
the early seventeenth). The state farmed out taxes to civic entrepreneurs
instead. Tax-farmers were, initially, less hereditary, more civilian; this
soon began to change, as indeed it had to – unarmed tax-farmers were
not always able to collect taxes at all. By the end of the seventeenth
century they too could have private armies, and be *de facto* hereditary.
Their most spectacular representatives became in the eighteenth century
derebeys, valley lords, controlling entire provinces and often groups of
provinces, in effect as hereditary princes of mini-states. More significant,
though, was the importance given by tax-farming and local influence to
an entire urban stratum, the local rich, still called *a'yan*, notables; this
stratum in the late seventeenth to nineteenth centuries was autonomous
from the state, maintaining its traditional intermediary role between state
and civil society. The *a'yan* were also the first to adapt to the possibilities
of capitalism in the outside (western) world. Under their influence, the
concept of the landed estate, *çiftlik*, reappeared in the Balkans and
western Anatolia in the eighteenth century, after centuries of eclipse, as
an organizing device, oriented towards commerce: a notable concession
to privatized control, and, significantly, in the areas most open to the
West. But the state had not given up. Mahmud II in the 1820s to 1830s
moved against these decentralizing forces; he overthrew or curbed the
derebeys, he confiscated much *a'yan* land, he reassumed all surviving
timars. His success was not complete (Muhammad 'Ali, himself from the
a'yan, was almost completely successful in a similar politics in Egypt, by
contrast), but it was substantial. The nineteenth century proceeded with
a continual struggle between state and notables as to how far private
property law should be accepted, and whom it should benefit; but even
the weakened (and commercially undermined) Ottoman state of the late
nineteenth century could at least hold the notables to a standoff until the
First World War.[29]

29 The analysis closest to mine is that of Islamoğlu and Keyder (1977), who also stress
ideology and commerce, themes I am ignoring. They see the Ottomans as 'Asiatic', as

Of course, the feudal elements in this are obvious. The Ottomans could not hold on to an entirely centralized power-network in so underdeveloped an empire, even in the Turkish heartlands. The tendency to privatization implicit in all decentralized local power was a tendency, as elsewhere, towards direct personal control of the land, the feudal mode. But it was not complete; in fact, genuine feudal appropriation barely began before the late eighteenth century. And the Ottoman state was always strong and sophisticated enough to be able to reassert its power, in the late fifteenth century, the mid-seventeenth, the early nineteenth. It never lost its control over the rules of political legitimacy. Its local rivals, though strong, never managed to establish local power-structures that were anything other than versions and perversions of the powers delegated to them by central government. The classic article on nineteenth-century urban notables by Hourani, though it emphasizes their substantial autonomy, also points up the informality and ambiguity of the political arena in which they were operating, in between the 'state class' and the urban commoners and peasantry. Their power was the manipulation of the state; it did not establish itself with its own political terrain, unlike notable power in Saljuq Khurasan, or gentry power on the Yangtse. Feudal landed power was too weak; the patronage potential of the state too vast to allow deviation from it. Real local independence was once again only possible by usurping the powers of *central* government – and, in Muhammad 'Ali's Egypt, actually using them more effectively (Hourani, 1968).[30]

That this was a matter of power rather than legal form is best seen by looking to nineteenth-century (Qajar) Iran. The Safavids and Qajars also seriously claimed rights to the ownership of all land, though their legal justification for this ran back to an increasingly hard interpretation of Islamic law, rather than to the state's occupation of all the land, as in Turkey. But they could not maintain it. Iran was too underdeveloped; its communications were too sketchy. Aristocracies, based on *tuyuls*, could rise or be pulled down, but the state always in practice had to recognize them as real landowning aristocracies, and they acted themselves as if they were. The politics of urban notables, as a recent study of Maragheh in Azerbaijan shows, were in principle independent of the state and, quite simply, functional to landowning. Even *tuyuldars* were now often

does the more quirky Divitçioğlu (1969). General social development: Inalcik (1973: 104–18); Gibb and Bowen (1950, I.i: 235–75), Beldiceanu (1980: 743–53), Inalcik (1977); articles on A'yan, Derebey, Kara 'Othman-oghli, in *EI²*, s.v.v.; Owen (1981: 10–44, 58–64), Karpat (1968).
30 Inalcik, too, for the previous century, stresses that *a'yan* are informal – when given official posts, they cease to be *a'yan* (1977: 32). Cf. also Owen (1981: *passim*), e.g. for Egyptian contrasts.

Chris Wickham

seen as landowners not tax-farmers, and the sources show that there had also, somehow, by the nineteenth century come to be landowners with close to full private title once more. The state had to negotiate; it could not dominate, for its army and bureaucracy were too weak. One has to recognize that the Qajars, and even their shortlived eighteenth-century predecessors, did this rather well, controlling local elites with intelligent brokerage, and maintaining the existence and influence of central power and taxation through a period of increasing penetration of capitalism, and right into the twentieth century; but the pattern of relationships is more reminiscent of Iran in the eleventh century than Turkey in the nineteenth. Legal title or no, the Iranian rulers had to recognize that landlordship was feudal, and defend their tributary power--base accordingly.[31]

Turkey and, to a lesser extent, Iran were the Asian states best known to Marx's predecessors. Marx knew India better, and indeed India seems to me to fit into this array of patterns without difficulty. But Marx's conception of Asian state power was largely formed from the second-hand images he received of Ottoman power and legal rights. The absence of private property in land seemed to him an extraordinary representation of the most primitive of social forms. And so, maybe, it is. But it should be clear that only an unusually *developed* economic and political system was actually capable of maintaining it. Only the 'Islamic state' at its most centralized and sophisticated, at its most uncompromising, was able even to try to stop landed property from being *de facto* privatized, from falling back into feudalism. The Ottomans could do it; the Qajar state, far less politically and economically developed, could not. Tributary states thus normally co-existed with feudal ownership; they had no choice. The extreme social forms of the Ottoman world that underlay what Marx sometimes called the 'Asiatic' mode were in fact at the opposite end of the run of human history from where he supposed. 'Static' is the least adequate adjective for the development towards the Ottoman state.

I have so far concentrated broadly on 'socio-political' history, rather than

31 This analysis, I have to admit, is contested; I am using Lambton (1969: 105–77; 1977), Abrahamian (1974), M.-J. DelVecchio Good's local study (1977), and, for the similar problems of the Safavids in the sixteenth century, Aubin (1959). Against, there are the 'anti-feudal' analyses, varying in approach, of Ashraf (1970), and Katouzian (1981: 7–26), an extreme proponent of the 'all property is precarious' school (and why do so many people, studying in all parts of Asia, harp on about partible inheritance inhibiting the establishment of aristocracies – thus here, p. 15? – it didn't stop anyone in early medieval western Europe). I owe much insight on Iran, as well as references for nn. 29–31, to discussions with Joanna de Groot.

'socio-economic'. Peasants have not appeared as often as they might. This is not because historical development *lies* in the history of the state, as Anderson would sometimes imply. It is because, first, the problem of characterizing Asia has always lain in the remarkable coherence of its state structures ('despotism', as it is still, astonishingly, often called, without any pretence of analysis of what this might mean – indeed, the very word represents an abstention from sociological analysis). It is because, second, the problematic of the tributary mode of course concentrates on the state; and because, third, the way state exploitative mechanisms persisted amazes me as a westernist, and it is the reasons for this that I originally sought to explore. I have tried to characterize one particular opposition, between tax (the state) and rent (private feudal landowning), principally at the political level of my various social formations. The rest has gone by the board, particular, the real productive and commercial developments in these very different societies that give the lie to most of them being economically static in any sense.[32] Neglected, too, has been the ideological level of state dominance, over what is now often called 'reproduction'. This is unfortunate, but inevitable in view of the space it would take to describe such articulations; it would anyway be presumptuous of me to try to dot the t's of descriptions of societies all of whose primary evidence, and an increasing amount of whose secondary analysis, is written in languages I cannot read. I will finish with two problems. The first is the real difference between tax and rent, as keys to the characterization of modes with separate economic logics; the second is the general one of the survival of the state. The first is the presupposition for my whole argument, of course; the second is the locus of my original interest.

The problem of tax versus rent is twofold. The first is their surface aspect: the two are sometimes difficult to tell apart, and sometimes, as in the Ottoman state, even fused. The second is the latent reason for this: that both are modes of surplus extraction based on peasant production, individual or collective. Seen existentially from the peasant standpoint, there might seem not to be a lot of difference between them in that they are both unnecessary outgoings enforced, ultimately, by extra-economic coercion of various kinds. The peasant's perception of this equivalence is most evident when he is also the tenant of a landlord, for in most tax-raising societies (though not all), tax under these circumstances is passed

32 Cf. Elvin (1973) and Anderson (1974: 520–46), for China, and the points raised by Hirst (1975: 452–3). Feudalism did not produce capitalism; it produced capitalism *first*. But the dominance of the feudal mode lasted well over a millennium; to allow the tributary mode two millennia or more does not seem to prove that it is static in any absolute sense. (Let us hope that these timescales do not represent some unrecognized economic law for the dominance of all modes.)

on by the landowner, who has extracted it in the rent-taking process. As a result, there is a strong if varied body of experts who do not distinguish between tax and rent at all, or, to be more exact, who see them as centralized and decentralized (public and private) variants of the same economic system, which most of them call feudal. A good percentage of Soviet scholars would say this, for example; so would Amin, though he calls the whole mode tributary; so, from different positions, would the French Byzantinist Éveline Patlagean.[33] This is certainly a better stance than that of those who have a much more Western-based definition of feudalism, and try and fit Asia to it, even though almost all of world history would thus come under the same heading. But the major problem about this formulation is that its presupposition is that all extra-economic surplus extraction from a peasantry has to have the same economic form; has to be the same mode of production. Is this really true?

I have excluded and will continue to exclude political and legal definitions from my counterpositions. Public versus private is a convenient shorthand, but it derives from the ideological superstructures of a social formation, and cannot define an *economic* opposition (tenth-century western Europe, for example, surely the society where the feudal mode was more overwhelmingly dominant over all rivals than ever before or after, certainly maintained a clear notion of the public). The formal constitution of the state, and the legal characterization of landed property, are equally superstructural, although they can at least give us guides as to where to look. What matters for the constitution of states, as I have emphasized, is not so much law as power, and its origin, the nature of the state's economic resources; only by studying this can the separate identity of state(/tax) *vis-à-vis* landlords (/rent) be explored.

States do not only tax peasants; they characteristically tax landlords too, at least in that they take a percentage from the surplus the landlord has extracted (not always a massive one, we may recall). One arena in which tax is thus very definitely opposed to rent lies in the structural antagonism there is between the state (unless it is itself a feudal state[34])

33 Dunn (1982: esp. 20–2), a warning against this tendency by Kovale as early as 1931; Petrushevsky (1968: 514–15, 536–7), Amin (1976: 15–16), Patlagean (1975). Cf. Hindess and Hirst (1975: 223–5), who see the equivalence, but show that it is different from their feudal mode. Wolf (1982: 79–88) sees the differences between centralized and decentralized state systems, but too easily subsumes them into a single tributary mode covering Europe, Asia and much of the rest of the world. His analysis is highly sophisticated, however, and is strong on commerce, which I have left out of this article.
34 As the Absolutist states were in the early modern West, on which see the sharp synthesis of Anderson (1974: 15–59). They taxed, of course, as did many feudal states from late Saxon England and the Italian communes onwards. Such taxation is generally regarded as a concentrated version of feudal rent, and no one doubts the general dominance of the feudal mode in such societies, but it seems to me inescapable that some of my discussions should be relevant to them.

and the landed aristocracy, or – with the Ottomans – the would-be landed aristocracy. Take a very small tributary state, a city-state, say, and a large private landed estate. Social relations in these two are very different – indeed, ironically, the reverse of the traditional Asiatic:feudal opposition. It is in the latter that there is one sole owner and power-focus; in the former, there will characteristically be independent exploitative powers, landowners, inside and subject to the tax-raising state apparatus and its associated state class. A tributary state is thus both economically and socio-politically more complex than a feudal estate. This is at least a more solid contrast that the legal one. The feudal mode can exist without the tributary mode, but the tributary mode cannot exist without the feudal mode, except in extreme circumstances, when it continually has to fight off the feudalization of some of its local institutions; its history is the history of the resultant antagonisms.

The political contrast between East and West could even stop here. But if we are to establish a *modal* difference between tax and rent, then it must lie in the relationship between the alternate exploiting groups and the peasantry. [This is a rough restatement of the classic formulation that the mode of production is an articulation of productive forces and social relations of production, though the level is a little different: peasant production and peasant society certainly cannot be reduced to the level of technique and the simple appropriation of the products of the soil, that constitute the productive forces – see, most clearly, Cohen (1978: 28–62).] The contrasts in such relationships lie in social distance and in control.

Taxation by a state is mediated and formalized. The state needs surplus, but in a fairly abstract manner. That is, not so abstracted that any surplus will do: cash is now needed, and now kind. The state may intervene to keep peasants on the land, cultivating and paying taxes; but it is not in the state's purview to control the process of production. If it does, it does so in a very generalized way: the semi-mythical 'hydraulic state', for example, or the organization of colonization and clearance, or the periodic redistribution of land that underpinned the armies of the early T'ang in China. The actual *production process* is not touched by these: neither what is grown, nor the social organization of production. The lack of structural relationship between the state and the presuppositions of production is well illustrated by the state irrigation system of Sassanian Iraq, maintained by the early Arab state, but allowed to fall into disuse from *c.*900 onward, with the resultant abandonment of large parts of the region. The state, here actually the creator of the conditions of existence of a peasantry, seems to have ceased to care, as a contemporary put it, whether or not the land was in cultivation (Adams, 1965: 71–89, 87–9). The distance of the state from civil society is here clear. States can sometimes benefit the lives of subject peasantries;

equally, and more often, they may tax so heavily, or (as in tenth-century Iraq) administrate so ineptly that the country is laid waste, without their coming close enough to their subjects to notice it, or without their understanding global economic processes well enough to realize that it is ultimately counter-productive.

Hindess and Hirst attacked the 'Asiatic mode' as a concept, largely criticizing traditional elements of the mode, such as the absence of property-owning, which I have already rejected. But they are particularly hostile to the idea that a mode can be coherent if it allows for more than one set of productive forces to articulate with a set of relations of production (or vice versa). This definition of a mode must be rejected as too restrictive. (Indeed, it caused them so many problems that they now oppose the concept of mode of production altogether.) The tributary mode as I define it certainly allows peasants in their villages to organize production however they like, in the same way as it allows landlords to co-exist with it. There can thus be a whole variety of types of co-operation persisting in such villages, arrays of organization of production from the individual to the totally communal that could often have pre-existed class exploitation, but are now systems in articulation with, and dominated by, the tributary state, as part of the whole social formation. The state does not need to control the economic and social lives of its subjects; it just needs the funding that enables it to pursue its chosen objectives. It is in this area that we find class struggle between the state and its peasantry (and indeed its landowners): in the amount of tax payable, especially when it is felt that there are no adequate returns.[35]

Landowners relate to peasants more closely. Their interest is not just in the amount of surplus, though this is important enough; it is in the recognition of local power, local control. Indeed, the major test for whether the local representatives of a state class have become feudal is whether this local control has become more important for their wealth and self-definition than has their relationship upwards to the state. But this control is not just political, that is coercive; it extends to involvement in production itself. This involvement is structural rather than necessarily conscious; landlords are not always, or even frequently, *interested* in production. But their control very typically extends to some of the crucial presuppositions for production – mills, sometimes plough teams in the West; canals in Iran or China. Sometimes, surplus-product is extracted under quite tight supervision, for example through demesne-farming, although this supervision tends to be counterbalanced by peasant

35 Hindess and Hirst (1975: 193–200): cf. Hindess and Hirst (1977), and Asad and Wolpe (1976: 482–4). The state absorbing and exploiting pre-class relationships is nicely discussed for the Incas in Godelier (1977: 63–9) – setting aside the problem of the exactness of Godelier's empirical categorization of the Incas, which is contentious.

customary practice. And, everywhere, landlords control access to the land, even if in practice how much power this gives them is very variable, and largely dependent on the strength or weakness of peasant resistance. These last two points show that landlords do not have uncontested powers over their peasants. Indeed, when they do try to influence production, they do not always succeed; it is the peasant, after all, who actually does the producing under feudalism. Recent work tends rather to emphasize the autonomy of peasants and village communities *vis-à-vis* landlords, even – and especially – with respect to the process of production. But the peasants have to fight for it. It is thus in this arena that class struggle tends to happen between peasants and landlords; over the control of the productive processes, and, at a more mediated level, over the conditions in which one side or the other might be able to exert such control: protection of local customs on the one hand, judicial subjection on the other (Hilton, 1973: *passim*; Brenner, 1976; cf. Hindess and Hirst, 1975: 233–55). Sometimes they fight over the amount of rent, too, as in the arena of tax; but it is over the control of production that the dynamic of class struggle in feudalism is most acute. In fact, at points of economic conjuncture for other reasons, such struggle can lead out of feudalism altogether. When peasants lose, they can be reduced to the total subjection of plantation slavery, or the total economic control represented by capitalist agriculture based on wage-labour (or, in the latter context, they can be expelled from the land altogether, to form the proletariat of the expanding cities of eighteenth-century England); when they win, as in twentieth-century Albania or China or Cuba, socialist relations can ensue (in the earlier period, peasant victory was rare; in late medieval Switzerland, success resulted in a partial return to *pre*-class, not *post*-class, relations of production).

The focus of class struggle is a pointer to the internal economic logic of modes. The state under pressure will attempt to increase the intensity of exploitation; the landlord is as, or more, likely to attempt to increase his influence over the productive process. Landlords are also more likely to respond to opportunities, as well as pressures, by increasing surplus extraction – so in Kula's Poland, early modern lords responded to a developed grain market by maintaining as high a degree of control over agriculture as they could, through demesne farming. (Pre-capitalist states were, by contrast, very reluctant to expropriate surplus so as to put it on the market, except for redistributive purposes, such as when both Rome and China moved grain around to alleviate famine, not always very effectively.[36]) In one sense, one can say that the difference between the

---

36 Kula (1976). So feudal lords were more receptive to market forces than were tributary states. They were also less able to control and ideologically englobe merchants and the

ruling classes of the feudal and the tributary modes is between the relative separation of the former and the near-total separation of the latter from the processes of production (just as, on the other side, the capitalist mode entails total control by owners over such processes). But this does not mean that the tributary mode involves no economic relationship at all between ruler and ruled; the link is not just arbitrary, based on the motiveless extraction of surplus. The state has economic objects, and its taxation can increase or decrease according to its success in achieving them. Warfare is one of the most obvious examples. Offensive war is, as has often been pointed out, an economically productive resource for a successful state; defensive war is one of the few activities of the state that is genuinely regarded as useful and necessary by its subjects. And indeed, it is after military failure that struggles over tax-paying tend to be the most acute; when, that is to say, the state is not fulfilling a major function. The difference between feudal and tributary is not, then, one between presence and absence of structural relationships, economic logic versus lack of economic logic; there is a *positive* contrast in the methods and aims of economic interventions inside the two modes. And it is for this reason, too, that state tax-raising and coercive rent-taking by landlords cannot be conflated. They represent two different economic systems, even if they can come together in some exceptional circumstances. Their differences, their antagonisms, lie in their divergent interventions in the peasant economy, just as their convergencies lie in the fact that both are rooted in it. The same productive forces, however, can be seen as giving rise to two separate modes of production.

Finally, let us return to the survival of the state in Asia: to the maintenance of the dominance of the tributary mode in various social formations, despite its continual undermining by feudal relations. We have seen how in China a reserve of free peasantry to whose surplus only the state had access is one of the keys to how tax-raising could survive even in adversity; otherwise, it largely dominated through the fact that landowning was small scale (although in many areas globally extensive), so that the patronage network and military protection of the state was always of greater value to local gentry than any uncertain local independence might have been. The Arab and post-Arab states were perhaps more complex, and explanations are anyway not helped by a greater vagueness in the modern historiography; but, as we have seen, decentralization certainly led to an accumulation of states on a smaller scale rather than to the abolition of state structures themselves. Even though the processes of tax-raising devolved to local tax-farmers, states

artisanate than Asian states were, though they certainly tried to do so when they could. These factors have obvious links to the classic issues around the rise of capitalism.

always maintained the power to recentralize them periodically, or at least to ensure that they were not privatized out of existence. Some states found this a lot easier than others (Mamlūk Egypt, sixteenth-century Turkey, nineteenth-century Egypt, as against Iran in most periods), but all found it *possible*.

I have not discussed the origins of these various versions of tributary social formations, and the problem would not be closely relevant to the patterns I have been trying to delineate. But origins may be of relevance to the one obvious failure among these secular successes: the Roman empire in the west. The historical origins of the Roman empire lay in the difference between the city as an institution and the countryside, expressed initially, in the early Republic, in the existence of public landed property, to be enjoyed by all citizens, in opposition to the private property they also possessed. This is the core of the ancient mode, which was (at least ideally) a pre-class economic system; but when the Romans began to conquer everybody else, the public part of the state, originally largely in land, came to include tribute as well. In the context of Mediterranean economic history, this can be treated as the ancient mode in its class aspect, the city exploiting the countryside and, indeed, other cities, who were exploiting their countrysides in turn (Hindess and Hirst, 1975: 106–8; Wickham, 1984, for all that follows.) But from an Asian standpoint, there is certainly no structural, modal, difference between this and the classic tributary states. The only organizational difference is that in the ancient mode tax-raising was devolved to local public bodies, the nominally independent cities of the Roman empire. The specific city-state origins of the tributary mode in the Roman empire thus left their trace in a particular institutional identity, which is sufficient for the characterization of the ancient mode as an identifiable subtype. The decentralized city society of the empire was the key not only to tax-raising, but to the whole society and ideology of the ruling classes, straddled between their access to state patronage and their local landowning, which in the west could be very great indeed. Cities were the foci of taxation; and also the centres of all aristocratic life, with formal institutional autonomy. In all these respects they were very unlike Chinese cities, or indeed Arab and Iranian cities, which, although major social foci, had no autonomy or tax functions.

In these respects, even the most autocratic of Roman systems, the later empire of the third to sixth centuries, was more decentralized than any eastern state. And it is these respects, in particular the local control over taxation, that were most fatal to the Roman empire. When it hit military crisis, in the fifth century, the empire in the west broke up, in effect, into its urban components; and each component was controlled by aristocrats who no longer had the economic interest to participate in raising taxation

that did not benefit them (for Roman armies were being defeated) and
which was being taken largely from their own estates. Late Roman urban
aristocracies in western Europe were civilian and conquerable, once the
central government of the empire began to fail, just like eleventh-
century aristocracies were in Khurasan, by Germans and Turks
respectively. But local Roman aristocracies as organized bodies, that is as
a (feudal) class, had their hands on the very structures of tax-raising;
local Iranian aristocracies, despite some individual involvement in tax-
farming, did not. The Romans sabotaged the whole system; by the time
the Germans established organized successor-states, taxation was barely
possible. The feudal mode *had* to dominate henceforth. It is scarcely
surprising that when the surviving east Roman (Byzantine) state faced its
own crisis in the seventh century and held it off, at least partly because its
landowners were smaller, one of the casualties in reorganization was the
decentralized city-based tax network. Byzantium henceforth headed
down a road more like that of the Arab states, with the antagonism
between tax and rent expressed in terms of centre versus periphery; and
this enabled it to survive for centuries. Tax-farming was dangerous to
states, because of its localizing feudal potential; but it was not as
ultimately fatal to their survival as the *institutional* decentralization of
taxation, and the consequent entrusting of tax-raising powers, auton-
omously, to the very people most structurally opposed to it, the feudal
aristocracy.

In returning to the problem of the survival of states, through a
recognition of the differences inherent in the Roman empire, I have put
the problem in a different perspective from that standard for Westernists:
it is survival that is the norm, failure that is the deviation. Indeed,
Westernists must respect the empires of Asia for their recuperative
powers, against the extraordinary inbuilt disadvantages of their vast size
and appalling communications; we are not entitled to use this as a stick to
beat them with ('Oriental despotism', 'stasis', 'stagnancy'). What their
peasantries thought is a different matter, of course. But the basis for their
survival was their continuing force as motors of surplus extraction, even
in the presence of structurally antagonistic feudal aristocracies, more or
less ready to replace them in a hierarchy of dominance, if it ever became
possible (and it seldom did). It is at the posing of this antagonism that my
analysis has been directed.[37]

37 A fair amount of empirical work on the topics covered in this essay has been published
since I wrote it in 1983, but I have not seen anything that contradicts my basic arguments.
As to theoretical work, I should like to draw attention to an important and useful critique
by Halil Berktay, 'Is "tax vs. rent ′ necessarily the product and sign of a modal difference?',
Journal of Peasant Studies, xiv (1987).

References

Abrahamian, E. 1974: Oriental despotism: the case of Qajar Iran. *International Journal of Middle East Studies*, 5.

Adams, R. M. 1965: *Land Behind Baghdad*, Chicago.

Amin, S. 1974: Modes of production and social formations. *Ufahamu*, 4, no. 3.

1976: *Unequal Development*, Hassocks.

Anderson, P. 1974: *Lineages of the Absolutist State*, London.

Ardant, G. 1965: *Théorie sociologique de l'impot*, 2 vols, Paris.

Asad, T. 1979: Equality in nomadic social systems? Notes towards the dissolution of an anthropological category. In *Pastoral Production and Society*, Cambridge.

1980: Ideology, class, and the origin of the Islamic state. *Economy and Society*, 9.

Asad, T. and Wolpe, H. 1976: review of Hindess and Hirst (1973), *Economy and Society*, 5.

Ashraf, A. 1970: Historical obstacles to the development of a bourgeoisie in Iran. In M. A. Cook (ed.), *Studies in the Economic History of the Middle East*, London.

Aubin, J. 1959: Études safavides I. Sah Isma'il et les notables de l'Iraq persan. *Journal of the Economic and Social History of the Orient*, 2.

1966: L'Aristocratic urbaine dans l'Iran seldjukide: l'exemple de Sabzavar. *Mélanges R. Crozet*, 2 vols, Poitiers, vol. 1.

Bailey, A. M. and Llobera, J. (eds) 1981: *The Asiatic Mode of Production*, London.

Beattie, H. J. 1979: *Land and Lineage in China*. Cambridge.

Beldiceanu, N. 1980: Le Timar dans l'état ottoman. In *Structures féodales et féodalisme dans l'occident méditerranéen*, Rome.

Beldiceanu-Steinherr, I. 1976: Fiscalité et formes de possession de la terre arable dans l'Anatolie préottomane. *Journal of the Economic and Social History of the Orient*, 19.

Bois, G. 1976: *Crise du féodalisme*, Paris.

Bosworth, C. E. 1973: The Ghaznavids, 2nd edn. Beirut.

Brenner, R. 1976: Agrarian class structure and economic development in pre-industrial Europe. *Past and Present*, no. 70.

Bulliet, R. W. 1972: *The Patricians of Nishapur*, Cambridge, MA.

1978: Local politics in eastern Iran under the Ghaznavids and Seljuks. *Iranian Studies*, 11.

Cahen, C. 1953: L'évolution de l'iqta' du IXe au XIIIe siècle. *Annales E.S.C.*, 8.

1954: Fiscalité, proprieté, antagonismes sociaux en haute-Mesopotamie. *Arabica*, I.

1954–5: Le Régime de la terre et l'occupation turque en Anatolie. *Cahiers d'histoire mondiale*, 2.

1968, *Pre-Ottoman Turkey*, London.

The Cambridge History of China 1979 (*CHC*): vol. 3, ed. D. C. Twitchett, Cambridge.

Carandini, A. 1979a: *Archeologia e cultura materiale*, 2nd. edn, Bari.

1979b: *L'Anatomia della scimmia*, Rome.

98   *Chris Wickham*

Chang Chung-li 1962: *The Income of the Chinese Gentry*, Seattle.
Christensen, A. 1944: *L'Iran sous les Sassanides*, 2nd edn, Copenhagen.
Cohen, G. A. 1978: *Karl Marx's Theory of History, A Defence*, Oxford.
Compte rendu des séances de la société d'étude de féodalisme, 1979–80, nos 3–4.
Cook, S. 1976–7: Review of Hindess and Hirst (1973). *Journal of Peasant Studies*, 4.
Crone, P. 1980: *Slaves on Horses*, Cambridge.
DelVecchio Good, M.-J. 1977: Social hierarchy in provincial Iran: the case of Qajar Maragheh. *Iranian Studies*, 10.
Demetriades, V. 1981: Problems of landowning and population in the area of Gazi Evrenos Bey's waqf. *Balkan Studies*, 22.
Dennett, D. C. 1950: *Conversion and the Poll Tax in Early Islam*, Cambridge, MA.
Divitçioğlu, S. 1969: Modèle économique de la société ottomane. *La Pensée*, 144.
Dunn, S. P. 1982: *The Fall and Rise of the Asiatic Mode of Production*, London.
Eberhard, W. 1952: *Conquerors and Rulers*, Leiden.
1977: *History of China*, 4th edn, London.
Ebrey, P. B. 1978: *The Aristocratic Families of Early Imperial China*, Cambridge.
Elvin, M. 1973: *The Pattern of the Chinese Past*, London.
Encyclopaedia of Islam 1960– (*EI²*) Leiden.
Gibb, H. A. R. and Bowen, H. 1950: *Islamic Society and the West*, Oxford.
Godelier, M. 1972: *Rationality and Irrationality in Economics*, London.
1977: *Perspectives in Marxist Anthropology*, Cambridge.
Habib, I. 1978: Economic history of the Delhi Sultanate. *Indian Historical Review*, 4.
Hilton, R. H. 1973: *Bond Men Made Free*, London.
1979: Towns in English feudal society. *Review*, 3.
Hindess, B. and Hirst, P. Q. 1975: *Pre-Capitalist Modes of Production*, London.
1977: *Modes of Production and Social Formations*, London.
Hirst, P. Q. 1975: The uniqueness of the West. *Economy and Society*, 4.
Hobsbawm, E. J. 1972: *Bandits*, 2nd edn, London.
Hourani, A. 1968: Ottoman reform and the politics of notables. In Polk and Chambers (1968).
Hsu Cho-yun 1965: *Ancient China in Transition*, Stanford.
Huang, R. 1974: *Taxation and Governmental Finance in 16th Century Ming China*, Cambridge.
Ibn Khaldun 1958: *The Muqaddimah*, trans. F. Rosenthal, 3 vols, London.
Inalcik, H. 1973: *The Ottoman Empire*, London.
1977: Centralisation and decentralisation in Ottoman administration. In Naff and Owen (1977).
Islamoğlu, H. and Keyder, C. 1977: Agenda for Ottoman history. *Review*, 1.
Johnson, D. 1977: The last years of a great clan. *Harvard Journal of Asiatic Studies*, 37.
Karpat, K. H. 1968: The land regime. Social structure and modernisation in the Ottoman empire. In Polk and Chambers (1968).
Katouzian, M. A. H. 1981: *The Political Economy of Modern Iran*, London.
Kennedy, H. 1981: Central government and provincial elites in the early

'Abbasid Caliphate. *Bulletin of the School of Oriental and African Studies*, 44.

Kula, W. 1976: *An Economic Theory of the Feudal System*, London.

Lambton, A. K. S. 1947–8: An account of the Tārīkhi Qumm. *Bulletin of the School of Oriental and African Studies*, 12.

    1967: The evolution of the iqta' in medieval Iran. *Iran*, 5.

    1969: *Landlord and Peasant in Persia*, 2nd edn, Oxford.

    1977: Tribal resurgence and the decline of the bureaucracy in the 18th century. In Naff and Owen (1977).

Lapidus, I. M. 1967: *Muslim Cities in the Later Middle Ages*, Cambridge, MA.

Le Tranh Khoi 1972: Contribution à l'étude du mode de production asiatique: le Viêt Nam ancien. *Studi storici*, 13.

Lewin, G. 1973: *Die ersten fünfzig Jahre der Song-Dynastie in China*, Berlin.

Løkkegaard, F. 1950: *Islamic Taxation in the Classic Period*, Copenhagen.

McKnight, B. E. 1971: *Village and Bureaucracy in Southern Sung China*, Chicago.

Marx, K. 1964: *Pre-Capitalist Economic Formations*, London.

    1971: *Capital*, vol. 3, London.

Maspéro, H. 1959: Les régimes fonciers en Chine. *Recueils de la société Jean Bodin*, 2.

Mottahadeh, R. P. 1975: Review of Bulliet (1972). *Journal of the American Oriental Society*, 95.

    1980: *Loyalty and Leadership in an Early Islamic Society*, Princeton.

Mukhia, H. 1981: Was there feudalism in Indian history? *Journal of Peasant Studies*, 8.

Naff, T., and Owen, R. (eds) 1977: *Studies in 18th Century Islamic History*, Carbondale.

Nomani F. 1976: Notes on the origins and development of the extra-economic obligations of peasants in Iran, 300–1600. *Iranian Studies*, 9.

    1977: Notes on the economic obligations of peasants in Iran, 300–1600. *Iranian Studies*, 10.

Owen, R. 1975: The Middle East in the 18th century. *Review of Middle Eastern Studies*, 1.

    1981: *The Middle East in the World Economy 1800–1914*, London.

Patlagean, E. 1975: 'Economie paysanne' et 'féodalité byzantine'. *Annales E.S.C.*, 30.

Perkins, D. H. 1969: *Agricultural Development in China 1368–1968*, Edinburgh.

Petrushevsky, I. P. 1960: *Zemledeliye i agrarnyye otnošeniya v Irane XIII–XIV vv.*, Moscow.

    1968: The socio-economic condition of Iran under the Īl-Khāns. In J. A. Boyle (ed.), *Cambridge History of Iran*, vol. 5, Cambridge.

Pigulevskaja, N. 1963: *Les villes de l'état iranien*, Paris.

Poliak, A. N. 1936: La féodalité islamique. *Revue des études islamiques*, 10.

Polk, W. R. and Chambers, R. L. (eds) 1968: *The Beginnings of Modernisation in the Middle East*, Chicago.

Rabie, H. 1972: *The Financial System of Egypt 1167–1341*, London.

Richards, D. S. (ed.) 1973: *Islamic Civilisation 900–1150*, Oxford.

Rodinson, M. 1974: *Islam and Capitalism*, London.

Sahlins, M. 1974: *Stone Age Economics*, London.

Schafer, E. H. 1954: *The Empire of Min*, Tokyo.

Shaban, M. A. 1970: *The 'Abbasid Revolution*, Cambridge.

1976: *Islamic History: A New Interpretation*, vol. 2, Cambridge.

Sofri, G. 1973: *Il modo di produzione asiatico*, 2nd edn, Turin.

Soviet Studies in History 1966: vol. 4, no. 4.

Turan, O. 1948: Le Droit terrien sous les seldjoukides de Turquie. *Revue des études islamiques*, 16.

Twitchett, D. C. 1962: *Land Tenure and the Social Order in T'ang and Sung China*, London.

1966: Chinese social history from the 7th to the 10th centuries. *Past and Present*, no. 35.

1970: *Financial Administration under the T'ang Dynasty*, 2nd edn, Cambridge.

1973: The composition of the T'ang ruling class. In A. F. Wright and D. C. Twitchett (eds), *Perspectives on the T'ang*, New Haven.

1976: Varied patterns of provincial autonomy in the T'ang dynasty. In J. C. Perry and B. L. Smith (eds), *Essays on T'ang Society*, Leiden.

Wang Gungwu 1963: *The Structure of Power in North China during the Five Dynasties*, Kuala Lumpur.

Wickham, C. J. 1984: The other transition: from the ancient world to feudalism. *Past and Present*, no. 103.

Wolf, E. R. 1982: *Europe and the Peoples without History*, Berkeley.

Wu Ta-k'un 1952: An interpretation of Chinese economic history. *Past and Present*, no. 1.

Zakythinos, D. A. 1976: *The Making of Modern Greece*, Oxford.

5

China as a Counterfactual

Mark Elvin

This brief chapter makes a single theoretical point about explanations that have been offered, and could be offered, for the appearance of 'modern' economic growth in Europe during the eighteenth and early nineteenth centuries. Its essence, expressed abstractly, is that it is both necessary and possible for historians to be more precise about just what it is that has to be explained than they have been hitherto, and that explanatory theories must be explicitly related to this explicandum. The procedure by which the increase in precision is achieved is a comparison with China at two points in time, *circa* 1100 and *circa* 1800. This is because Chinese economic culture at both these points, though in ways that have important differences, possessed most of the characteristics that are commonly thought necessary for an endogenous 'modern' revolution in the means of production, but did not in fact have one at either date. The delicacy of the theoretical problem raised by the need to separate the European and Chinese cases is then illustrated in specific terms by a study of mechanized spinning.

Assumptions

'Improved' technology is the one indispensable component of a revolution in production. It is neither a sufficient cause in itself, nor does it arise independently out of previous technology. In virtually every case there is an interplay of cause and effect between it and other social, political, economic and cultural conditions. But it is, so to speak, the eye of the needle through which progress must pass. The concept of 'improvement' is not easy to define in any ultimate sense, because of

Mark Elvin

practically unforeseeable feedback loops. These can occur in production
(for example, environmental degradation and technologically generated
hazards to health), in destruction (for example, the shift in military
relationships from the defence/defeat spectrum to the deterrence/
catastrophe discontinuity), or in life-conservation (for example, the
overuse of antibiotics causing the unintended selection of resistant
strains of bacteria), or between these three sectors. For convenience in
exposition, 'improvement' will be taken in the naïve sense of the creation
of more output per some unit of input (whether labour, capital, energy or
a resource such as land). 'Technology' will be taken broadly, including
even organizational capacity, Liebenstein's X-efficiency, and the like.
Essentially it will be thought of as the point of juncture of the abstract
and the concrete (e.g. the relationship between blue-print and working
machine), and of economic and other social forces on the one hand and
conceptual capabilities on the other (a view which tends to see crisis and
opportunity as the parents of invention).

China *circa* 1100

By about 1100 the Chinese economy had what was, by the standards of
the rest of the pre-modern world, an advanced agriculture. There was
virtually no fallowing. There were crop rotations, multi-cropping, and
seeds selected for varying environments and maturation cycles. There
were extensive irrigation systems, both gravity-fed and machine-fed, and
a variety of agricultural machines such as seed-drills. The population
supported by these means was, according to recent estimates, well in
excess of 100 million. Where geographically feasible, both riverine and
sea transport were highly developed, as a result partly of improving
natural rivers and building hundreds of miles of canals, and partly of
advances in ship construction, such as water-tight bulkheads and the use
of iron nails, and in navigation, such as the use of the mariner's compass.
The economy had a high level of monetization (including the use of
fiduciary money). There was a network of markets based preponderantly
on exchange-generated exchanges rather than on the spending of money
derived through taxes and coercion-rents, though both of these of course
also existed. There were widely used practices involving written contract
and mercantile credit. Urbanization was high by mediaeval levels
(perhaps 6 to 7 per cent in cities of over a hundred thousand), and the
largest cities may have had close to a million inhabitants at times.
Woodblock printing of books and the civil-service examinations seemed
to have sustained a respectable if unquantifiable level of literacy; and
works published on everyday mathematics, and the spread a couple of

centuries later of the rod-and-bead abacus, suggest a measure of useful popular numeracy. Military technology in East Asia at this time advanced rapidly under the pressures of the multi-state system. The Chinese and their rivals innovated in the military use of iron, gunpowder, flame-throwers, siege-engines and the like. Chinese science and scientific instrument-making had a number of triumphs, such as hydraulic astronomical clockwork.

The implication of this picture is that Chinese economic culture had already passed through most of the barriers that may be thought of as 'difficult'. By any reasonable definition it was to a high degree rational, based on quantified calculation, and contractual-transactional. The important exceptions were a somewhat unpredictable state disciplinary system in place of what we would recognize as a proper legal system, and substantial areas of tenant-serfdom in the rural economy. But the extensive presence of rational, free, market-based behaviour shows that this latter is merely a precondition for a 'modern' type of economic growth, not a unique precursor of it, from which it can be assumed to grow almost automatically in due time.

The second implication is that the use, by historians, of the attribution of virtually unchanging cultural characteristics as the key to discriminating between China and Europe as regards patterns of long-term economic growth must be ruled out. The same set of characteristics cannot be held to be responsible for China both (1) having on most counts the most advanced, as well as the largest, economy in the mediaeval world, and (2) having failed thereafter to develop of her own accord in most qualitative respects. This is in no way to rule out cultural characteristics as elements in an explanation, but merely to insist that they are likely to have changed somewhat over time or to have had different effects at different times because embedded in different complexes of other factors, economic, political, and so forth, at these times.

In brief, statics have to be rejected in favour of dynamics, a style of analysis much harder to handle.

The Chinese Economy *circa* 1800

Major technical advances ended in China after the early fourteenth century, but from the sixteenth to the early nineteenth there was a flow of small improvements and importations from outside. Examples are humidity-conserving spinning-cellars, wind-driven pumps, oilcake ferti-lizers, the flywheel cotton-gin, large egg-incubators, reading-glasses, and New World crops such as maize and sweet potatoes. If anything, these modest changes were a stabilizing factor, for example by reducing the pressure of a growing population to some extent. Quantitatively there was a massive growth. In demographic terms, the Chinese population of 1800 was of the order of four times that of 1100.

The main factors that can be easily identified as having changed in China between the two dates seem to have been these. (1) Because of the expansion of the population and earlier resource-exploitation, easily accessible resources per head had declined (not just farmable land, but wood, coal, and iron as well). (2) Most pasture had been 'arableized', and this had led to what was certainly a relative decline in the numbers per person of large animals (the forerunners of inanimate engines), and possibly an absolute decline, as pastures vanished. (3) The external stimulus from war had declined once the Mongols had been expelled, and China less and less existed in a multi-state system, but instead dominated her neighbours. (4) The social repression of women increased (the spread of foot-binding being both a symbol and symptom of this phenomenon). One can only speculate, but it is not unreasonable to suspect that this may have adversely affected the intellectual formation of children during their early years.

China around 1800 was more or less caught in two complementary traps. The first, which is shown in figure 1, was the familiar low-level

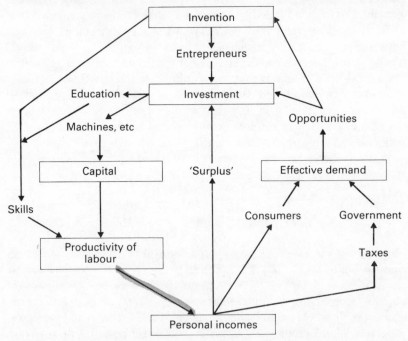

Figure 1 The low-level productivity equilibrium (relative to labour)

productivity equilibrium, though Chinese markets were much larger than exponents of this theory usually regard as normal. The diagram is most conveniently read starting with the 'productivity of labour'. If this is 'low', it is clear that 'lowness' spreads through the rest of the system in a self-reinforcing fashion.

The second trap was the less well-known pre-modern high-level technological equilibrium, which is shown in figure 2 for the crucial case of farming, though an analogue was applicable also in the case of inland water-transport.

The basic assumptions behind this theoretical construct are: (1) that there is a technological discontinuity between 'pre-modern' and 'modern' farming techniques (the main criterion being scientific and industrial inputs); (2) that China in 1800 had come close in most regions to the per-hectare maximum for pre-modern farming; and (3) that, with the exception of Manchuria, there was no significant amount of accessible but still unused land of farmable quality. The argument then goes on to postulate that invention and innovation are most commonly induced by a rapid change in demand (whereas a slow rate of change often permits incremental adjustments within existing technologies), and

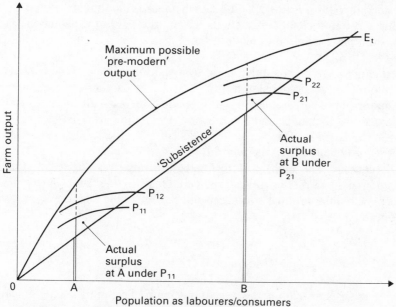

Figure 2 The high-level technological equilibrium trap (relative to farmed land, assumed constant)

are facilitated by a rapid rate of change in supply (notably the provision of raw materials). Where agriculture is the predominant sector, as it was for China in 1800, as population growth pushes the farming system towards the point of high-level equilibrium (E_t), the maximum possible increase in surplus above 'subsistence' (defined in any of the ways reasonably possible), which is achieved by raising the level of actual practice to universal use of the best available technology, drops first in per caput terms, then in absolute terms, and finally becomes zero. Thus both the stimulus to technical change (considered here as taking the form of rapidly increasing demand) and the capacity to support it when it originates in other sectors (especially by supplying extra raw materials) grow weaker and then vanish. Capital formation also becomes more difficult, though not impossible (in a sustained fashion) until E_t is reached. Exploitation – in the form of taxes, rents, and other levies – may also perhaps tend towards or oscillate around an equilibrium point at which the extra output resulting from the extra hours worked by farmers (at least at peak periods) beyond what would be their leisure-preference point in an unexploited economy is offset by physical weakness due to reduced food supply and impaired health, which reduce output. There is no obvious way of testing whether this was or was not the case historically, but if it was it would clearly block off an important possible source of rapid change, namely increasing the level of exploitation (as, for example, Stalin did in modern times with increased inputs of labour in the USSR).

It should also be noted that the growing absolute scale of the Chinese economy in late-imperial times, and probably its share of the world economy up to some time after 1800 made it increasingly impervious to the external demand-stimuli and supply-facilitation afforded by foreign trade. This trade was, of course, much of the time subject to various forms of limitation by state control.

Eventually the high-level technological trap was broken by the introduction of modern Western technology in the later nineteenth century, but the residual effects can still be seen in the Chinese economy even today.

Mechanized Spinning

If the focus is turned up, the case of mechanized spinning can be shown to illustrate many of the general points made in the previous sections. Figure 3 shows the water-powered belt-drive hemp-spinning machine described by Wang Chen in 1313, and the 'filatorium' or 'torcitorium' shaped like a rotating lantern equipped with fliers that was used for

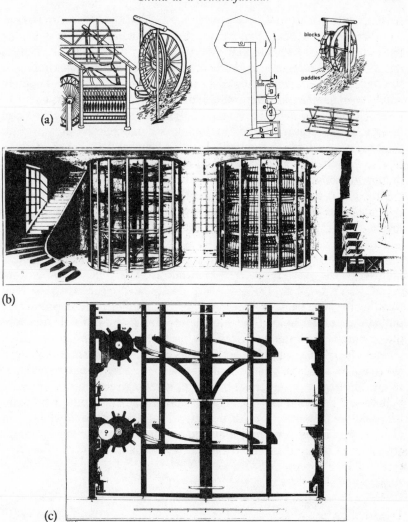

Figure 3 (a) A large water-powered hemp-spinning machine described by Wang Chen in 1313. Redrawn from Wang Chen, *Agricultural Encyclopaedia* (1313), and M. Elvin, *The Pattern of the Chinese Past* (London, 1973). (b) General view of two lantern-shaped silk-twisting engines (*filatoria*) driven by the water-wheel visible at the right and linked to their shafts on the floor below (not shown). From Diderot, *Encyclopédie*. (c) Schematic view of the transmission systems in a *filatorium*: the reeling-frames are rotated by curved strakes pressing against pegs set around their circumferences, and the shafts of the spindles (extreme left) are rotated by the pressure of the flat leather-shod wheel rotating at the bottom of the lantern. From Diderot, *Encyclopédie*.

twisting silk thread in Lucca and Bologna at about the same period.
(The illustration is an eighteenth-century one, however.) It is clear that
both in mediaeval Italy and in mediaeval China the major 'difficult' steps
of the machine revolution had already been taken. More specifically, (1)
the movements of the hand had been mechanized, (2) the number of
hand-movement-replicating units had been multiplied, (3) a source of
inanimate power was being used, and (4) different motions were derived
from a single power-source. In both cases the purely technological
progress required for an industrial textile revolution was slight compared
to what had already been achieved. In Italy there followed some centuries
of slow development, including the extension of the technique to flax,
culminating in a stimulus imparted to Britain, where the real breakthrough
was made in the eighteenth century. In China the hemp-spinning
machine entirely disappeared, no effort being made to adapt it to cotton,
which increasingly became the chief clothing fibre. Figure 4 shows the
only sort of analogous machine that survived in China, namely the linear
multi-cone silk-twister, powered by hand or water. The picture is from
Wei Chieh's book of 1899, but the device was regarded as of long
standing by this date. A Piedmontese flax-spinner, whose prototypes
probably date back to the sixteenth century, is also shown for the purpose
of comparison (see the next section).

Any theory that seeks to explain the occurrence of an endogenous
industrial revolution in Europe and its absence in China has – in addition
to meeting the requirements set out in preceding sections – to account
both for the development of mechanization in China up to this point, and
for its failure to develop any further after this stage. This is, obviously, an
extremely exacting criterion, and one which no existing theory seems
able even to begin to meet. Nor can it be avoided.

Techno-cultural Style

The case of spinning suggests another way in which the questions that
historians ask might be more sharply focused. This is the pattern of
differences in technical style between China and Europe. By no later
than the late sixteenth century there are at least four respects in which
the European style differs markedly from the Chinese. (1) The Chinese
are remarkably miserly as regards the use of energy and materials. This
point is well illustrated by the ergonomics of the Chinese flexible
carrying-pole or of the fish-tail oar, or indeed by the use of the wooden
collar or 'cangue' as a cheap form of punishment. The Europeans, in
contrast, tend to be profligate with energy and materials. (2) The
Europeans have a flair for accuracy. This can be seen by contrasting the

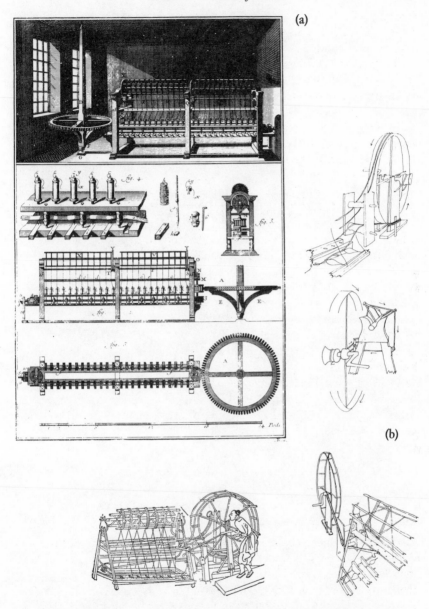

Figure 4 (a) General view and details of the Piedmontese type of flax retwisting engine. (b) Chinese engine for twisting silk thread from Chekiang province depicted in Wei Chieh, *Ts'an sang ts'ui pien* (1899), but of much earlier origin, and provisional reconstructions of the mechanism by the present author, based on the text as well as this picture.

Figure 5 (a) European technological megalomania: the design of a machine hitherto unknown for bringing a fully equipped man-of-war into or out of harbour by means of the strength of a single hand resting upon a lever. From Besson, *Theatrum Instrumentorum et machinarum* (1582).

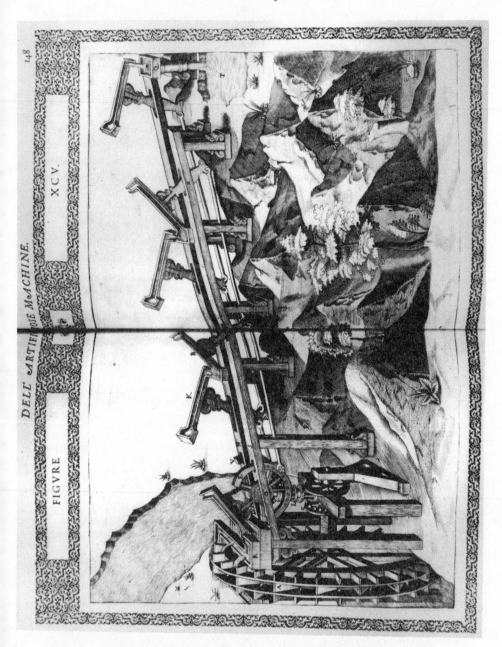

Figure 5 (b) European technological fantasy: a spectacularly inefficient device using half-lantern gearing and a reciprocating system of wooden flumes to raise water up a hillside. From A. Ramelli, *Dell'artificiose machine* (1588).

Chinese and European diagrams in figures 3 and 4, and many practical examples can also be adduced. (3) The Europeans have a vein of precisely visualized mechanical fantasy, which is illustrated by the ridiculous but ingenious devices shown in figure 5. The Chinese are at times susceptible to the romance of machinery – one early-nineteenth-century novel has an account of a 'flying-carriage' whirring with hundreds of wheels – but they are not capable of this disciplined imagination. If anything, they are too severely pragmatic. (4) The Europeans have developed a sort of X-ray vision that enables them to see machines as geometry in motion, and hence to analyse them with a view to perfecting them. Even in 1800 the Chinese remain at the level of the artisan's intuitive adaptations, often effective but inherently limited. These four contrasts are either not present or present only in weak form in mediaeval times. It would be useful to examine how and why they developed over time. Would this need for development perhaps also offer clues to another problem, the slowness with which the implications inherent in the Italian machines were realized?

References

More detailed information supporting the factual assertions made in the text may be found in the following:

Blunden, C. and Elvin, M., 1983: *Cultural Atlas of China*, London.

Elvin, M. 1972: The high-level equilibrium trap: the causes of the decline of invention in the traditional Chinese textile industries. In W. Willmott (ed.), *Economic Organization in Chinese Society*, Stanford.

1973: *The Pattern of the Chinese Past*, Stanford.

1975a: Mandarini e macchine. In L. Lanciotti (ed.), *Sviluppi Scientifici, Prospettive Religiose, Movimenti Rivoluzionari in Cina*, Firenze.

1975b: Skills and resources in late-traditional China. In D. Perkins (ed.) *China's Modern Economy in Historical Perspective*, Stanford.

1982: The technology of farming in late-traditional China. In R. Barker and R. Sinha (eds), *The Chinese Agricultural Economy*, Boulder, Colorado.

1984: Why China failed to create an endogenous industrial capitalism: a critique of Max Weber's explanation. *Theory and Society*, 13.

Endrei, W. 1968: *L'évolution des techniques du filage et du tissage du moyen âge à la révolution industrielle*, Paris and The Hague.

Needham, J. 1954–: *Science and Civilisation in China*, Cambridge.

Shiba, Y. 1970: *Commerce and Society in Sung China*, Trans. M. Elvin, Ann Arbor, Michigan.

6

The Mamlūk Military System and the Blocking of Medieval Moslem Society

Jean-Claude Garcin

The social and economic development of Europe has for a century been thought of by Europeans as the flowering of humanity through a form of civilization that was the most suitable for achieving progress. Thus other civilizations, seen as less adequate, have led to a failure or to the blocking of their evolution among the human groups in which they have developed. Sometimes for the historians most favourable to the Arabo-Moslem group, 'the Islamic moment in the history of the world' (Lombard, 1971: 235) came to an end very early in what is conventionally termed the Middle Ages, in the eleventh century, or at least with the 'great discoveries' and the beginning of 'modern times'.

The success of Europe, as demonstrated by colonial expansion, was perceived to lie in the upsurge of its economy and the development of capitalism. The possible opposition to such an economic upsurge by the principles guiding other great civilizations has been seen as the main cause of their failure. Since the Arabo-Islamic world was one of the areas where endogenous capitalist development did not occur, the reasons for the blockage were to be found in the precepts of Islam, which may have prevented such an evolution. But the conclusions of Rodinson (1974) are well known. A pre-capitalist sector, which he terms 'capitalistic', existed in the Moslem Empire, and Islam did not stand in the way of its development. Studies carried on in parallel concerning the economic foundations of this Mediterranean society – the first Islamic society – based on the documents of the *Geniza* at Cairo (Goitein, 1967) or on the ordinances laid down by Islamic law concerning economic matters (Udovitch, 1970) have shown that such an analysis is well founded. However, these authors study such development at a stage of evolution when in fact the society of the time was multiconfessional, pluralist, liberal, and not yet entirely Islamized. Such a society has been favourably regarded by many Orientalists up to the present day. But Rodinson's study concerning the possible connections between the absence of any real take-off of capitalism in Moslem countries and in Arabo-Islamic culture does not deal especially with this first period in the social evolution of Moslem countries. More generally, Rodinson denies that the absence of the entrepreneurial spirit in this field is the result of a taste for magic or of a lesser degree of rationality, whose evil effects had been denounced at the time in post-classical Islam (Rodinson, 1957). According to him, if in the Moslem Empire, as in the Far East, people continued to put their money in land, it was because it remained a factor of wealth and prestige, and Islam does not come into it.

In the 1960s attempts were likewise made to lay the responsibility for the blockage at the door of one of the most characteristic social actors of the Arabo-Islamic world, the Bedouin (Planhol, 1968). The expansion of Islam allegedly brought about the spread of Bedouinism. And it is understandable that a lesser agricultural development may possibly have contributed to the backwardness of Moslem countries. However, it very quickly appeared unjustified to historians to establish a link between the great advances of nomadism and Islamization, which would have been to acknowledge 'a kind of general vocation, *a priori*, of Islam to nomadism' (Cahen, 1973). Later research carried out on 'pastoralism' has led one to hesitate between highlighting the positive contribution of a 'Bedouin moment' in the history of pre-capitalist civilizations (Vignet-Zunz, 1979) and the recognition of the harmful role played by Bedouin values, ascribing to the Bedouin 'in the end, the origins of slowness to develop of the Arabo-Islamic economy and society in its competition with Western Europe' (Vignet-Zunz, 1983). Despite the ambiguous nature of such analyses, it does not mean that without Islam 'Bedouinization' would not have existed, but that the adoption of Bedouin values by Arabo-Islamic culture was harmful. A closely parallel evaluation of the phenomenon has led even to detecting in the religious Law 'a profound hostility to settled States' (Crone, 1980: 62): there may have been at least a compromise on the part of those who formulated the religious law with what in the long run was to lead to a blockage. The connection between this blockage and the specific nature of Islam is in that case no longer totally ruled out.

But, besides the Bedouin, another social actor, the soldier of slave origins, or the Mamlūk (moreover, often springing from a population that was still nomadic), is now, just as much and even more so than the bedouin, held responsible for the stagnation. 'It should, however, be pointed out that the penetration of the Mamlūks had been much more far flung than that of the nomad hordes': this is the way it was expressed by D. Ayalon (1976: 204; see also 1963, 1975, 1977) in a study that counts among the efforts made to pinpoint the origin of a phenomenon to which that eminent historian had devoted the greater part of his life. These efforts were completed by the work of P. Crone, *Slaves on Horses*, which was followed shortly after by D. Pipes, *Slave Soldiers and Islam*. The idea that the development of a military class in Islam from the tenth century onwards was prejudicial to the development of Moslem society is not novel, and Rodinson, without dwelling unduly upon the subject in his *Islam and Capitalism* (1974: chapter 3), admits that it doubtless prevented the rise of a powerful bourgeoisie, and thus hampered the possible development of capitalism. Furthermore, Western historians have up to now not dealt tenderly with the Mamlūk state that was set up in the Middle East about the middle of the thirteenth century and that lasted right up to the Ottoman occupation at the beginning of the sixteenth century. The political game that went on in it has been seen as a succession of intrigues, acts of treason and crimes, in a merciless struggle for power. The economic decline, in the context of a process of general impoverishment, was merely the predictable consequence of an iniquitous social and fiscal system. (An example of this type of analysis is to be found in Ashtor, 1981.) But the books of Crone and Pipes go farther, inasmuch as, for these authors, the appearance of such a regime is not a matter of chance: it is the result of a failure in the political organization in the Islamic city, which occurred from the ninth century onwards, and for Pipes, who shows that such a regime exists only in Islam, this setback would necessarily even have come about because it is connected to a wholly inapplicable conception on the part of the *'ulamā* as to what constituted the legitimate authority. Thus there is a specific relationship between Islam and the slave in arms, one that 'has almost nothing to do with material circumstances (geographic, economic, social, political, technical and so on) but follows from the needs inherent in Islamicate [*sic*] civilization' (Pipes 1981: 100). From this last viewpoint, which is peculiar to Pipes, taking into account the harmful effects usually attributed to the Mamlūk system, it may be thought that the blockage was inevitable. In an indirect way we are therefore brought back to an evaluation of the role of Islam in social and economic evolution that is fairly close to the one that prevailed before the publication of Rodinson's work. The Islamic or 'Islamicate' background, Pipes would say (1981: xiii–xviii, 93–9), is indeed responsible.

There can be no question here of being able to resolve in a few words a problem that will doubtless be discussed for a long time yet. We will therefore confine ourselves to suggesting a few elements for reflection.

We know the circumstances that gave birth to the regime of the Mamlūks in Egypt, one Monday in April 1250, between Damietta and Manṣūra. We know that the Ayyūbids, the descendants of Saladin, had established, over those countries formerly subject to the Fatimid Caliphs and the lords of the Latin states of Palestine, a kind of family confederation in which power was shared between princes related to one another and installed in numerous scattered capitals. Family tensions had led certain of these princes, among them the prince of Egypt, to set up personal armies loyal to them, constituted from the purchase of prisoners, whom they had instructed in the profession of arms: the Mongol advance in the east then caused many captives to be available for sale on the market. When the Ayyūbid of Egypt, who was attempting to oppose the progress of the army of Saint Louis that had disembarked at Damietta, died of illness among his army, which was encamped, facing the enemy, and after his son, a violent and inexperienced young man, having been urgently summoned there, had wished to rid himself of that personal army, which meanwhile had just given victory to Islam at Manṣūra, the Mamlūk regiment decided to do away with the young prince. Thus there came into existence, amid the chances of the resistance to the Crusade, a political regime that had at the beginning been merely a defensive movement on the part of soldiers threatened by the dangerous plans of an imprudent prince. Perhaps at that time these soldiers had not even had a clear idea of how the crisis might be solved after they had accomplished the murder. Messire de Joinville, a captive with Louis, the King–Saint, had been present at the events, and, horrified, has naïvely recounted how afterwards the mutinous emirs had come to propose to the King of France that they elect him Sultan of Egypt. To his great astonishment the King told him that 'forsooth he would in no wise have refused' if it had been genuinely offered to him (1952: 287)! Underlying the derisive nature of the gesture, of which the good Joinville seems to have had no inkling, one can nevertheless perceive how improvised the revolt had been. Taking into account the fact of the existence of other Ayyūbid princes, the movement had scarcely any chance of success. It could not fail to be wiped out by force or won over again by the establishment of links that in one way or another bound the leaders in revolt to Ayyūbid legitimacy. The history of the ten years that followed shows that progress was being made towards the latter solution when the Mongol invasion, by abolishing all constituted authorities in the Near East – from the Caliph of Iraq to the principal sultans of Syria – impelled the junta that had been precariously instituted to become what these men in the beginning had doubtless not dreamed of, a purely military system functioning with no other justification save the necessity of defending itself against new and redoubtable enemies.

Intentionally, we have just insisted on the unexpected character of the chain of circumstances in which was born this regime that was to survive for over two centuries, but which only gradually discovered the rules under which it would function as it went along, and which doubtless beforehand was never conceived of or sought after as such. To state this is not to deny the importance of Ayalon's effort to discover in the political past of the Islamic Empire the first examples of that strange phenomenon of the Mamlūk. Crone's book, so magnificently documented, has attempted to show that if a military aristocracy (such as the West has known) had developed in the 'Abbāsid era, the constitution of regiments of a slave origin might have been avoided: from this era onwards the prince preferred it to his client subordinates. The work of Pipes clearly proves, just as do the articles of Ayalon, that military training within the bonds of slavery (which was a legal status and not necessarily a social stigma) was on many occasions a military imperative for the medieval Moslem princes eager for military effectiveness, and that the existence of these armed groups (as also that of troops made up of free men) was not without influence on political life. Yet all these reasons, which, according to Pipes, should have made the Mamlūk 'an institution implicit in the Islamicate order' (1981: 194), and which are at work from the ninth century onwards, were not sufficient to give rise to this regime: the Crusade and the Mongols were more effective. To write that 'the achievement of the various Mamlūk societies may well represent the achievement of the Muslim world as a whole' (Ayalon, 1976: 223) leaves one reflecting that there were in Islam the seeds of an evolution which was ineluctably to lead to that state, provided that the circumstances were favourable, and that the Mamlūk regime is truly the coming into existence of that which the city of Islam bore within itself. Likewise this investigation into the antecedents of the phenomenon seems to imply that there was a necessary connection (in the facts and in the mind) between the existence of Mamlūk troops in the armies of the classical era and that of the Mamlūk regime in Egypt. The installation of this regime, according to Pipes, was allegedly the consequence of a sublime act of treason on the part of the *'ulamā'* who despaired of ever seeing the realization of the impossible political ideal of the Caliphate, defined as the sole valid ideal by the religious law – and who therefore abandoned scornfully to the armed slave (as moreover they had done in the past to other military authorities) the care of public affairs. This regime was allegedly the outcome of the fundamental political failure of the Caliphate. But was this failure really felt to render impossible the application of the religious law in society? We have ourselves insisted enough upon the importance of the need for political legitimization in the Mamlūk regime (Garcin, 1967), which brought about the reconstitution of a formal 'Abbāsid caliphate in Cairo between the thirteenth and the sixteenth centuries, for us not to underestimate that institution. However, we must limit to three centuries at the most (between the end of the tenth and the beginning of the fourteenth centuries) the period in which the application of the imperatives of Islam seems to the theorists to imply that such an ideal state should necessarily be led by a Caliph.[1] As Crone clearly perceived, the application of the Law was always a matter of prime importance for the '*ulamā*'. And not often has it been linked to a precise form of state.

In fact, much more than the sense of an institutional failure within Islam having then led to that abandonment of the city to slaves, it is the sense of the danger from without that seems to dominate mentalities. The Moslem world into which the Mamlūk state was born is a world that is disputed and attacked from all sides. When the great traveller Ibn Baṭṭūṭa, still a young man, began in 1325 his long journeyings with a pilgrimage to the Holy Places of Islam, he passed through Egypt. Like many Maghribians of the time he sought to reach the Ḥijāz not via Suez and a fairly easy route, but via Upper Egypt, embarking on board ship at a very southerly point on the Red Sea. This is what so many holy personages of the Moslem West had done in former times, when the Latin States of Palestine barred the northerly route, and the Ḥijāz could only be reached freely from the south. There was virtue in this. The tracks of the deserts of the Thebaid were long, ill supplied with water and hardly safe when a crisis broke out between the state and the tribes. What is more, the passage of the Red Sea, with its coral reefs and its greedy ferrymen heeding little the pilgrim's safety, constituted an ordeal that was often fatal. It was at the end of one of these tracks that Abū'l-Ḥasan al Shādhilī, the great inspirer of a moderate form of mysticism, had met his death about the end of the year 1258. Thus the pilgrims who still wished to take this route were taught the very beautiful 'Prayer of the Sea' that Shādhilī had composed. Ibn Baṭṭūṭa had also learnt it and handed down the text (Defremery and Sanguinetti, 1854:

---

1 It is known that the Caliphate was initially a *de facto* institution, and not Koranic, from which certain Moslem historians have argued that, in the true sense of the term, it lasted only a short while. Cf. Rosenthal (1958: 98, 241 n. 52, 303 n. 44). Later on the *ulamā*' never hesitated to oppose the caliphs every time that the interests of Islam seemed to demand it. It was only at the end of the tenth century and in the eleventh century, when the first military regime had imposed itself on the authority of the caliphs, that the first theory of the Caliph Imamate appeared (Rosenthal, 1958: 59; Laoust, 1970: 16–18). From Ghazālī onwards, at the beginning of the thirteenth century, the necessity of the caliphate is no longer affirmed with the same insistence (Laoust, 1970: 237–9). At least from Ibn Taymiyya, at the beginning of the fourteenth century, the important matter is first the application of the Law (Rosenthal, 1958: 59, 61, 214), and the terms 'sultan' and 'Imam Caliph' have a tendency to become interchangeable (Rosenthal, 1958: 217, 302 n. 28).

vol. I, 40–4). In its long invocation the pilgrim asked God to subdue the elements for him and to grant him safety of body and soul during the passage of that redoubtable sea, the symbol of our whole journey here below. Before the traditional formulas of the Koran, the prayer finished with a pathetic supplication for God to wipe out all enemies: 'may they not be able to advance and come unto us' – but had not believers already received divine succour in sufficiency by the handing down of the Revelation? If this prayer were indeed composed by the holy mystic, as tradition would have it, one cannot help recalling that the East had already in his day been thrown into turmoil and that when he died Baghdad had already been for some months in the hands of the barbarians. This prayer was recited for a long while after the abandonment by the last pilgrims of the southerly route, and not only among members of the Shādhilī brotherhood. It is still to be found today printed in the cheap little collections of prayers sold on the pavements of Cairo. From the middle of the thirteenth century Islam felt itself under siege. The Mamlūk regime cannot be understood outside this context.

Yet can one speak of a 'Mamlūk regime'? 'It has justly been stated that "the fighter on horseback is the expression of feudal society". No less accurately can one say that he is its progenitor. In the East the Mamlūk and the janissary are the disturbers of Moslem political life. Ferdinand Lot sums up fairly well, in these lines placed at the end of his book *L'art militaire et les armées au Moyen Age* (1946: vol. 2, 449), what modern Western historians have thought about the Mamlūk sultanate: the installation of disorder, and murder raised to the dignity of being a normal instrument of political life. Even so, in the first period in which the system functioned, which lasts until about the end of the fourteenth century, there is occasionally acknowledged to be a certain dignity, because a kind of dynasty seems to have succeeded in constituting itself, and the members of one family have been for a while raised to the sultanate. But very quickly it appeared that this dynastic constitution was a failure and, under the last Mamlūks, who were of Circassian origin, the return to the vying for power added to other signs testifying to the disorder and decline of the sultanate. Thus it was not without great embarrassment that for a long time the historians of Islam, after the happy days of classical Islam, tackled the shameful recollection of those decadent times when, in a way that was unjustifiable, the destiny of the Moslem world had been abandoned for more than two centuries to former slaves.

The Mamlūk system was built up in an empirical manner, at the beginning with the sole purpose of continuing to exist, at a time when every other political organization had been destroyed in the Near East by the Mongols. Since at first it was the seizure of power by an army regiment made up of one age group, the regime functioned afterwards regularly according to age groups, each one elevating to the sultanate the one who appeared to be most fitted to assume the position, and he, once he had become sultan, built up by purchase from distant places a reserve of power that was a new human basis for the political body that had been merged with the army. One can understand how, in this system where solidarity arose within the 'mint' of the barracks, heredity had no place:[2] the initial act that had founded the regime had been the murder of the son of the dead sultan. In our view the dynastic achievements that there were in the fourteenth century were dynastic only in appearance or, on the other hand, during the forty years that followed the Great Plague, they were the sign that the system was no longer functioning normally;[3] in the fifteenth century the return to stability is marked once more by its functioning on a non-dynastic basis. Very recently P. M. Holt recalled the pithy epigram written by an Egyptian 'Abbāsid on the investiture diploma legalizing the installation of a sultan: 'Kingship is childless' – or 'cannot engender' (1984: 505). This signifies that the system was founded on the continual supply of men who had been imported to be trained physically, militarily, socially and religiously in the slavery of the barracks. Moreover, their sons, born as Moslems and consequently not able to be subjected to the mould of slavery, could not by this very fact later inherit the power of their fathers and had to be gradually integrated with the mass of subjects. We can realize that it is hardly adquate to evaluate according to the dynastic criterion the success of a regime founded to the very end upon the political elimination of the sons.

To acknowledge that there is in a system a logic that allowed it to function is not enough to justify it or to exclude it from the numerous signs of the decadence into which it is held that the Moslem world had fallen from this era onwards. Lot again writes about the Mamlūk system: 'It goes without saying that this system could have no counterpart in the West. It could only inspire astonishment mingled with horror in kings, in the ranks of chivalry, and in the entire Christian population' (1946: vol. 2, 440). And this horror of the slave become master that was felt in the West is expressed again by Crone when she writes that this system 'bespeaks a moral gap of such dimensions that within the great civilizations it has been found only in one' (1980:81). Pipes's vast enquiry

2 This vision of the political evolution of the system has been expressed in Garcin (1981, 1985). This seems to fit in well with the work of Ayalon.

3 It is upon the analysis of the situation during this special period (which can in fact lead one to overestimate the importance of the dynastic factor in the Mamlūk regime), that is based the fine study of Harmann (1984).

indeed allows us clearly to state that the system is to be found only within the Moslem lands, and that, for example, we could not find in the Roman world this compatibility between slavery and the service of arms that we deem scandalous. Yet what can we say about the administration of imperial Rome, which for a while was entrusted to those imperial slaves and freed men, as they have been studied by G. Boulvert (1970, 1974) and P. R. C. Weaver (1972)? Many of those traits that are connected with the origins, power, career and social status of these Roman financiers and administrators can justify their being compared to the armed servants of the Mamlūk State. Was it by chance that, as Crone has indeed shown, the constitution of a military aristocracy of the Abbasids failed because the prince preferred to administer the state and dominate it through his freed men and slaves? Perhaps the attitude of the Moslem *'ulamā'* when they were confronted with the ever-strange phenomenon of power is less one of unjustifiable abandonment than a realistic appreciation of the public interest (cf. Garcin, 1986). Should one really think that it was as the sole result of human cowardice that this fortuitous regime, born amid improvisation and danger, lasted more than two centuries? The advice once given by Ayalon (1976: 196) not to evaluate the Mamlūk phenomenon too negatively seems to be still valid.

We shall therefore unhesitatingly take the opposite view to Lot's assertion. The Mamlūk emir is not the disturber of Moslem political life in this era and, not unlike the role of the fighter on horseback in the West, he is the holder of social and political power, and above all of economic resources. But the state has not disappeared, and Cahen (1953) has shown that the appropriate distinction to make is that between the Western fief of a feudal society and the fiscal allocation – or *iqṭāʿ* – that ensured the wealth of the emirs. As we have seen, the system normally prevented the constitution of a lineage: the son of the Mamlūk will not inherit the *iqṭāʿ* of his father and will have to think for himself about ensuring his own means of subsistence. However, there were evidently ways of mitigating the effects of this constituting principle of the system, and in particular of avoiding the confiscation of property by the state upon the death of the Mamlūk as sometimes occurred. The Mamlūk could constitute as entailed property, or *waqf*, the estates acquired in his lifetime through the resources available from the *iqṭāʿ*: in this way the family was constituted as the administrator of the property so long as there were descendants, and disposed of the revenues from it, which had to revert in their entirety to works of piety when they had died out. The *waqf* documents (which can of course emanate from persons other than Mamlūks) thus play somewhat the same role as wills, although they are of a totally different kind. When one consults the *waqf* documents of the time, it can be seen that this wealthy class used mainly to invest in sumptuous private residences and public buildings (in this case of a religious kind) on which, somewhat as in the Roman world, very detailed inscriptions indicated to the passer-by who their constructor was; these prestige investments ensured the renewal of the urban structure. But such men also invested in goods that brought in wealth: apartment blocks for letting, or *rab‘*, on a standard plan that was very modern in style, baths, markets with small shops ready for hiring, mills and ovens, oil factories, sugar cane presses, premises housing up to several dozen looms to spin silk, and so on. A whole complex of types of dwelling or useful buildings were perfected at that time in the large Mamlūk towns, and these served right up to modern times. The existence of these models for building leads one to assume that demand must have been brisk (Garcin, 1982). Moreover, reading the *waqf*, one does not get an impression of economic stagnation but is led to wonder whether the existence of a powerful bourgeois class was really an indispensable condition for expansion. We still do not appreciate fully the real economic mechanisms that allowed this society to function (Petry, 1983).

Shall we therefore say that the economic progress of the West at that time first took place through the upsurge in agricultural production, arising from modest technical improvements, from the presence of the nobles on their lands? Shall we believe that the Mamlūk military class, essentially urban, whose investments brought about the beauty of the towns, merely in this way caused the ancient domination over the countryside by urban groups who squandered their wealth to be perpetuated? Is the Moslem town of this time, so closely connected to the mounted emirs (Garcin, 1984a), merely a 'consumer town', as has long been said of the towns of antiquity (although this now seems to be less certain: Leveau, 1983, 1985)? In short, might it be not a true bourgeoisie, but a feudal system that was lacking in the Moslem world? Here again the testimony of the *waqf* gives one an inkling that in Mamlūk society there was no lack of interest in the land, particularly up to the fifteenth century when the structure of the towns, which had largely been opened up, does not yet evince the division that occurred later between urban and rural. Among the entailed goods that are detailed in the *waqf* records, there are lands (owned previously in outright freehold, the legal condition indispensable for their constitution as a *waqf*), and certain emirs had a reputation for being interested in their farms. One must not indeed jump to the conclusion that ownership of land was non-existent from the fact that the main resources of the active military class were derived from tax concessions, or *iqtā‘*, provided principally by revenues arising from the tax on land. It must again be said that the revenues from the *iqtā‘* ceased to be paid over on the death of the Mamlūk, and even diminished considerably when his age meant that he was retired: only estates that had been acquired could be retained, particularly if they were to be protected from confiscation by being recorded in the *waqf*. This does not mean that landowners resided on their lands: although certain of them must have gone regularly to visit them, the prestige attached to living in the town very clearly played its part. But it is an indication not to transform the whole of the Mamlūk military class into a dominant group that was necessarily isolated, and that only tax-bleeding of a quasi-colonial type linked the town to the country. Thus it does not seem to have yet been demonstrated that the nature of the socio-political system of the Mamlūks constituted in itself an element of blockage making impossible the normal functioning of agriculture and artisan trades. It is impossible to see the two and a half centuries that the Mamlūk regime lasted as a long decline in civilization.

In general one places very far back chronologically the point in time when the decline of the Moslem world began – often, it has been stated, in the eleventh century. From then onwards the evolution of these by then truly Islamicized countries seems more foreign to us, less easy to understand. The handy criterion of the functioning of the Caliphate state is no longer capable of being applied. The historian can wear himself out cataloguing the proliferation of innumerable authorities, as common as they were unjustifiable. But it took a long time for our Western ancestors to cease being impressed by the strength of Islam. It posed for them, until a much later date, a quasi-theological problem: how had the true God permitted such a triumph? When in 1549 the Venetian printer Matheo Pagano published the very fine, already ancient, plan to Mamlūk Cairo, he preceded the engravings of this superb work with a very well-informed introduction in Latin concerning the history of Islam; the success of the 'Turkish' peoples, from the Saljuks to the Ottomans, including the Mamlūks, was justified in the Christian scheme of Providence by attributing to them a Jewish origin and claiming that they were the descendants of the lost tribes of Israel, and thus also inheritors of the promise made by God to the descendants of Abraham (Blanc et al. 1981).

In the preceding century, Westerners came in large numbers to Egypt, among the men who were of a thoughtful cast of mind, such as Joos van Ghistele (1976), of Burgundian origin – the future counsellor of Maximilian of Habsburg – who passed through it in 1482–3, or Emmanuel Piloti, a Venetian merchant from Crete, who lived more than twenty years in Egypt at the beginning of the fifteenth century (Dopp, 1950) – these men appreciated the power of the Mamlūk state and the orderliness of the regime, even if they could not approve of all its aspects. For them, also, the strength of this state needed explanation: they sought it – sometimes carrying matters to the absurd – in the diversion of vital forces that normally belonged to the Christian world, namely in the continual importing of future Mamlūks, all of whom, in their eyes, had sprung from Christian countries and were consequently renegades. For Fabri, the Dominican monk, the Mamlūk state was therefore described as an organization of the Devil founded upon apostasy, indefatigably transforming former Christians into the enemies of Christ (1975). We know, moreover, the enthusiastic lines written by Ibn Khaldūn (Dār al Bayān, n.d.), concerning this system, which was for him also an act of Providence that had caused Islam to shine forth again with the lustre of youth, thanks to this unceasing recourse to unspoilt human beings whose nature had not yet been perverted by civilization (and, according to him, even less so, it must be added, by Christianity). These fanciful evaluations contradict one another. Nevertheless all seem to demonstrate the level of the analyses undertaken by contemporaries concerning the foundations of power: the offspring of a race, the availability of a number of men, an arithmetic of human bodies rather than a mastery of things, to which we became sensitive later on (Garcin, 1984b). They appear also to us, through their dim appreciation of reality, to point up the demographic drama through which that world was passing at the time.

Undoubtedly the supply of men to the Mamlūk army represents a very special case. Whilst Europe was building its uncertain hopes upon an alliance with Prester John – perhaps the Mongol Khan – the Mamlūk horsemen, men of the steppes placed in the service of the Mamlūk state, were attempting to bar the way to invasion: right up to the end of the first quarter of the fourteenth century the Near East lived in fear of the Mongols, and their return in strength at the beginning of the fifteenth century, under the leadership of Tamberlaine, showed that the danger could arise once more when one no longer had it in mind. Up to the Ottoman conquest this fear sustained a deep mistrust of everything coming from the East. This assumed the maintenance in the Egyptian 'sanctuary' of a military society of roughly the same size as that which Philippe Contamine estimated for the kingdom of France at the end of the Hundred Years War,[4] but for a population doubtless two to three times smaller in size. In the geopolitical context in which the Moslem peoples were living one can conceive how the need for soldiers was often pressing long after the vanishing of the Jihād spirit, and how, whereas the Roman world used its slaves, apart from domestic service, for material

4 Contamine (1972: 316). In a totally different context the definition of the conditions for the existence of a military society adopted by Contamine (1972: 542) would be useable for the Mamlūk state.

tasks and in the management of goods, the Islamicized peoples often employed theirs in the profession of arms. But the burden that the maintenance of these forces represented for these countries, often excessive in proportion to the resources available, became even heavier when the number of men who were the producers of wealth diminished. It is understandable that in such circumstances the importing of the Mamlūks was perceived, wrongly but tentatively, as the borrowing of external forces that the country would have been unable to supply, whereas it was rather the production of resources that served to pay for this importation that was in jeopardy.

The demographic history of the period in which the Mamlūk state survived from the Black Death onwards is indeed a very sombre one. If the effects at first were less than in Europe, the production of wealth had already considerably diminished (it was from this era that there dates the development of the 'dynastic' experience of the Mamlūk state), and the country was badly disturbed. A new crisis in 1375, combining both famine and plague, was considerable enough to modify in a lasting way the use of space in the Mamlūk territories (Garcin, 1974). There then ensued the collapse of the years 1403–6, resulting from the cumulative effects of Mongol invasion, drought, famine and plague. There followed from this an infinitely more serious breakdown than anything that the country had known since the great crisis of the eleventh century. At the beginning of the fifteenth century the political organization in its entirety almost disappeared. Hardly had this ordeal been precariously overcome when two new extensive epidemics again brought ruin: in 1415–17 and in 1420; and the list can be lengthened with the epidemics of 1427–8, 1429–30, 1435–7, 1443–4 and 1445–6. Afterwards Egypt experienced a certain respite, in spite of the deadly return of the sickness in 1467–70, 1491–2 and 1505–6.

These epidemics decimated town-dwellers and *fellahin*. Financial resources which, through the *iqṭā'*, ensured the maintenance of the military state, were henceforth no longer sufficient. It was then, at the end of the first quarter of the fifteenth century, that there were instituted those economic monopolies that alone allowed the sultans to keep the state functioning, especially the sultan's monopoly of the sale of spices to Europeans in a period when, through the chances of the Mongol wars, the traffic was concentrated on the Red Sea routes, to the maximum advantage of Egypt. It is these monopolies, often presented as indissolubly linked to the Mamlūk regime, that have sometimes been held responsible for the economic decline. One must indeed acknowledge that the Egyptian historians of that time (who were firm supporters of freedom in a trade in which the social group to which they belonged had up to then invested heavily) saw in these measures merely the immoral

greed of the sultans. It is nevertheless likely that it was thanks to these
monopolies that the Mamlūk state in the fifteenth century recovered
once more an equilibrium that the crisis at the beginning of the century
had put at risk. If there was a blockage by virtue of the existence of such
monopolies (which does not seem to have yet been demonstrated) should
we make the Mamlūk state responsible for this or take into account the
essentially demographic reasons that, among other things, led to these
measures for survival?

Another consequence of the demographic decline in settled populations was the development of the Bedouin powers. From the end of the
fourteenth century onwards, and for a long time afterwards, Bedouin
authorities were constituted. In Egypt, if these generally formally
acknowledge the authority of the established state and do not dream of
taking over the sultanate, in reality they enjoy great autonomy (Garcin,
1976: 468–98). In them we find the other main party allegedly
responsible for the blockage. In fact, much could be said concerning the
harmful effects of the Bedouin: the Mamlūk state that existed before the
crisis had succeeded in finding a role for the tribes and in getting them to
contribute to the smooth workings of the social and economic body, even
if injudicious acts were committed that had to be paid for later. On the
other hand, a region such as Upper Egypt experienced afterwards,
during the eighteenth century, a period that seems to have been very
prosperous under the authority of Bedouin emirs (Garcin, 1976:
359–410, 1978; for the post-medieval situation in Upper Egypt, see
1976: 514–31). Generally the Egyptian Bedouins were not all lacking in
culture (here of course we have in mind the Bedouin emirs), or
indifferent to the interests of agriculture and trade. However this may be,
the Bedouin phenomenon took on a great extension in the East from the
second half of the fourteenth century onwards, and we know that the
same held good for the Maghrib. It is in the light of this phenomenon
that one must read the detailed expositions of Ibn Khaldūn concerning
the strength of the Bedouins as the driving force of history. One would
undoubtedly not wish to consider this situation of Bedouin expansion as
due to the demographic crisis, seeing only in the ideology of Ibn Khaldūn
an additional proof of the fascination of Islamic culture for the Bedouin
way of life, and as the predestined source of so many woes. One must
then acknowledge that in his day people were especially fascinated, for he
is not alone in having been forced to take into account, one way or
another, the fact of Bedouin existence: the works of Qalqashandī or
Maqrīzī, his contemporaries, are testimony enough to this.

We shall refrain from reaching conclusions about what, from this time onwards, was able to seal for a long while the destiny of countries in which the development of capitalism did not take place. The Mamlūk military system did not then involve the whole of Mediterranean Islam, but the Near East was subjected to it for over two centuries. If one wishes to investigate the reasons for this blockage in what was the centre of the Moslem world of the time, one cannot help assessing Mamlūk responsibility.

The mechanisms of this regime, which seem to us to have been established in a very empirical way, evidently do not correspond to those that allowed the economic upsurge of the West. We are aware of these mechanisms; nevertheless only with difficulty can we evaluate their precise effects on economic activity. Most frequently we imagine what those effects were by analogy with what would be implied in the West from soldiers residing in the town but maintained by the tax yield derived from the rural areas; the absence of a true bourgeoisie endowed with political power; the proliferation of entailed property; the monopolization by the prince of important sectors of the economy, and so on. But we do not know how the production of wealth occurred in a context that was not Western, through institutions run by contemporaries in many different ways. To assert that in such a society there was neither a true bourgeoisie nor a true feudal system, is surely merely to affirm that it was a different society? Shall we say that these institutions and these mechanisms, arising from an historical evolution, could not lead to progress? But did they not function fairly well for a long time, allowing, for example, the era of prosperity at the beginning of the fourteenth century?

What part did Islam play in this blockage? Such social mechanisms are specific to Islam in so far as they were devised among peoples that had been Islamicized. How could it be otherwise? Doubtless one may desire to find in them the specific nature of Islam in its entirety, and to show that these mechanisms fit perfectly into a closed system which, with the passage of time, displayed the virtualities contained in its initial beginnings, and which is responsible overall for its stagnation. Attention to what is specific is undoubtedly a necessary attitude in the study of different societies, where the approach must be avoided of employing instruments designed for the West (for example, by confusing *iqṭāʿ* and fief); such an attitude is also the useful instrument for the diffusion of knowledge where large-scale markers are indispensable. Yet should we confuse the 'specific' method of approach and historical reality, and if the mechanisms devised in different civilizations are different, are we to believe that these suffice to neutralize the effects of large-scale general phenomena that man has only very slowly learnt to control? One would find in the pace of evolution of the states of western Europe and that of the Mamlūk state tempos that are analogous and problems that are similar, even if the working of the mechanisms is clearly different. This impels us to seek the reasons for blockage in these large-scale phenomena, such as the accidents of demography, beyond the mechanisms that are peculiar to each cultural entity. Another problem is to know how Europe overcame such a blockage.

However, are we to believe that if this blockage had not occurred there would have been, in addition, a 'Near East miracle', as it is said there was a 'European miracle'? Should we think that, with a large and active population, the Near East at the end of the Middle Ages could have been the area which sparked off an economic development based, like that of Europe, on an extension of practical knowledge and the exploitation of natural resources? When we investigate the origins of the 'European miracle', we rightly attribute great importance to the institutions and mentalities that allowed the phenomenon to occur. But from what moment can we esteem that the movement has become clearly enough visible for it to be distinguished from what is occurring elsewhere in the world? Had there not been necessary an accumulation of wealth, technical skills and tools devised out of the experience that had been acquired? I recall how impressed I was a few years ago, when I visited the museum of military arts at the Tower of London, by an exhibition of armour of the medieval West, the Moslem Near East and Japan. Beside the refinement, and even the slightly foolish ostentation, of the Eastern weapons of war, the European suits of armour at the end of the Middle Ages, with their jointed plates, their rivets and screws, already testified to a technical mastery in tools for working metal, which it was soon going to be possible to apply to more productive instruments. With what sort of iron would the Moslem artisans have been able to perfect their techniques? In what naval shipyards could they have been trained in discovering better designs for ships, when wood had to be imported very expensively as needed, and when it was a strategic material? What new kind of plough should have been invented, when modern instruments later occasionally proved to be too rough, and for what sort of agricultural surface? Egypt, the centre of the Moslem Empire, had at the time a utilizable land surface no larger than that of Holland. In such conditions, was a 'Near East miracle' conceivable? The end of medieval times highlights the worn-out state of this old world that was the inheritor of the ancient world, the scene in its day of so much progress, but now grown poor and bereft of the great resources upon which was to be built the power of Europe. Should we really be astonished if the next stage in human development came about in countries that were still new and vast, with abundant natural wealth that was almost untouched? Such an economic development in the Near East of that time would have truly deserved the term 'miracle' if it had occurred.

References

Ashtor, E. 1981: The Levantine sugar industry in the late Middle Ages: a case of technological decline. In A. L. Udovitch (ed.), *The Islamic Middle East, 700–1900. Studies in Economic and Social History*, Princeton, New Jersey.

Ayalon, D. 1963: The European–Asiatic steppe: a major reservoir of power for the Islamic world. *Proceedings of the 25th Congress of Orientalists* (Moscow, 1960).

——— 1975: Preliminary remarks on the Mamlūk military institution in Islam. In V. J. Parry and M. E. Yapp (eds), *War, Technology and Society in the Middle East*, London.

——— 1976: Aspects of the Mamlūk phenomenon, I. *Der Islam*, 53.

——— 1977: Aspects of the Mamlūk phenomenon, II. *Der Islam*, 54.

Blanc, B., Denoix, S., Garcin, J. C. and Gordiani, R. 1981: A propos de la carte du Caire de Matheo Pagano. *Annales Islamologiques*, 17.

Boulvert, G. 1970: *Esclaves et affranchis impériaux*, Paris.

——— 1974: *Domestique et fonctionnaire sous le haut empire romain*, Paris.

Cahen, C. 1973: Nomades et sédentaires dans le monde musulman du milieu du Moyen Age. In D. H. Richards (ed.), *Islamic Civilisation, 950–1150*, Oxford.

——— 1953: 'L'évolution de l'iqta' du IXe au XIIIe siècle. *Annales E.S.C.*, 8.

Contamine, P. 1972: *Guerre, Etat et Société à la fin du Moyen Age. Etude sur les armées des rois de France (1337–1494)*, Paris.

Crone, P. 1980: *Slaves on Horses: The Evolution of the Islamic Polity*, Cambridge.

Dār al Bayān n.d.: *Kitāb al-'ibar, ta'rīkh Ibn Khaldūn*, vol. V, pp. 371–4.

Defremery, C. and Sanguinetti, B. R. 1854: *Voyages d'Ibn Battûta*, vol. I, Paris.

Dopp, P. H. 1950: *L'Egypte au commencement du quinzième siècle d'après le traité d'Emmanuel Piloti de Crète*, Cairo.

Fabri, F. 1975: *Le Voyage en Egypte de Felix Fabri, 1483*, trans. J. Masson, Cairo.

Garcin, J. C. 1967: Histoire, opposition politique et piétisme traditionaliste dans le Ḥusn al-muḥādarat de Suyûti. *Annales Islamologiques*, 7.

——— 1974: 'La "méditerranéisation" de l'empire mamelouk sous les sultans Bahrides. *Rivista degli Studi Orientali*, 48.

——— 1976: *Un centre musulman de la Haute Egypte médiévale: Qûs*, Cairo.

——— 1978: Note sur les rapports entre bédouins et fellahs à l'époque mamluke. *Annales Islamologiques*, 14.

——— 1981: Los nuevos estados musulmanes del Proximo Oriente: los mamelucos (siglos XIII–XVI). In H. Salvat (ed.), *Historia Universal*, vol. 3, Barcelona.

——— 1982: *Habitat médiévale et Histoire urbaine a Fustat et au Caire*. In J. C. Garcin, B. Maury, J. Revault and M. Zakariya (eds), *Palais et Maison du Caire*, vol. 1, Paris.

——— 1984a: Toponymie et topographie urbaines médiévales à Fustat et au Caire. *Journal of the Economic and Social History of the Orient*, 27.

——— 1984: Aux sources d'une idéologie, la force empruntée de l'Islam. In J. Lafitte (ed.), *Le miroir égyptien, rencontres mediterranéennes 1983*, Marseille.

1985: L'Egypte dans le monde musulman (du XIIe siècle au début du XVIe siècle). D. T. Niane (ed.), *Histoire générale de l'Afrique*, vol. 4, Paris.

1986: Le sultan et la pharaon: le politique et le religieux dans l'Egypte mamluk. In *Hommages à F. Daumas*, Montpellier.

Ghistele, J. van 1976: *Le voyage en Egytpe de Joos van Ghistele, 1482–1483*, trans. R. Bauwens-Préaux, Cairo.

Goitein, S. D. 1967: *A Mediterranean Society*, vol. 1, Berkeley.

Harmann, U. 1984: The sons of Mamluks as fief-holders in late medieval Egypt. In T. Khalidi (ed.), *Land Tenure and Social Transformation in the Middle East*, Beirut.

Holt, P. M. 1984: Some observations on the 'Abbāsid Caliphate of Cairo. *Bulletin of the School of Oriental and African Studies*, 47.

Joinville, 1952: *Histoire de Saint Louis*. In A. Pauphilet (ed.), *Historiens et Chroniquers du Moyen Age*, Paris.

Laoust, H. 1970: *La politique de Gazali*, Paris.

Leveau, P. 1983: La ville antique, 'ville de consommation': parasitisme social et économie antique. *Etudes Rurales*.

1985: Richesses investissements, dépenses: à la recherche des revenus des aristocraties municipales de l'Antiquite. In P. Leveau (ed.), *L'Origine des richesses dépensées dans la ville antique*, Aix-en-Provence.

Lombard, M. 1971: *L'Islam dans sa première grandeur (VIII–XIe siècle)*, Paris.

Lot, F. 1946: *L'Art militaire et les armées au Moyen Age en Europe et dans le Proche Orient*, vol. 2, Paris.

Petry, C. 1983: A paradox of patronage during the later Mamluk period. *The Muslim World*, 73.

Pipes, D. 1981: *Slave Soldiers and Islam: The Genesis of a Military System*, New Haven.

Planhol, X. de 1968: *Les fondements geographiques de l'histoire de l'Islam*, Paris.

Rodinson, M. 1957: *Classicisme et declin dans l'histoire de l'Islam*, Paris.

1974: *Islam and Capitalism*, London.

Rosenthal, E. 1958: *Political Thought in Medieval Islam*, Cambridge.

Udovitch, A. L. 1970: *Partnership and Profit in Medieval Islam*, Princeton, New Jersey.

Vignet-Zunz, J. 1979: A propos des Bédouins: une réévaluation des rapports 'nomades-sédentaires'. In *Pastoral Production and Society*, Cambridge.

1983: A propos de la bédouinisation en Afrique du Nord. Déterminations culturelles et niveaux des techniques agricoles. *Techniques et Culture*, 1.

Weaver, P. R. C. 1972: *Familia Caesaris*, Cambridge.

7

Islam: A Comment

Michael Cook

How is an Islamicist to respond when summonsed before a conference on 'the European miracle' to show the cause for the non-occurrence of a similar miracle in Islam?

One response might be to enter a plea of 'no case to answer'. There is a good deal to be said for this course. If the outcome of European history is stipulated to have been miraculous, then by implication Islamic history has kept within the bounds of the laws of nature; and such conformity hardly stands in need of explanation. To put things this way is, of course, to trade too much on the metaphor of the miracle. The point of the metaphor is that the outcome of European history has been extraordinary, and it is a point that deserves to be taken. Its corollary, then, is that the course of Islamic history has been relatively ordinary. Yet the plea of 'no case to answer' still seems in place: the ordinary hardly cries out for explanation.

On the other hand, there are doubtless many things in the world which are open to explanation without actually crying out for it. So it may still make sense to ask why Islamic history did not have an outcome comparable to that of European history. But if it makes sense to ask the question, does it really make sense to attempt to answer it? It could do – but only if we are prepared to make one crucial assumption. We have to assume that, but for some fairly specific circumstance which we can hope to identify, Islamic history would indeed have had such an outcome. Less abstractly, what we have to assume might be dubbed the 'Dynorod model': the view that somewhere in Islamic history there was a blockage,

This chapter is a slightly revised version of some remarks I made at the 'European Miracle' conference as discussant of Professor Garcin's paper. It is not an attempt to come to grips with the Islamic aspects of the issues raised by the conference as a whole.

the removal of which in counterfactual speculation would enable an Islamic miracle to gush forth. Now Islamic civilization is in several ways a remarkable *cultural* phenomenon. But there is not much about it to suggest that it was pregnant with the greatest *material* change that has affected our species since the neolithic revolution. The Sinologist is in a different position: he can at least point to plausible instances of the miraculous falling victim to abortion or infanticide. Not so the Islamicist. And if we reject the 'Dynorod model', we are left with the thought that Islamic history might have had a different outcome if things had been different; but any attempt to *specify* the differences will be highly subjective.

A second response an Islamicist might make would place him in less danger of being found in contempt of conference, and is more in keeping with Islamic notions of received authority. Assuredly Islamicists do not *know* the causes of the European miracle, but they can always be *told* them – and for any given cause, they will usually be able to come up with an Islamic alibi. The alibi for which Islamicists are most often asked relates to the role of predestinarian doctrine in concentrating the capitalist mind. But on this occasion, refreshingly, the focus is different. The question to which our attention is directed is the distinctiveness of the European state – or more precisely, the peculiar relationship of at least *some* European states to the societies they ruled. The idea to which we are asked to react is that there is something interestingly paradoxical about the European state. On the one hand it is remarkably strong: in terms of the penetration of society, it may be said to reach the parts that other states don't reach. And on the other hand, it acts very weak: it does not make use of its strength to engage in arbitrary and predatory behaviour; rather, it is somehow constrained to respect, or respond to, the interests of large segments of the society it rules. It is this paradoxical phenomenon which John Hall refers to in his chapter as 'the organic state', and argues is a significant element in the causation of the European miracle. Here, at least, the Islamicist can provide an alibi with some assurance.

The basic point in the Islamic alibi is a simple one: the systematic tendency for military force in Islamic history to be imported from outside civil society. Two major processes are involved here. One is the import (or invasion) of tribesmen, frequently nomads; and the other is the import of *mamlūks* – military slaves from beyond the frontiers of the Islamic world. With regard to the first, Islamic civilization owes its existence to a tribal conquest of the Middle East in the seventh century, and tribal conquest remained a persistent theme thereafter. It is rather as if the Young Pretender's adventure of 1745 had represented a recurrent mode of successful dynastic change in English history. With regard to the *mamlūk* phenomenon, we have to do with a pattern that has again been remarkably prominent in Islamic history – it lasted from the ninth into the twentieth century, and in its heyday extended from Spain to central Asia. It is rather as if the core of the Hanoverian troops at the battle of Culloden had been black slaves, freshly imported from West Africa in each generation.

This is, of course, a simplified picture, and open to extensive qualification. But such qualification has its limits. To put the point the other way round: it is remarkably hard to find in Islamic history instances of what might be called citizen armies – armies locally recruited, by a state identified with the area in question, from a settled population that was not tribal. (One of the rare exceptions is perhaps the military basis of the Ṣaffārid state in ninth-century Sīstān.)

Equally, we have begged the question *why* the import of armies is so salient a feature of Islamic history. In the case of the *mamlūks*, the answer is tricky; but there has to be one, since the phenomenon is virtually unattested outside the Islamic world. (See, in particular, Crone, 1980.) In the case of tribal armies, part of the explanation at least is obvious: the Middle East is sandwiched between the world's two great domains of pastoral nomadism.[1] But for our present purposes all that matters is that the import of armies dominates Islamic history as it dominates that of no other great civilization.

This prominence of imported armies has obvious and drastic implications for relations between state and society. It is of course the case that an army fully representative of the society it defends is (in the context of a territorial state) a democratic day-dream. Equally an army uncompromised by any linkages to the society which maintains it, and totally subordinated to the purposes of the state, is a despotic day-dream. But Muslim armies clearly lie towards the despotic end of the spectrum. What this creates, then, is a marked degree of disjunction between state and society – between central military power and local economic power. This disjunction, though inevitably blurred in many particular contexts, is familiar to any Islamic historian, and obvious to any observant comparativist.[2] I shall not attempt a serious analysis of it here; but I will illustrate it with a single historical example.[3]

1 To pick up a point made by John Hall in his chapter in this volume, there was a Great Wall of China to keep out the nomads of the steppes, and there could perhaps have been a Great Wall of India for the same purpose; but no set of walls could have secured the Middle East against the nomads of the steppes to the north and the deserts to the south.
2 See Mottahedeh (1980: esp. chapter 4) for an example of the former, and Wickham's chapter in this volume for an example of the latter.
3 Barthold (1928: 272, 291). In Barthold's source, the story is placed in the mouth of the cadi of Nīshāpūr some thirty years later, at the time of the Turcoman conquest of Khurasan.

In the early eleventh century the civil society of the city of Balkh in Central Asia experienced some rapid political changes. Balkh was under the rule of the Ghaznavids – a typical *mamlūk* state. But while the Ghaznavid ruler was away making war on the Indians, Balkh was taken off him by the Qarakhānids – a typical tribal state. Soon after this, however, the Ghaznavid ruler returned and repossessed Balkh. Now the people of Balkh – perhaps unusually – had not remained passive through these events. They had vigorously resisted the Qarakhānid invaders, with considerable loss of life and property – some of it belonging to the Ghaznavid ruler. What then was the reward they received for their loyalty when the latter returned? What the Ghaznavid ruler did was to treat them to a homily on the importance of minding their own business. Warfare, he admonished them, is for rulers, not for subjects; it was their duty to pay their taxes to whoever had them in his power. The notables of Balkh duly apologized for their misconduct, and promised not to repeat it. The Ghaznavid ruler was not, then, a leading theorist of the organic state; and in this, I suspect, he spoke for Muslim rulers as a whole.

At this point I may perhaps comment directly on the argument of Professor Garcin's chapter. For the most part he concentrates his attention on a single, but classic example of the *mamlūk* phenomenon: the Mamlūk sultanate which ruled Egypt and Syria from the thirteenth to the sixteenth century. The drift of his argument is to defend the Mamlūk regime against the implied charge (implied, that is, by the agenda of the conference) of obstructing the occurrence of a miracle. Now we are agreed, but on different grounds, that the Mamlūks ought to be acquitted on this charge. In my own view, they should be acquitted for lack of evidence of any miracle in the making which they could be deemed to have frustrated. In Professor Garcin's view, by contrast, the burden of the defence is that the Mamlūks, though a rough lot, were not all bad. This is doubtless true enough. In political terms, it would seem that many Mamlūk civil wars were more pacific occasions than an English football match. Economically, as he shows, their record is not one of consistent neglect; and if it was worse after the middle of the fourteenth century, so also were the times. But none of this shakes my conviction that the Mamlūks, whatever else they were doing, were not in the business of running an 'organic state'. In other words, it seems to me entirely plausible that, had there been a miracle delicately poised to happen in fourteenth-century Egyptian society, the existence of the Mamlūk regime could have blocked it. At least, it is hard to feel confident that an eighteenth-century English society dominated by an imported West African soldiery would have delivered the Industrial Revolution.

There is, however, a point raised by Professor Garcin's concluding remarks which bothers me. Does it really matter, he asks, not to have a true feudality or a true bourgeoisie? Not that I am about to sketch a hypothetical route to the miraculous unassisted by the presence of either of these macro-historical agents. What we come back to here is the element of tautology in the observation on which our conference is based: that the European miracle happened in Europe (and happened in a manner which precluded the spontaneous occurrence of any comparable miracle elsewhere). How varied is the set of hypothetical miracles which could in principle have issued from human history? And how diverse are the routes which could hypothetically have led to them? These are questions which are probably best left to the more up-market writers of science fiction. But in the absence of more constrained answers, there is bound to be a good deal of arbitrariness in our attempts to distinguish the essentially miraculous from the contingently European features of the process of transformation we are trying to explain.

References

Barthold, W. 1928: *Turkestan Down to the Mongol Invasions.*
Crone, P. 1980: *Slaves on Horses: The Evolution of the Islamic Polity*, Cambridge.
Mottahedeh, R. P. 1980: *Loyalty and Leadership in an Early Islamic Society*, Princeton.

8

The Modernization of Japan: Why has Japan Succeeded in its Modernization?

Jacques Mutel

This question assumes that one can define exactly what is understood by 'the success of modernization', and by 'why'. Now, modernization is a vague concept. We may note that if, at the present time, the Japanese economy were not so obviously successful, the modernity of Japan would hardly be a subject of discussion. This implies, firstly, that the economic element, and particularly the industrial one, is fundamental to our perception of modernity. Yet since the notion of modernity has been defined exclusively on the basis of the European or American experience, one is tempted to think that only the resemblances between Japan and Europe are significant, and that Japan (or Europe . . .) could not have a special form of modernization of its own. Provisionally, in examining the Japanese past, we shall here keep to well-known criteria that have already been observed in Europe: mobility, individuality and secularization. We shall admit that the investigation of these criteria cannot be limited to the Meiji period and ought to go back, on the one hand, at least to the eighteenth century, and on the other, since modernization is a continual adaptation to techniques that are rapidly evolving, go right up to the present day.[1]

Next we come up against the problem of the distinction between the why and the how. Can one explain the success of Japanese modernization in any other way than by expounding recent Japanese history, since this

I should like especially to thank Professor Ronald P. Dore for his suggestions and remarks.

NB Japanese names are quoted in the Japanese fashion: surname first, and forename afterwards.
1 Upon the problems of Japanese modernization, cf. firstly, the five basic volumes, *Studies in the Modernization of Japan*, Princeton, 1965–.

has had as the desired and organized result that very modernization? It is only on a provisional basis that this distinction will be held to be legitimate. Yet if we have thought of analysing the success it is because we think that failure was possible. The present example of countries that are euphemistically termed 'developing' demonstrates to us that the hopes of governments are often disappointed. We must therefore clearly indicate what divides Japan from these countries. The Japanese Marxists of different shades of opinion, who are numerous in Japanese historiography in universities, argue that there is absolutely no question to be answered (Shiota, 1978). The exploitation of the peasants by the confiscation of surplus value necessarily gives rise to the appearance of a capitalist society. The special characteristics of this confiscation are interpreted in numerous archaic ways that make it a semi-feudal capitalism. There is an immanent and implicit necessity for its transition to industrial capitalism, and it is unnecessary to pose further questions on anything other than the degree of archaism in that society and the moment it will collapse, which is constantly pronounced to be imminent. Even assuming that one succeeds in gaining a clear and distinct idea of a concept such as that of capitalist society, which is termed fascist because it is at one and the same time at the highest stage of its development and also riddled with feudal archaisms, this historiography is of little assistance for our purpose, for it devotes itself to seeking out the causes of failure, not success. It believes failure to be imminent, the 'natural' development of historical evolution. None the less the reasons for the absence of failure in the Japanese case poses a striking problem for the historian. At every moment one is drawn back to the role of the contingent in the formation of reality, a reality that might have become something different from what we know, from what the leaders wished or hoped for. The useful part played by such temptations offered by theories is to warn us against the determinism of necessity.

Modernity and Tradition in the Tokugawa Era

The Japanese society as found by Westerners in the middle of the nineteenth century is certainly not an industrial society similar to their own, but neither does it resemble an agrarian or 'traditional' society. It may be noted that Thünberg, working for the Dutch in 1775–6 at Nagasaki and going as far as Edo, felt none of those great psychological shocks that go with being plunged into a radically different world. He does not remark any surprising state of backwardness or poverty – nothing save certain areas of scientific and technical ignorance that were, moreover, common in Europe itself. The social organization does not

astonish Thünberg, who in no way dreams of terming it 'feudal': it seems
to him one to be taken for granted, for it differs little from what he had
already experienced. On the other hand, strangeness, exoticism in time
and space, pervade the accounts of journeys in the 1860s. One can
legitimately wonder whether it is not between the middle of the
eighteenth and the middle of the nineteenth centuries when the
evolution of Japan and that of Europe have diverged at an increasing rate.

   The authoritarian state of the Tokugawa *shōgun* is defined by a series
of contradictory terms, for the great withdrawal into itself during the
seventeenth century did not rest upon the destruction of centrifugal forces
by an all-powerful centre, but on a compromise between disparate
forces. Japan is at one and the same time centralized and decentralized.
It is sufficiently centralized to feel its cultural and institutional identity.
To tell the truth this fact dates from the origins of the Japanese state
when a pioneer vanguard of relatively homogeneous populations moved
towards the north. During the Tokugawa period every Japanese is aware
that his country exists and has a religious centre – the region of Kyōto-
Nara – and a centre of power – the regions of Kantō, Kamakura and
present day Tōkyō (Edo) – and that this duality is of ancient origin.
There are no ethnic problems as in contemporary Africa; the racial
mixing of the various populations goes back to a period that pre-dates the
formation of the Japanese state, and the differences in origin are not
perceptible. Nor do we note any religious differences that might generate
hostility. Moreover, the *shōgun* insists on periods of residence in Edo for
the *daimyō*, the great lords; when these *daimyō* are authorized to return to
their fief, they are replaced by their family. In so doing the *shōgun* merely
wished to ensure his safety by the linked procedures, well tested in many
societies, of the court and hostages. All this functioned very well, and
Japan, which was emerging from centuries of civil wars, for the first time
experienced a long period of peace that lasted two and a half centuries. It
should be said that such a long period of internal and external peace is
exceptional in world history. It constituted the absolutely necessary
precondition for the development of the forces of production: war
quickly eats up the meagre surpluses accumulated in preindustrial
economies, and forms of agriculture relying on irrigation are even more
precarious than others. The installations that they presuppose require
much more than one annual cultivation cycle in which to be constructed
and very little time to be destroyed. But these alternating periods of
residence also stimulated the mixing of populations from the different
regions in the town of Edo; thus there arose a national market for labour
and for products, and a feeling of the unity of this market. It was all
accompanied by a continual traffic on the roads that converged upon
Edo, the most famous of all being the *Tōkaidō* road that goes from Kyōto

to Tōkyō. In this way this market in Edo had ramifications over the whole country. Finally, in order to pay for their stay, the *daimyō* were obliged to negotiate the sale to the merchants, principally those coming from Ōsaka, of the levies of rice they had made on their peasants, receiving monetary payments in exchange. Ōsaka was becoming the centre, on a national scale, for financial and banking institutions. We can therefore note a similarity to the European situation: there exists a sufficiently extensive market within a cultural area that is conscious of its unity, and within this area there exists a plurality of competing markets. Yet, in order to define the organization of the large fiefs, we can also speak of decentralization, and this allowed a large number of political experiments and the training of administrators and personalities playing the role of ministers of state, which led to the stepping down of the *shōgun* government after 1868. For example, the fiefs of Chōshū and Satsuma, in the first half of the nineteenth century, carried out policies of financial recovery that were absolutely opposed to each other, the contradictory aftermaths of which are to be found later in the tendencies of the Meiji era, with mixtures of *dirigisme* and deregulation of the economy, or the alternation of both.

In its hierarchical organization this state can be said to be at the same time both civilian and military. The cadres of the administrative and political power are indeed warriors, but they exercise that power in offices and by the written word, the edict or circular. Moreover, they derive their means of existence not from the revenue of land held as a fief, but from a remuneration paid in rice. They proudly lay claim to the ethic and conduct of the warrior, but have no possibility of fighting and have no fixed roots in a special, privileged place outside the region controlled by their suzerain, the *daimyō*, who alone possesses this kind of fixed origin. The leaders have no possibility of using their revenues for the purchase of lands, for the lands are not for sale. Capital cannot therefore be tied up in this way, in contrast to China. The result is also that any kind of political change can only be made in the name of this *daimyō*, and must include a somewhat extensive area. And, as in all bureaucracies, subordinates can exceed their powers under the cover of a hierarchy that had been overtaken by events. A good example is provided by the tumultuous decade that preceded the beginnings of the Meiji era. Thus men not paralysed by the extent of their responsibilities have enough power to act in favour of innovation. There likewise results a paradoxical outcome: elites, since they are not recruited, as in China, by a competitive written examination, are not subjected to the intellectual conformity that such competitive examinations suppose, and are therefore capable of demonstrating their creative intelligence. Not having been rendered impotent by the intensive practice of repetitive and

normative exercises of an academic kind, but being well educated, highly
literate, attentive to realities, and sensitized to the problems of an
armed defence that had been revolutionized by the technical changes
that Westerners had brought with them, they busy themselves immediately with gun foundries, naval arsenals and all the innovations of this
kind,which they learn about through the Dutch in Nagasaki. If the *shōgun*
forbid the diffusion of Western publications it is only because he wished
to reserve exclusively for himself a knowledge whose decisive importance
he understands. This world of warriors, as a whole, like the Chinese
literati, indeed considers that the thought of China alone brings wisdom,
and this wisdom is the most important thing in the conduct of affairs. But
they do not deduce from this that European techniques only produce
playthings to amuse the curiosity of the idle passer-by; the narrow-
minded are on the side of the intellectuals who wield the writing-brush
and not of those who trail a sabre. Another result is that the warrior
group has no rival for the political government of the country. The
merchants are not an autonomous bourgeois class; they remind us rather
of the Germanic *Hofjudentum*. As the forced intermediaries of the
daimyō, they are part of the system. Thus a modernization of Japan does
not necessarily end in revolution, and a civil war will be limited to a
few actors without profoundly disturbing the country's production
mechanism.

One of the essential aspects of the policy of pacification followed by
the Tokugawa consisted in closing access to the country as a general
rule, opening it only selectively, in order to prevent the upheavals
brought by Christianity, by European trade and also by the Japanese
diaspora that had been active in the conquest of south-east Asia since the
sixteenth century and which could have returned in strength to the
archipelago. Geography makes this closure and self-sufficiency possible:
like China, which was likewise sealed off at that time, Japan benefits from
its climatic zones, which are in close proximity to one another because of
its situation in the middle latitudes on the eastern shelf of the Eurasian
continent. Over a small area are concentrated a great variety of vegetable
and animal products, both on land and sea. Among other consequences
there is the fact that the originality of the Japanese is reinforced and that
they are faced with the necessity of ensuring their mastery over the
population forced to live in their archipelago.

The feeling of originality is given a theoretical basis from the
eighteenth century onwards with the school of Mito, which is one of the
origins of the 'Meiji renovation' (*Meiji Ishin*). China ceases to be the
obligatory reference point and certain persons, even proclaiming the
superiority of Japan, invent nationalism. Now, this nationalism, in the
long term an ideology of modernization, is in its beginnings turned

towards the past, with hankerings for dynastic legitimacy – the Hegelian cunning of Reason, heteroclitic or serendipitous. In the daily life of the people as a whole their tastes and customs, and everything that springs from *shimaguni konjō* (an insular state of mind, even a siege mentality) date back to this time and have been raised to the dignity of traditions. In this we can find the roots of what Nakane Chie (1984) has called the 'vertical society', certain aspects of which, moreover, are strangely modern and are adapted to *The Organization Man*. Chapter titles of this book by William H. Whyte Jr (1956), directed to the American 'affluent society', seem made for the Japan of those days, and not only of today: 'Belongingness' (chapter 4), 'Togetherness' (chapter 5), 'The Well-rounded Man' (chapter 10), 'The Fight Against Genius' (chapter 16) and so on. The same remarks might apply to the seasonal fads and fashions that have favoured the consumer society, and which do not spring from it, as the European example might lead us to believe. The psychological unity ran no risk of being altered either by foreign immigration or by Japanese seeking broader horizons, and could sustain a nationalism lived by a whole people from the very moment when that people became aware of its being different – if the country were opened up. Of the three means of reacting to social conflict – emigration, violence and withdrawal into a homogeneous group – the first is impossible and the second is very dangerous, for even if peasant or urban revolts have been very numerous, they were all successfully repressed. Only the third remains. But minorities that accept the existence of a society, although not its present mode of functioning, bring with them the possibility of innovation. This possibility in particular was accompanied by a strong sense of injustice among men sure of their own worth, and rightly so, such as Fukuzawa Yūkichi. One cannot help thinking of Barnave before the French Revolution. Passing from emotion to theory, certain samurai assert that in time of peace there is no longer any natural selection, and therefore it is appropriate to question the hierarchy of elites. In the case of the samurai this consisted in changing those in power. If this is not necessarily the way to modernization it is assuredly a spur to change.

On the other hand, the impossibility of responding to demographic pressure through emigration constrained them to try to overcome this pressure. There are two cases to be considered. Firstly, it does seem that the rural population remained roughly stable, through the concerted means of limitation in the number of births, infanticide and flight from the countryside, despite various government prohibitions. The urban population increased, but without any lasting disturbance of the social peace, for the flight from the countryside benefited from the network of towns established between 1580 and 1610 by the great feudal lords. Even today the large towns of Japan have their origins in these *jōkamachi* (towns under the castle), and the roads that are the most used today are by and large the same as at that time (Hall, 1955). Japan has never known the uncontrollable expansion of the gigantic metropolises of the Third World today, nor even the perilous situation of London at the beginning of the Industrial Revolution. At the end of the nineteenth century the total population increased rapidly, but at a slower pace than that of productivity. One can discern in this the continuation of the age-old habits of population control, one that was perhaps made easier by an intensive form of agriculture practised over limited areas, in a situation where the boundary that could not be crossed was clearly and continually indicated. Japanese and Russian topography contrast strongly in this respect. The mean annual growth of the Russian and Japanese populations between the end of the nineteenth century and now is roughly the same: over 1.1 per cent for Japan, and almost 1 per cent for Russia. But whereas the use of an exponential function allows the Japanese progression to be very precisely adjusted, and it was possible to extrapolate the size of the 1980 population from estimates made before 1914, the Russian population is not amenable to any analytical adjustment save that of orthogonal polynomials, that is it increases and decreases at times and in orders of magnitude that are equally unforeseen. The idea of a 'black' distribution as a social remedy is utterly foreign to Japan, and thus the poverty of the Japanese peasant could not be a source of revolution. Japanese solutions have consisted in the development of activities unrelated to rice cultivation, that is not taxed by the tax administration: cottage industry intended for current consumption, cultures such as that of the mulberry tree for breeding the silkworm. The existence of towns provided a national market for production and consumption. The opposition between an intensive Japanese economy and an extensive Russian one is therefore one of ancient origin. And mercantile capital sustained the distribution of all manufactured products in both town and country. Whether small entrepreneurs, who were originally small- or medium-scale agricultural developers, were concerned, or merchant bankers who lent to the feudal lords and speculated in rice, the first accumulation of capital, as contrasted with Europe, owed nothing to a distant overseas trade. This is proof, if one were needed, that one has overestimated, if not the place, at least the necessity of such trade in the birth of modern society. We are therefore led to make the comparison with the financial crisis in the large fiefs and the decrease in the *shōgun* gold stock between the eighteenth and nineteenth centuries. The normal course of production brought about an initial redistribution of capital: official amassing of wealth has partly given way to private investment, precisely because closure from the outside world meant that the exodus of capital was negligible. Thus linked to the closure were its cadre structures, the stability of the population and economic progress. But in no way does it seem that these connections necessarily arose from one another.

In this closed society there was an opening up of minds. Since the work of Ronald P. Dore (1965) we know that on the eve of the Meiji era 40 per cent of boys and 10 per cent of girls had received an education outside the home, rates that can be compared to those in Europe. Because of the rigidity of the hierarchies, it remained only for everyone to attempt to rise within his own group. Education in Japan reconciles the collective ethic and individual ambition by legitimizing the latter. For the working classes this means increasing the market value of individual labour. Education does not lead exclusively to entry into the public service, so gratifying and so lucrative for individuals, and so harmful for society as a whole, as in underdeveloped countries, nor to entry to minor office in the king's service or into the prebends of an established church, as in absolutist Europe. The question remains why so many Japanese made such efforts to obtain an education from the eighteenth century onwards, whilst so many peoples in a like situation fatalistically accepted the status quo. One might hypothesize that the desire is present, sometimes openly avowed, and backed up by quotations from classical Chinese authors, to overtopple the social hierarchy, fed by memories of the civil wars of the sixteenth century. But this feeling did not necessarily come about through the modernization of society. The socially downgraded *samurai* provided warriors in the troubles that led to the disappearance of the Shōgunate. Yet this does not explain everything: most of these *samurai* are not intellectually inclined, whilst at the same time not being without education; they are nationalist, opposed to a modernization that they view as Westernization, whereas a Fukuzawa, of a very modest rank, is favourable to modernization and trusts the Shōgunate to bring it about, whilst detesting its bureaucracy. So as to complicate everything, there is the case of Itō Hirobumi, a *samurai* of the lowest rank, who, before becoming the great statesman of the Meiji era, took part in violent anti-foreign movements before being converted to the virtues of modernization after a journey in Europe. In the case of the peasant entrepreneur the problem was similar: the desire for technical knowledge can spring from the desire to grow wealthy, but there would still have to be explained the will to make the effort and to take the risks of enterprise.

The content of this education is as contradictory as the motivation for it. In this movement of transformation the temptation must be resisted to insist unduly upon the role of books coming from Europe. There are to be found technical works whose applied knowledge may have as its source either Chinese tradition or Dutch innovations. Their diffusion among the peasantry, for example, is only explicable because new economic activities were being undertaken for which there did not exist already in every village technicians, already of proven worth, who were capable of training apprentices: knowledge came from the written word. From the eighteenth century onwards a large number of self-taught people tried their luck, and their adventure was the same as that of the introducers to Japan of the steam engine and the railway in the nineteenth century, whose task was thereby facilitated. To these works, socially neutral – at least in the short term – are added Chinese and Western scientific and ideological works that mutually exclude each other. We should group together books about ideas and books about science, not only because an historically fixed scientific knowledge is more or less consciously linked up to an epistemology and a metaphysics, but because Chinese thought is above all a cosmology from which are deduced a 'naturalist' morality and politics. To dissect a corpse with the help of a Dutch textbook, and to perceive that the Chinese tradition was mistaken, comes down to effecting a mental revolution. This is what Sugita Gempaku and Maeno Ryōtaku did in 1771, and they were not wrong in perceiving in this the beginnings of a new era. That Western science which the Japanese term 'Dutch science' (*Rangaku*) is found to be the direct and precise origin of the modernization of techniques, in particular for the arming of the great fiefs. But the indirect and widely diffused effects are to be found right up to the end of the nineteenth century. (On the whole question of the problem of values, see Bellah, 1957; Keene, 1969; Jansen, 1980. A basic book is Blacker, 1964.)

Modernization is not always set in train by personal interest and an 'invisible hand'. Ronald Dore (1959) has clearly demonstrated that, taking into account the customs that regulated the taxing by agricultural levies, it was of no consequence to the beneficiary from these levies whether the crop increased permanently or not. The principal motive that had impelled certain privileged persons to adopt measures for the modernization of agriculture in the Meiji era was the tincture of physiocratic theories that they had acquired. What is subsumed under the generic term of Chinese thought has its part in the movement. Sugita Gempaku, for example, wrote that if he had been able to understand the Dutch books, he owed it to his classical intellectual training. The fact that this Chinese thought represents a 'Summa' in the medieval sense of the term and that in this way it trains intellectuals practised in argument and reasoning cannot be neglected: these intellectuals are capable of understanding other systems of thought. Yet this does not necessarily mean that they took an interest in them, and the case of China reminds us of this. Now, this Chinese thought constitutes for the Japanese a borrowing, and is felt as such. From the eighteenth century onwards, in particular, it is relativized and intellectuals can admit the idea that other borrowings are possible. Furthermore, Confucianism, or what for the sake of convenience is classed under that term, allowed both for the praise of rationality and, for inferiors, the duty to rebuke their superiors: transformations of every kind could be justified – if one desired to do so. But this aspect is even more strongly emphasized in the rival thought of the official Confucianism of Chu Hsi, the school of Wang Yangming. The latter, which gives pride of place to intuition and the individual, enjoyed the favour of all the opponents of the *shōgun* regime, and even today still nourishes a current of thought that contests the established order.

Yet, in spite of its conformism, the role of official Confucianism in modernization is no mean one. As Ronald Dore (1965) has noted, without the habits inculculated by a more or less diffused Confucianist teaching there would have been many more broken machines or goods spoilt through not having scrupulously respected the instructions that had been given. Furthermore, this Confucianism caused the minds of people to see the importance of the common good. This does not go unaccompanied by hypocrisy, as is underlined in a famous text of Natsume Sōseki in the twentieth century, in which the novelist makes one of his characters remark that, if it is for the good of the country for one to grow wealthy, he is quite willing to sacrifice himself for his country in this way. But the hypocrisy is never absolute, and permanent cynicism is not a very common state. Above all, since the general spread of this moral Confucianism, the efforts made to improve one's lot by improving the production of marketable goods are neither ignored nor condemned by public opinion. On the contrary, they receive the eulogistic approval of the whole of society. This approbation doubtless facilitated all such proto-industrial attempts. If one adds to this a collective passion, nationalism, then indeed one truly enters into modernization.

There remained to be resolved the antinomies between Chinese and Western thought. The term *kyūri* in both cases did indeed signify science, but not at all with the same meaning. Fortunately this was not immediately perceived, and later on the repeated misinterpretations of ingenuous pedants compounded it by forging the concept of the ideal union between Western science and Eastern morality. Perhaps one might find something even more profound that favoured the entry of Japan into modern society, something whose extensiveness would demand a separate series of reflections. In 1922 Jacques Maritain, in the 'Antimoderne', emphasized that modern thought was stoutly immanentist, and the dominant German thought even more so than elsewhere in Europe. This he linked to the glorification of the state and material success as the ultimate goal of man. Now, Sino-Japanese thought is likewise pervaded with immanence, and in this way would be favourable in its basic principles to the implicit philosophy of modernization and to any material change increasing the domination of the state and society.

To single out only the characteristics of a country that account for its later evolution is to run the risk of falsifying the impression of the whole. Undoubtedly there exists a considerable homogeneity in Japanese civilization, and a national identity whose profound originality will strike foreigners as much as the Japanese themselves, when both groups have occasion to enter into continuous contact, and this is still true. Yet we should not draw the conclusion that Japan in its entirety achieved a national consensus that at the same time facilitated the governance of men and a policy of adaptation to the modern world. On the contrary, Japan has always been a land of conflicts, and in the nineteenth century the great debate (and the great struggle) within the dominant groups was precisely that about modernization. Modernization had as many reasons to come about as not, and its opponents believed that they had carried the day with the victory of the supporters of the Emperor in 1868. Investigating Japanese society before the Meiji era, we find all the ambiguities of an entity in a potential state, in the realm of the indeterminate, *to aoriston*, and not that of the predestined and necessary. The explanations of contemporary Japan through its values, culture and traditions, or more generally through its past, are not sufficient. But they are necessary. Often we misinterpret the pioneer work of historians in the 1950s and 1960s concerning the *shōgun* eighteenth century: their aim was not to account for, but to demonstrate – and this was the great, the novel idea – that the transformation of Japan had begun well before the contact with Europe in the middle of the nineteenth century, and that Japan was better prepared for this contact than the other countries of East Asia. We must therefore propound, but only after this, other ways of making intelligible the success of Japan.

'An early case of late development'[2]

The moment of contact with the West, and the types of organization that result from it, provide an additional locus of explanation for the achievement of modernization – that of the 'conjuncture'. And we can

2 The title of this section is an expression used by Dore (1979: 369). References on economic growth include: Allen (1983), Ohkawa (1957), Rosowsky (1961), Smith (1977), Nakamura (1966, 1974), Waswo (1974).

clearly see how striking are the differences from the Third World. Underdevelopment is a concept that is only relevant when applied to a population increasing uncontrollably, finding itself up against industrial consumer economies. The latter impose their patterns of behaviour through their prestige, but afford no possibility of catching up with their level of productivity, so far are they ahead. Japan did not experience this situation. Thus Dore's expression clearly takes into account the complexity of the situation and the importance of chronology, by situating Japan in its international context in the nineteenth century and in the ranks of countries that have effected the greatest transformation ever achieved.

The moment when the two entities came together was not exactly a matter of chance, in the strict sense of the term, for the nineteenth century is the great period of Western expansion. For Japan, the problem had already arisen since the beginning of the century, with the Russian push forward from eastern Siberia and Alaska (bought back from the Russian by the Americans just one year before the beginning of the Meiji era). It was posed with increasing urgency after the opium war, which had provoked in Japan a flood of pamphlets and polemics concerning the 'white peril'. The meeting is rather a good example of the *Cournot effect*, whose methodological importance has been clearly highlighted by Raymond Boudon (1974): a conjunction of independent determinisms which spark off a series of infinite regressions of which it is impossible to conceive. Firstly, as was noted by the Iwakura mission of 1871–3, the time-lag of Japan was only two generations behind continental Europe. And Japan arrives on the international scene at a time when progress is beginning to accelerate, but only *beginning* to do so. Thus technical progress is integrated into the Japanese world without destroying it. Or Japan welcomes this progress at the same time as the West, as in the case of electricity or the internal-combustion engine, and it is neither better nor worse prepared for this than the rest. Japanese technicians can even carry out original work, for example in the armaments field – so very important for security – very early on under General Arisaka (1897), and then General Nambu (from the 1920s onwards). Nowadays no under-developed country would be capable of manufacturing its own modern armaments – the cases of China and India would be worth discussing in this respect. In any case the Japanese try to adapt imports to local conditions: thus in machines they replace expensive steel by cheap wood. Or indeed these techniques existed already, but were very recent. In the years 1860–70 the breech rifle and the centre-fire cartridge are on the point of revolutionizing tactics, but only on the point of so doing; Japan can buy a little of this modern material, whilst retaining, in spite of everything, defences that were on the whole outdated. But Westerners would not have been able to conquer the country cheaply, and the *samurai* are not seen to be abruptly outclassed, with a loss of their esteem as an elite, through their technical backwardness. Moreover, the 1860s are those of triumphant liberalism in the West. This means firstly that it is the 'nadir of imperialism': the Great Powers no more desire to take possession of Japan than of China, but only to open them up to trade. It is true that the leaders of Japan and China believe the will exists to destroy them, because they themselves do not conceive of international relations in terms of the *jus gentium* and *mare liberum*. Capitalists readily lend money to those countries whose state systems are responsible (and occasionally to the others also), and if they wish for foreign experts there is no difficulty. If Japan made better use of this than did China the sole reason for this that comes to mind relates to their previous situation. The Japanese are very sensitive to what they call *taisei* – the spirit of the times – because they are moved by habit to desire to find a harmony with the world and to blend with what is in process of development. The spirit of the times, then, represented a liberalism, tempered by a sense for the contingencies and practice of realities that impelled them towards a provisional form of mercantilism, a suffrage based on wealth, and a Prussian-type administration. The Iwakura mission had in fact concluded that the case of Germany was the most interesting one because of its relative delay in establishing a centralized government and its military policy, which guaranteed independence. Now, these solutions had been tried and tested in the nineteenth century, whereas the popularity of a planned, authoritarian socialism in the twentieth century among the leaders of underdeveloped countries is due to its being spread among young students in Europe. The same phenomenon occurred again after the defeat of 1945: the reconstruction and capital monetary reform of 1949 owes much to the cooperation between Japanese and American classical economists, for on the Japanese side there were no Marxist economists to hand, and on the American side the businessmen and financiers entrusted with these problems had little taste for the Keynesian inspirations of the New Deal. Thus ideologists have never at any time had the upper hand in the economy. We may also add that at the end of the nineteenth century, trade union stipulations or compulsory social security charges did not arise to burden the budget of burgeoning, but still fragile, undertakings. Today, although a job is cheaper to establish in an underdeveloped country than in an industrial one, that employment costs much more than in the nineteenth century because there is a minimum wage recognized by international consensus. In the nineteenth century poor countries could avail themselves to the full of their comparative advantages. As regards colonial policy, the delay in modernization in Japan had the same consequences as for Germany.

Latecomers on the scene, the two countries did not have the benefits, but neither the burdens, of colonization and decolonization. The balance of profit and loss to be struck concerning colonial policies constitutes a difficult problem, but it is notable that these two countries have had in common for a century both an absence of colonies and particularly strong economic growth. Under this political regime the problem of the renewal of the ruling classes did not depend upon public opinion but on an oligarchy, and the latter had ended up by being in favour of the modernization of the country. Yet it did not follow that this renewal would come about through physical elimination, once the period of fighting and plotting was over. Undoubtedly the tradition of the *sōshi*, those patriots whose patriotic zeal went as far as assassination, never entirely disappeared, but remained what it had been before the Meiji era, a technique reserved for the opposition; state terrorism as a means of government did not become an institution, as might have been feared after the 1860s. Social stability thus lowers the cost of modernization by avoiding a wastage in men.

Serious obstacles of a conjunctural nature continually blocked the ambitious plans of the oligarchy that led Japan. Among the obstacles successfully overcome, three may be singled out that owed much to the world economic situation, and were thus shared with other countries. They therefore require comparison. The take-off in the Meiji era was quickly upset by the Great Depression of the 1880s; then the world crisis of 1929 hindered exports; finally, the general collapse in 1945 left the Japanese economy totally dependent upon the American dollar. In any case, a bad economic situation can only be overcome by decreased consumption, coupled with an increase in production. Moreover, this must not give rise to disturbances that prevent the normal functioning of society, in which case the remedy is worse than the disease. But the Japanese found themselves well prepared, through their past, for such kinds of ordeal. It so happened that the beginnings of the modernization concerted by the Meiji government coincided with a deflationist phase, in a world-wide pile-up of production. The failure could have been foreseen because of the difficulty in exporting and in stabilizing the finances necessary to pay for new modern institutions such as the army and the new school system [out of the state budget]. Firstly, massive recourse to the minting and printing of money destroyed the currency (Mainichi, 1975); then the deflationary policy of Matsukata in 1881 ruined the first entrepreneurs and worsened living conditions for everybody. But, in contrast to the Balkan or South American countries of then and now, or present-day socialist bloc or underdeveloped countries, economic reconstruction did not allow itself to take the easy route of bankruptcy. International loans were later made easier because of this, as well as the abrogation of unequal treaties, and Japan could enter the respectable club of the gold standard, whose members had the right to large-scale international trade. But in point of fact Japan resorted to such loans as little as possible, and the external debt swelled above all at the time of the wars against China (1894–5) and Russia (1904–5) – for exceptional political reasons, and not in the normal functioning of the state and the economy. In this are to be found the rules of classical, stringent financial management. ~~The Japanese rely above all upon themselves~~: the gross internal formation of capital amounts annually on average for 1892–1901 to 195 million yen, and the net balance of foreign wealth is then at −29 million yen; the relationship between the latter and the former figures is especially unfavourable for 1897–1906, a situation which is never to recur. Japan used in a most felicitous way the rules of the international game of parities fixed by the gold standard. At the time of the 1929 crisis the rules were changed, and a retreat to a zone of monetary and political domination, with the creation of money and the build-up of armaments, allowed a policy of full employment, with the certainty, in the medium term, of international upheavals. Japan was also ready for that situation, through its nationalism and its desire to dominate Asia in order to 'protect' it from the perverted West. Finally, the post-1945 reconstruction boded very ill. In 1949 one of McArthur's advisors prophesied: 'The Japan of the next three decades . . . may be self-supporting, but with internal political, economic and social distress, and a standard of living gradually approaching the bare subsistence level.' Only the material factors of production were taken into account, and human ones not at all. Japan turned to its advantage its non-dominant but indispensable situation in the capitalist world. In particular, since the United States was peculiar in being the only country where the harsh reality of squaring the balance of payments did not obtrude, either in the short or medium term, Japan exported to it without opening up either its commercial or financial market, and accumulated dollars that it reinvested afterwards in its production equipment. Also, the yen that was fixed at 360 to the dollar in 1949 was soon undervalued, and became increasingly so. Japan likewise used its geographical position to pay for its protection by the American taxpayer, without allocating a proportional share of its revenue to the defence of the region. Furthermore, it needed to show itself capable of building a modern economy; this it did by assigning to the dominant American economy, and, to a lesser degree, the economies of industrial Europe, the role of a Third World country that exports its raw material and imports manufactured products; with this difference – and it is enormous – that the United States or Europe could pay.

Comparisons with other countries come inevitably to mind. These comparisons, moreover, loomed large with the political actors of the time, and it should be said that the examples from elsewhere were hardly encouraging. For example, Tani Kanjō resigned from the government in 1887, and wrote a memoir to denounce his colleagues' corruption, and the world of politics, predicting that Japan was set to experience the same fate as the Egypt of Mehemet Ali. Nor was he alone in viewing the situation pessimistically. For example, in 1906 the Frenchman La Mazelière wrote a sort of chronicle of contemporary Japan, in which its fate was envisaged as hardly better than that of China. In China's case, at the end of the nineteenth century, its backwardness can partly be explained by the lack of capital and by unequal treaties that did not favour burgeoning industries; on the other hand, it had the advantage of low salaries. Now, Japan had also experienced unequal treaties up to 1889–94, but did not see its economy ruined through them (despite what the Japanese press said at the time); it succeeded in having them revised to its advantage. One may concede that the payment by China to Japan of a war indemnity benefited enormously the latter's investments; it also proves that China possessed capital funds, or could borrow them, but did not know how to use them for its own modernization. Pakistan has possessed for a long time a very special cottage industry – the copying of firearms by artisans among the north-western tribes, now revived in connection with Afghanistan – could have resulted in a powerful mechanical industry. Such artisan production was exported abroad, for example to the Philippines in the 1960s and early 1970s. Thus this was something vastly different from a picturesque local activity. There were to be found in it certain characteristics of the first Japanese exports: products of middling quality copied from the West, but preferred by a local clientele because they were cheaper, without there being, strictly speaking, any competition, for the European or American originals sold at prices that reflect another economic world and a different purchasing power. Despite everything, such cottage production does not improve or develop into a modern industry. Now, the Japanese used such production from the Meiji era onwards for manufactures intended for the army, but as subcontractors. There were arsenals directing and advising these artisans, organizing them as a whole. Furthermore, the state had favoured the creation of modern steelworks and, under its control, permitted delivery to the artisans of more or less finished steel through these arsenals. Such a situation assumes that the state has no fear of an armed uprising and has confidence in its capacity to maintain order: we are taken back once more to a certain political tradition. It also assumes that the state wishes to coordinate modernization. In the use of the economic situation by Japan everything comes back to a central body that organizes, for many other countries have known, at one time or another, situations analogous to this, but the consequences have been different.

The predominance of large centralized organizations in Japan is so notorious that occasionally the modernity accomplished is ascribed to them alone (as in official propaganda since the Meiji era). This predominance is to be found in any late modernization that sets out to proceed at top speed, and is proportional to the degree of tardiness. The state has played a strategic role by causing public opinion to accept two founding myths. According to Machiavelli's expression, to govern is to cause to believe. The first myth is that of *Tennō*, the divine emperor, but whose divinity is immanent on earth and to the Japanese people in such a way that every subject can share in it. Political stability, designated as the historic permanence of the dynasty, implanted in the very nature of the country the social peace necessary for the great transformations that were planned. Nationalism spread from the warrior classes to the whole people, and justified itself with pride – in the field of compulsory education, for example – in an archipelago that had never known foreign invasion and in a people springing, so to speak, from its own soil. Japan enjoyed historically a collective 'immaculate conception', like the Athens of the Greek tragedy writers or the proletariat of Marx; this clearly presages a unique destiny. With humility, in down-to-earth fashion, nationalism was justified by the geography of a country smaller than California that lacked cultivable land and was obliged, in order to survive, not only to seal itself off from other peoples but also to install itself among them. This nationalism caused a 'grand design' to be accepted by the whole people, which thus constituted itself as a nation, not *proprio motu*, but under the influence of an oligarchy. This great design was summed up in the slogan *fukoku kyōhei*, a rich country and a strong army. Through this emotional 'New Deal' passionate feeling was aroused in everybody, and what had been merely a *samurai* quarrel became a matter for the entire people. No great change can happen without the support of all social groups united together. And the men in the middle echelons, present in great number, capable of handing down the modernization that had been organized at the top, and even of taking personal initiatives, had existed for a long time, thanks to the effort made in moral and technical instruction, which had already become rooted in habit. (On the origins of the leaders, see Yoshimoro, 1984.)

The second myth was just as durable and viable: that of the competence of those elites having the sanction of the authorities. And these new elites were for the most part the ancient ones. The *samurai* families represented 6 per cent of the population, but roughly half the governing elite in the Meiji era. Later on the prestige of the great universities took over, but the process of social renewal was always very slow. We can doubt whether the control of modernization alone justified the power of these elites. We doubt it, firstly because of the permanent factors involved. We doubt it equally when we examine the types of studies that gave entry to the leading elite. One would expect to see the leading Japanese cadres educated for the most part in the sciences, because of their performance in industry. Now, 32 per cent – and this is the most numerous group – from the top 500 companies came in 1970 from the University of Tōkyō, and in particular from the law faculty. And it is well known that this percentage is even exceeded in other sectors. But law is of hardly any importance in Japanese society, as contrasted with the United States and France. This percentage can be compared to the 34 per cent of polytéchnique graduates at the head of the 100 top French companies in 1968. The temptation might be felt to rationalize these choices if this did not go against the economic realities. It clearly seems that in both cases authority is legitimated by its own existence, on condition that it does not reveal irremediable deficiencies. It is perfectly true that Japan owes much to its education system, but this must be understood in a very broad sense. We do not mean that the economic successes of Japan and its modernization are proportional to the number of those qualified in disciplines that are directly involved in the production of material goods, and that it is necessary and sufficient to increase the amount of scientific studies if one wishes to implement modernization. Japanese leaders are not drawn from the scientific track. The cadres as a whole work in teams, and these teams are homogeneous in their level, although coming from different forms of training; except for specialized tasks, those with a literary background are recruited as well as scientists and economists. Finally, technical education has always been of very minor importance, with companies preferring to enrol recruits when they leave general education, themselves giving the necessary technical knowledge at the appropriate time. The system functions well because public opinion as a whole believes in the validity of the forms of prestige conferred by universities. The beginning of modernization and of the establishment of state examinations that aimed at a meritocracy coincided chronologically. Public opinion could link the two, and believe that the sufficient condition to rise in the social scale was to pass examinations. This belief in equality of opportunity contributed, and continues to contribute, to awakening the ambition to transform the country at the same time as it reinforces the founding myth of the state. Major qualifications behave as does a currency that circulates only if there is confidence in it, but which cannnot hold up very long in the face of bad results. Next, work in differentiated teams prevents everybody making the same error at the same time. Furthermore, training on the job follows closely and leads rapidly to developments in techniques.

Thus society accepts the validation of competence effected by the great centralised organizations – the state and the large firms. Yet this does not mean that it was these large organizations that realized the modern take-off of Japan. They organized it by bringing to it their prestige and their models. If we consider the realities, leaving aside attitudes and aptitudes, we have to state that for a long time heavy industry represented merely a 'show' modernization: the net added value of the metallurgy industry in 1929 was a little below that of the ceramics industry and only a quarter that of the textile industry. Moreover, this statistic ignores the share of undertakings that employed less than five persons, numerous in these two sectors.

The increase in goods available is essentially due to individual entrepreneurs in agriculture, traditional manufactures and light consumer industries. In them is to be found the precocious character of this development. Such industries are labour intensive, and the state lacks the capital to launch a vast heavy industry (Lockwood, 1978). Furthermore, there is no thought of holding back this light industry, because of a lack of an ideology to rationalize economic progress. There is no controversy such as the Bukharin–Preobrazhensky controversy in Russia in 1925. The question was not even raised. Agricultural production increases more rapidly than the population and pays heavy charges in the form of taxes and rents. The farm feeds the town and pays for the factory. The difficulty consists in measuring the size of the development. Nakamura (1966, 1974) reports already very high productivity before the modernization by the Meiji government and therefore thinks that progress attributed to the policy of the time must be put down to the efforts of the peasantry, whilst insisting on the endogenous aspect of these transformations. According to Nakamura, the rate of agricultural growth may be from 0.8 per cent to 1.2 per cent per year in the Meiji era. Okawa (1957), on the other hand, puts the emphasis on the transformations wrought by the Meiji oligarchy and suggests 2.5 per cent per year. The problem is doubtless insoluble, for land records and agricultural statistics are even less reliable than the others, which is saying a great deal. In any case these rates exceed those of population growth and allow consumption to be improved as well as savings to increase. After 1920 the picture perhaps deteriorates, and there is recourse to imports from Taiwan and Korea. The food situation among the Koreans plainly becomes difficult. But if Japan proper is considered, given an index of 100 for 1910–14, in 1935–9 the population index stands at 141 and food production at 161. Japan has not known famine, as contrasted with the Soviet Union, Maoist China or the 'developing' part of Africa. But life remains harsh in the countryside. Rent dues payable never go below 50 per cent. The result is riots in the 1880s, when compulsory military service – i.e. a levy of men – and increases in taxation or rent charges are both felt at the same time: too many painful innovations occurred together. But these isolated disorders did not last. More serious, precisely because they did last, are the incessant quarrels between farmers and landowners, which come to a head between 1935 and 1937. Their persistence had struck the movements of Young Officers who were in close contact with recruits of rural origin. The 'Shōwa Restoration' programmes, which were both revolutionary and reactionary, and in any case subversive, and whose implementation was accompanied by assassinations of ministers and financiers, or by bloody attempts at a *coup d'état*, have clearly some connection with this situation. But by then the modern state was no longer in process of construction, the imperial mythology had been assimilated by everybody, and institutions, like civil peace, survive very well despite the death of a few leaders. Much was asked of agriculture, but it was not sacrificed: in this is to be found the reason for success.

Light industry and artisan trades do not disappear in the face of large-scale industry – on the contrary, they progress. In general there are two to three times more small-scale than large-scale undertakings. Thus, in 1909, out of 15,400 industrial undertakings, only 6700 were using motive power. Modernization occurs during a period of growth without overturning and ruining what had gone before. The reason is to be found in the persistence of consumer tastes. One had to wait until 1906 for salaries, employment and productivity (the three elements being linked by the rates of marginal productivity) in the modern sector to increase markedly more rapidly than those in the traditional, non-mechanical sector. Yet this latter sector, even if it is overtaken, does not disappear, and the labour market is not upset. In the building industry, for example, there is to be found an astonishing continuity: 92.53 per cent of houses in Tōkyō were built of wood in 1886, 93.08 per cent in 1938. Nowhere is this situation to be found in underdeveloped countries, whose leaders want to live as do their counterparts in the industrial countries, and, in a desire to imitate upward social mobility, all strata of society attempt to possess some of the goods their country does not manufacture, whose importation ruins the economy. We must not transpose in time this fascination for a life-style founded upon consumption. Europeans understand fairly well this attitude of the Japanese – before 1945 they had only somewhat incredulous commiseration for the first indications of the affluent society in the United States. For this there must undoubtedly be a certain national pride, a naïve but rewarding assurance that refinement and the quality of life belong distinctively to your own tradition. But it is indeed true that the Japanese tradition offered 'the pleasure of living' sufficient to enter into competition with the Western way of life, which, all in all, owed a good part of its attractions to the pre-industrial aristocratic, luxurious life. The weight of the new production techniques did not make itself felt with the same intensity as today. Through a paradox that is common in history, the desire to change nothing allows one to opt for change, whilst the desire to change everything leads only to upheaval.

The Japanese example affords the possibility of verifying the generality of very plausible theories concerning modernization, which have not been elaborated to take into account the case of that country. The need for external financing at the beginning for an economy in the process of modernization, either slowly by external trade, or rapidly and voluntarily by means of international loans, according to the view of Nurkse (1963), is called very much into question. Yet one cannot maintain that these international loans ruin such countries on every occasion. It is not true that a state that is transforming itself rapidly by opening itself up to the outside world has especially to bestow privilege on its armed forces and police by granting them material advantages; it will depend on the patriotic attachment to common interests, and on the strength of national unity. And if Raymond Boudon (1974, 1984) has already demonstrated that one cannot count on the school to ensure social mobility, because this lies in the domain of politics, as much might be said of modernization: it cannot be summoned up by decree, even in the long term. To enlarge the place given to the physical and mathematical sciences in order to facilitate industrial production is not based on any necessity, for such production, once a certain technical level has been attained, depends above all upon the way the undertaking is organized. On the other hand, Japan demonstrates extremely well the validity of the criticisms made in 1969 by David S. Landes of certain illusions, illusions that were even more widespread at the time he wrote than they are now: it is not true that backward economies grow more quickly than others and that we are consequently moving towards a global equalization; nor is it true either that the dominant factors for growth are heavy industry and modern machines. If credit is dear and labour cheap, machines of an older type allow one to utilize the comparative advantages afforded by the place and time; and the choice of heavy industry is a political and not an economic one, for it occasions costs without giving a return.

At all times, from the eighteenth century up to now, modernization and increase in production have been talked about, emphasizing the fact that the population made sacrifices and worked and saved. Clearly we cannot deny the influence of Confucian ideology, of the habits of frugality, and of the ideology of feudal loyalty. Doubtless we can also rely on the traditional attitude of *menjū fukuhai*, that seeming obedience which is accompanied by resentment and manipulation of one's superiors. Occasionally an argument has been advanced against the importance of value systems, and in particular, of Confucianism, in the transformation of Japan. It was pointed out that China and Korea, which shared Confucian values, if not the war-like and feudal ones, did not become modernized. Now, the persistent economic success of Singapore, Taiwan and South Korea, which the global economic crisis has highlighted since 1973, proves the importance of these value systems. This proof is reinforced by the patent failure of North Korea, continental China, Vietnam and Cambodia, in so far as they conform to other models and other values. But these are negative factors that can account for the absence of grave disturbances, but do not explain why the Japanese did not react, when faced with being deprived of the fruits of growth and with the very palpable corruption of the elites, by a general 'go-slow' strike or massive emigration, modes of behaviour that exist in other societies. A passion, an emotion was necessary. Nationalism provided these, and in the most extreme form, that of a feeling of being encircled by a hostile, non-Japanese world, and that it is, in spite of everything, necessary to accept the abuses of that society without trying to change them, because of the emergency that exists. Doi Takeo (1971) has dubbed this sentiment, which for him is a fundamental constituent of Japanese culture, *higaisha ishiki*, the feeling of being victimized. It is a powerful means for the mobilization of the masses, but a very dangerous one when applied for too long a time. It served in the military sphere to preserve the unity of the nation in the Meiji era, but it led to the hostility of the other great powers, and was abandoned in this sphere after 1945. We now perceive, and for the same international reasons, that it must also be abandoned in the economic sphere. In Japan the search is on for what is to replace it, and for what 'grand design' to give society. The impression is clearly that this problem is not one exclusive to Japan and that the whole of the industrial world is confronting it. Since these emotions in Japan were fed in their origins by means of myths, especially that of Tennō and state Shintōism, we may doubt the importance of secularization and rationality as criteria of modernism. Success does not depend upon processes: its origins are drawn from the encounter of a prepared people with a passion revealed by imaginative and realistic leaders. If the expression did not evoke a body of clear-cut doctrine and ideological connotations, one might say that Japan affords an 'object lesson' in organizational empiricism.

References

Allen, G. C. 1983: *Le defi economique du Japon*, Paris.
Bellah, R. N. 1957: *The Values of Pre-Industrial Japan*, Glencoe, Ill.
Blacker, C. 1964: *The Japanese Enlightenment*, Cambridge.
Boudon, R. 1974: *Education, Opportunity and Social Inequality*, New York.
   1984: *Le place du désordre*, Paris.
Doi, Takao 1971: *Amae no kozo* [*The Structure of the amae*], Tokyo. (Numerous translations exist.)
Dore, R. 1959: *Land Reform in Japan*, London.
   1965: *Education in Tokugawa Japan*, Berkeley.
   1979: *Japan: A Comparative View*, ed. A. Craig, Princeton.
Hall, J. W. 1955: The castle town and Japan's modern urbanization. *Far Eastern Quarterly*, XV.
Jansen, M. B. 1980: *Japan and its World*, Princeton.
Keene, D. 1969: *The Japanese Discovery of Europe, 1720–1830*, Stanford.
Landes, D. S. 1969: *The Unbound Prometheus. Technical Change and Industrial Development in Western Europe from 1750 to the Present*, London.
Lockwood, W. W. 1968: *The Economic Development of Japan*, Princeton.
Mainichi Shinbun 1975: *The Hiro Hito Era*, Tokyo.
Nakamura, J. I. 1966: *Agricultural Production and Economic Development of Japan*, Princeton.
   1974: Incentives, productivity gaps and agricultural growth rates in pre-war Japan, Taiwan and Korea. In H. D. Harootunian (ed.), *Japan in Crisis*, Princeton.
Nakane Chie 1984: *Japanese Society*, London.
Nurkse 1963: *Les problèmes de la formation du capital dans les pays sous-développés*, Paris.
Ohkawa, K. 1957: *The Growth Rate of the Japanese Economy since 1878*, Tokyo.
Rosowsky, H. 1961: *Capital Formation in Japan, 1868–1940*, New York.
Shiota Shobei 1978: *Dictionnaire biographique du mouvement ouvrier international*, published under the direction of J. Maitron and G. Haupt, 2 vols, Paris.
Smith, T. C. 1977: *Nakahara: Family Farming and Population in a Japanese Village, 1717–1830*, Stanford.
Waswo, A. 1974: The origins of tenant unrest. In H. D. Harootunian (ed.), *Japan in Crisis*, Princeton, New Jersey.
Whyte, W. H., Jr 1956: *The Organization Man*, New York.
Yoshimori Masaru 1984: *Les entreprises Japonaises*, Paris.

9

The Russian Case

Alain Besançon

In a famous speech Pericles asserted that Athens was 'the school of Greece'. No country in Europe can claim such pre-eminence. The great nations of Europe – Italy, France, England, Spain, Germany – have always been successively, or at the same time, the pupils and teachers of one another, and each one of them has accomplished something unique and equally admirable in its own domain. The less great nations – the Low Countries, the Scandinavian countries, Portugal and so on – have shared their status, and their merit is proportionally no less. This is, in my view, the miracle of Europe. What are its geographical boundaries? How far did this 'miracle' extend to Poland, Romania, Finland and Russia? To answer these questions might be the object of another colloquium, because, to judge from the great majority of the chapters presented here, it is another conception of the miracle that appears to dominate this book: not the miracle *of* Europe, but the miracle *in* Europe, which might be the emergence of the modern world as viewed in the main from the economic angle. From this viewpoint the emergence occurred somewhere in England, and the question that is posed is to learn why it did not come about elsewhere, and why it was impossible for it to do so.

I do not believe that this other way of tackling the European miracle is the most fruitful or the most interesting one. Yet, having voiced this reservation, I shall adopt it as my general framework. The discussion has revolved round two points: the birth of capitalism, and the relationship established between the state and society that favoured this birth. I do not know what 'capitalism' is, but its usual connotation is with modernity, with a disenchantment with the world, with the reform of man, who becomes active, rational, capable of initiative within a society that is itself autonomous and free. It is in this conventional sense, laden with all these historiographical allusions that I shall use the word *capitalism*.

If we relate it to the historical entity of Russia, three questions must be posed:

1 Why was it radically impossible for 'capitalism' to be born in Russia?
2 Why was it born all the same, in spite of this impossibility – a birth that constitutes a sort of 'Russian miracle' within the European miracle?
3 Why was it so rapidly and completely destroyed, so much so that Russia is today farther from the European West than at any moment in its history?

If we go back to the list of conditions for 'the European miracle' that Professor Finer gave to us in our conference discussion – namely: law, citizenship, individuals, respect for property, limited government, religious consistency, counter-cultures – we note that nothing of this kind existed in Muscovy. Indeed two traits characterize the Russian world.

Extreme barbarity

If we consider the chain of empires that surround it – Europe, the Turkish Empire, the Persian Empire, India, China, Japan – the Russian expanse, as it presented itself in the eighteenth century, is the most empty and the most indigent. The agriculture is of a primitive type, close to that of Carolingian Europe. The peasant scratches the earth with a primitive plough. He has available as metal instruments only his axe and the point of his plough blade. There are almost no artisan trades. There are very few towns and these are centres for the authorities, and for the collection of taxes. Society is simple to an excess (a mosaic of estates held together by a primitive administration). The level of literacy is very low, culture almost non-existent, and the language still rudimentary, the technique of reasoning and thought elementary.

The Muscovite state: an additional obstacle

The Muscovite state is a mixture of Tartar and Byzantine elements that are not favourable to the flowering of capitalism. Moreover, the state finds ways of making them even more depraved. The Grand Prince of Moscow was for a long time a kind of vizir of the Tartar Khan. A loyalist, he obliged the Orthodox Church to offer prayers for the Tsar of Sarai or the Tsar of Kazan. In fact, the Tartar state enjoyed the legitimacy accorded to conquerors. But when the Grand Prince had seized independence, instead of considering that he had formed a polity with his people, whose monarch he was, he preferred to consider himself as the conqueror of his own subjects. When Fletcher asked Ivan III what the status of his subjects was, the latter replied: 'All are slaves.' At the same time the Grand Prince sought another legitimacy as the heir, not of the Tartar Tsar, but also of the Tsar of Constantinople. The Russian state is a liturgical one in which the sovereign spends the best part of his days in carrying out ritual acts. The confusion between the spiritual and the temporal power is absolute, with all the advantages lying with the latter. The form of Byzantism that has been borrowed is that of the empire of the ancient languages, shot through in its entirety with hatred of the Latins. Hence, after the fall of Constantinople, the siege mentality and Messianic ideas that arise in this 'third Rome' of Moscow.

The Russian state is a patrimonial one. Sovereignty is hardly distinguished from property. His subjects' goods belong to the prince. Law cannot evolve. The state is violent, predatory. By the end of the sixteenth century it has destroyed the aristocratic elites of the country in the unbelievable butchery that was the *Opritchnina*, and the sole commercial towns, half Hanseatic, that the country possessed – Novgorod and Pskov – had been wiped out. Of the three legends (Romanian, German and Russian) that depict, in the guise of Dracula, the reign of Vlad the Empaler, the Russian one alone sings the praises of this prince. Dracula is shown as a model, the Machiavellian prince that Russia needs.

Peter the Great made matters worse. For a century the people had been slowly entering into the bonds of serfdom: he tightened those bonds, and under his successors Russian serfdom was transformed into a slavery that included most of the population. Peter's state enslaved the whole of society, including the nobility, demands upon whose services were made from infancy until retirement, and finally the church, which lost what little autonomy it had been able to retain. Just as much as the Muscovite state, the Petersburg state was the destroyer of aristocracies. It persecutes and sets beyond the pale the Old Believers, that is the sole group which has any vocation for commercial and industrial enterprise, and in the eighteenth century it proceeds to undertake several 'purges' among the upper aristocracy. To carry out these purges, which are accompanied by the confiscation of property, the state enlists the help of the petty 'service' nobility, which regularly prefers equality under despotism to the freedom that goes with privilege. The chequered history of the dynasty in the eighteenth century, the *coups d'état*, the whims of its sovereigns prevent the Russian state from becoming a state governed by law.

Now, this Russian state, so archaic, so foreign to Europe, is a victorious one. In its foreignness it finds what enables it to conquer the three great military leaders that Europe sends against it: Charles XII, Frederick the Great and Napoleon. Its victory over the latter saves it from the forced modernization that had been undergone, or as a consequence, had been wished for, by a Europe that had been subjected to his domination. The Russian state, sanctified by its victory, as Karamzine had understood, progresses on its own lines at the end of the reign of Alexander I and throughout that of Nicholas I.

This is why Westerners and the Russians themselves have been struck by the incapacity of the Russian state to civilize the country because of the artificiality and the precarious nature of the results. Here are three celebrated quotations:

> The Russians will never be policed because this happened to them too soon. Peter had the genius for imitation. . . . He saw that his people were barbarians, but did not see that they were ripe for policing; he wished to civilize them when it was merely necessary to render them warlike. He wished first to make them Germans or Englishmen, when he should have begun by making them Russians: he prevented his subjects from ever becoming what they might be by persuading them that they were what they were not.
>
> (Rousseau)

> As well as the fascination, we see constantly reborn a scepticism that follows it like its own shadow, mingling its slight note of irony with the cries of peoples in agony, mocking the veritable greatness of Russian power, just like the attitude struck by a charlatan in order to dazzle and deceive. Other empires have, in their infancy, caused similar doubts to arise; but Russia became a colossus without having dispelled them. In history it offers the unique example of a vast empire which, even after achievements on a world-wide scale, continues to be considered a matter of belief and not one of fact.
>
> (Marx)

> Peter's reform was the struggle of despotism against the people, against its inertia. The Tsar hoped to awaken, by his wrathful power, both ardour and initiative in a society that was enslaved, as well as introducing into Russia, with the aid of the noble who oppressed the serf, the sciences of Europe, public education, and the conditions necessary for social productivity; he wanted the slave, whilst still remaining a slave, to act consciously and freely. The conjoint action of despotism and liberty, of civilization and slavery, is the squaring of the political circle, the problem that we have been seeking to resolve for two centuries, since Peter, and which has not been resolved to this day.
>
> (Klioutchevski)

Voltaire wrote that 'Jean Jacques had not seen that first of all Germans and English must be used to make Russians.' The argument concerns the fruitfulness of imitation. Up to that time Russia had imitated the barbarian hordes and Byzantium. Peter forces it to leave the system of the steppe empire and for two centuries links it to the European system. But what Europe should be imitated? There could be no question of imitating the older Western countries – rich, virtuous to a fault, populated and 'developed'. But it could imitate those European countries that imitated them. East of the Elbe there began another, poorer Europe, but which, at the end of the eighteenth century, is busy reorganizing itself. Sweden, Prussia and then Austria become military monarchies. The aim is to build up armies that could compete with those of France, despite their having a poorer land, a smaller population and a more primitive society. This was to be the task of the state which, by using to best advantage its limited resources, creates disciplined and technically developed armies. This in turn entails a reform of the state, into the *Polizeistaat*. The state, instead of being the sacred seal set upon a society that is organized by itself alone, becomes the driving force in that society and propels it on a planned and rational path. To do this a central administration must be constructed, and then a local one, with regularity in its methods and continuity in its action. Poland does not succeed in achieving this transformation to a military monarchy and a well-policed state: it is doomed. Peter the Great imitates Prussia and Sweden, not without the use of cruel means, which makes the imitation something of a caricature, something monstrous, causing some to believe that the imitation has failed. Now, with ups and downs, with pockets of barbarity that are all the more glaring because the barbarity is decked out and policed, imitation succeeds, but with a gap of roughly a half-century behind its models.

The key problem is that of installing military and administrative cadres. To deal with what was most urgent the Petersburg state imported a number of Westerners, usually Germans. On a more massive scale, it drew from the elites among the peoples of the western fringe that had been recently conquered: first the Ukranians, then the Baltic peoples, the Poles and the Caucasians. As regards the clergy, it adopted the Prussian formula. It imposed upon the church a quasi-Reformation, turning clerics into the cadres for the burgeoning system of education. Indeed the solution of the problem was the education of new elites that were Russian, trained in the secularized ideal of service to the state. Within the framework of the *Polizeistaat* it was useless and dangerous to make the masses – still caught up in the bonds of serfdom – literate. The target group was only the limited one of the nobility, under Nicholas I and comprising some 600,000 men. These, and these alone, were given a suitable education. The education system installed during the first half of the nineteenth century comprises some fifty Gymnasia with roughly 15,000 pupils, and six universities with some 5000 students. These are institutions of good quality, certainly inferior to their prestigious German models, but which, taking into account Russian underdevelopment, constitute a remarkable achievement.

Indeed – and this is the Russian miracle – the graft succeeded. From the end of the eighteenth century, under the reign of Catherine, the imitation begins to bear fruit. It will be marked, throughout the nineteenth century, by the progress (measured by European standards) of society, the state and the economy.

The nobility was freed from obligatory service to the state in 1762 and exempted from physical punishment. This nobility, returned to its own affairs and no longer fearing the lash, rapidly takes on the customs, manners, clothes, and even the languages of western Europe. It comes into physical contact with the West through the wars of the revolution and the empire. Madame de Stael believes that in Russia she breathes 'an air of liberty'; this is extremely exaggerated, but the aristocratic circles that receive her justify the illusion. Maistre in his 'Soirees de Saint-Petersbourg' does not fear to put words of good sense, and even lofty in tone, into the mouths of Russians. The Russian gentleman is accepted by the aristocracies of Europe.

Through imitation, such manners reach even wider circles. Education rather than birth, more even than service to the state, suffices in order to gain entrance to what in Russia is called 'society', that is the Europeanized section of the nation. The spread of education disseminates beyond the nobility the Westernized humane type of the nobility. The latter is to be found from now onwards in the traditional classes and castes (merchants, clerics), and in the new classes that have arisen from the general progress made. The proof that the graft had taken, that Russia is now in Europe, is given by the birth of a Russian literary culture, fully European in its genres and its rhetoric, and, moreover, successfully translated in the West, fully Russian, and giving to the young nation the sense of its own identity. By the end of the century one can speak of a Russian society that is diversified, complete and conscious of itself.

State progress lies firstly in the progressive installation of a state based on law. From Alexander I onwards, it becomes clear that the imitation of Europe can only be complete if the Russian state becomes honourable and respects persons and property in accordance with the norms of the civilization to which it aspires. Speranski regulates Russian law, introducing into it the modern notions of property, contract and society. Confiscation becomes the exception.

Justice, from 1860 onwards, was dispensed in forms that were approximately European. The 'juridical' obstacles to the take-off of 'capitalism' are thus removed.

Another handicap is eliminated at the same time: serfdom. This vast operation is carried out half a century later than in Prussia and Austria. Although the peasants do not acquire personal ownership of the land, remain confined within the stifling framework of the rural commune and must pay for the land at an exorbitant price, they now have the means of gradually entering civil society.

This fact enables society henceforth to stand up to the state, demanding participation in its affairs, and obtaining by means of revolution what Western civil societies have obtained, or what German civil society has obtained by means of compromise. The progress of the Russian state, the promoter of the Enlightenment, civilized by the Western education its cadres have received, thus brings with it its own crisis: the state of the *ancien régime* therefore sees approaching the prospect of a European-type revolution. It is in Europe, once again following the military monarchies of central Europe, that it seeks to ward this off: a compromise on Bismarckian lines, which seeks to bypass the elites to reach the masses, leaves the bureaucracy and the army in the hands of the sovereign, and concedes to civil society the beginnings of a right to representation.

Capitalism arises in Russia, even if its elements appear in the reverse order to which they had appeared in the West. The state had wished to build an economy capable of sustaining the military might of the empire. It had therefore taken the initiative in 'modernization', but, faithful to the European model, it had done so through the private entrepreneur. Large-scale industry arises first. It calls upon capital and Western technology. But in the pre-war decade (to 1914) the Russian economy develops through its own dynamism. Russian capital, assembled in Russia, takes over from French and English capital. A powerful banking system replaces the offices of the ministry of finance in their function of providing a framework. The state withdraws, and society takes over the reins of the economy. The unblocking and take-off of agriculture follows that of industry. The dominant factors are the progressive expulsion of the nobles, who are obliged to liquidate their estates, the break-up of the rural commune after the Stolypin reform, and, finally, the growth of the co-operative movement.

Foreign observers, judging the Russian economy on the eve of 1914, perceive its structural defects: the youthfulness and immaturity of the industrial system, the agricultural backwardness. Yet all see the powerful dynamism and the infinite range of prospects for development. Russia is advancing at top speed along the path of a Wilhelmine-style capitalism, and on a continental scale. As regards currency, finance and commerce, it is fully integrated into the world market.

Four years later all this is swept away. Capitalism vanishes like a dream, once and for all. Why? This is our hypothesis: in the same way as it was the imitation of Europe that had given rise to it, it is the imitation of that same Europe (but of something else in Europe) that condemns it to death.

Only recently created, and contending against the political tradition, the heritage of barbarism and the weakness of society, capitalism is fragile. However, the forces that seriously threaten it are neither political nor social. The state, albeit archaic, albeit of the *ancien régime*, has promoted capitalism, and when the latter has been strong enough, the state has learnt how to withdraw from the economic sphere: the ministers have read the liberal economists.

The social classes have opposed change by inertia, by passive forms of resistance, but not by any systematic, organized hostility. The rural nobility is the class that is most affected. Yet Europeanization and the raising of its cultural level seem to it to be a compensation for the progressive loss of its serfs and estates. Modern life offers surrogate outlets. The intelligentsia is becoming tamed. There is now a stratum of intellectuals who are integrated into society, who no longer define themselves in terms of moral and political dissidence, but in terms of professional occupation. Teachers, health professionals, the legal profession, the technical professions: they are white-collar personnel. The merchant class, formerly so very picturesque, lose their caftans and beards. The working class, in so far as it is allowed to go where it will, following the path of Jewish and Polish syndicalism, moves towards a kind of social democracy on the German model. The peasant class, delivered from the yoke of the commune, becomes more differentiated and rapidly organizes itself. In short, Russian society, launched in a brutal and authoritarian fashion by the state on the road to Westernization, takes a liking to it and on the whole would like to advance more quickly – if needs be against the state.

This at least is its instinct, its spontaneous impulsion. But it is deterred by the ideas that are insinuated into it, which find support in its immobility, its millenarianism, and its spirit of reaction and revolution.

These ideas originate in the most Europeanized sector of the Europeanized portion of the Russian world, and in direct imitation of Europe. They arrive by way of importation, in a narrow environment that acclimatizes them, adapting them to the country, to its real or imaginary difficulties, to the simplicity of a public which, residing in the most distant outskirts of Europe, is rarely capable of understanding such ideas in their complexity and their true dimensions.

These ideas imbue Russia with a consciousness of itself that proves an obstacle to its real evolution and even prevents it from seeing this. Here I cannot trace the history of Russian culture in the nineteenth century. But it can be classified around three great intellectual importations.

The first is religious. The eclipse suffered by the Orthodox Church, after the revolution of Peter the Great, creates a vacuum that is filled by European religious ideas, mainly German Pietism. Pietism, with its esoteric, Gnostic and Masonic doctrines, carries with it a speculative mysticism that, on condition that it is simplified, will spread in Russia. Shored up by idealist philosophy, this imported religiosity will find national roots, will invent an Orthodox genealogy and will be passed off as the spontaneous religion of the Russian people. It suffuses the literature of Gogol, Tolstoy, Dostoevsky and symbolism. It spreads disdain for the world, for secular values, for law and property, for customary moral observances. It propounds a moral and religious state of the sublime that is very appealing to the young and deters them from the 'this-world' asceticism that Weber judged to be linked to the success of capitalism.

The second importation is nationalism. There had always existed in Russia a violent national sentiment, but from the nineteenth century onwards it had been conceived of on the model of German nationalism. The latter had constituted, in opposition to the Anglo-French West, a radical cultural originality (a *Volksgeist*). Since culture was somewhat lacking in Russia, it was religion – that is the true faith the absolute truth – which took its place. The inventors of the national religion (a mixture of pietism and idealist philosophy in the guise of Greek patristics) were also the inventors of Russian nationalism. Slavophiles inaugurated a reasoning process that was afterwards imitated by nationalists in South America, the Arab countries, China and so on, and which is expounded as follows: we are not inferior (or backward) in comparison with the European West, We are different by nature. Now, Europe is bad, as it itself recognizes in its books, reviews and newspapers, all of which are extremely critical. Consequently we are better. The conclusion is that Europe must not be imitated, neither in the forms of its socio-economic life, nor in the forms of its political life. Bourgeois life, the bourgeois spirit, constitutional government, political representation, are condemned.

The third importation is the most directly anti-capitalist: socialism. In its first form of populism it produces a synthesis of religiosity and romantic nationalism, but by displacing to the left the themes and common values in these tendencies, that is by transposing them onto the plane of a revolutionary political struggle. In its second form of Marxism, particularly in its Bolshevist version, the religious and nationalist themes have vanished or are no longer directly recognizable. Yet the values subsist, concentrated and radicalized: a pure hatred of the social world as nature and history have shaped it, the aspiration to change it from top to bottom, according to principles and formulas that the doctrine knows to be absolutely right, with scientific certainty.

This gap between Russian realities and the Russian consciousness was not incurable. In fact it was rapidly diminishing. The revolutionary doctrines were losing their prestige. The nationalist sensitiveness, born of an inferiority complex, was disappearing in the face of the remarkable success of the Russian nation. Even in the religious domain a return to a more healthy orthodoxy was noted.

Nothing was fatal. Nothing obeyed an inevitable historical process, a *zakonomernost*. To decide the fate of the country an event was necessary, mysterious as all events are: World War One. Entry into the system of European states had been the first step in imitation, in the time of Peter the Great. Its entry into the war, in the time of Nicholas II, which was the ultimate imitation, the definitive adoption of Russia by Europe – and that by the most 'European' of Europes: France, England and Italy – this entry brought about in the space of a few years its definitive exclusion from it.

10

Political and Social Structures of the West, 300–1300

Karl Ferdinand Werner

The question to which I should contribute one part of the answer is simple: had that modern Europe, which sets itself apart from other great civilizations by accomplishing the 'European miracle', prepared itself to do so during the period with which I am dealing here, and if so, in what way? The key terms of our programme, 'dynamism' and 'stagnation', lead one to suppose that one period, that of modern dynamism, allegedly followed a period of at least relative stagnation, conventionally styled the 'Middle Ages'. In this perspective my problem would come down to the manifestation of a significant acceleration in a continent that had hitherto been relatively lethargic, and to reflecting upon the possible causes of this change. This would fit perfectly into the ideas of Max Weber and more recent authors who reveal to us the active man – at the same time a disciplined one – who in Europe becomes the creator of the world in which he lives.

To Max Weber belongs the merit of having perceived the importance of the renewal of an urban civilization, but also the importance of elements of religious origin, one which he sees as the passage from an economically unfruitful asceticism to an indefatigable and creative activity in the world. For him the decisive factor in modernization was rationalization and bureaucratization, the effects of which in the long run would prove dangerous because they lead to a heartless and impersonal routine that might threaten the liberty and dignity of man. He was even afraid of the death from 'hypothermia' of rational civilization because of an all-invading bureaucratization, 'in the manner of a late second Antiquity' (as quoted and discussed by Mommsen, 1974: 132, 137).

It is at that point we wish to begin a critique of the views that modern and contemporary thought has held about 'Antiquity' and the 'Middle

Ages'. These views were dominated by the ideas of the Enlightenment
and of an aestheticism that (in Gibbon no less than Nietzsche) saw the
Later Empire period as a doleful and sinister one, with responsibility for
the Christian defeatism that allegedly refused to fight in defence of the
Empire and its civilization (Werner, 1984: 22). To this image of a
declining and dying world may be opposed that of a Christian and
triumphant Empire, and, at its side, the Catholic kingdoms, likewise
triumphant, with the kingdom of the Franks to the fore. The Empire in
no way ends at Constantinople. In the west it will not be the heathens
that will dominate in Rome, but the Catholics, who will triumph on the
banks of the Elbe before evangelizing the Slavonic and Scandinavian
peoples. In these times the cross was a sign of victory. The field in which
the Empire had effectively failed, that of the economy, stifling under the
weight of taxation and of an ultra-privileged army, afterwards experienced
a visible improvement. The governing stratum of high public officials,
joining forces with the barbarian military leaders, retains its position and
still constitutes a burden, but one that is much lighter in an agrarian
society. State fiscality does not disappear either, and even the church
joins in it, but it ends up likewise by becoming less irksome. The reviving
Christian Empire succeeds in effecting a remarkable integration of the
ideas of the Old Testament, St Augustine and the Roman tradition, but
it cannot impede the full development of regional forces both within it
and without, namely, over the whole of Christian Europe. The new
'mother-countries' are consolidated, and the peoples that grow up within
their bounds vie with each other in every sphere. Instead of provoking a
disorder of wasted strength, this competition liberates extraordinary
energies. One might cite the towns of the Italian littoral, which, from the
tenth century onwards, set out on the path of renewal.

But the case of the Scandinavian countries is even more impressive
(Musset, 1979: 57–75; Sawyer, 1982). Coming late into the Catholic
world, they become a dynamic factor of the first order, extending
their influence and action throughout England, Ireland, Iceland and
Greenland as far as America to the west, but also to the east into the very
depths of what was to become Russia, where they create a wide-ranging
system of commerce and taxation among the conquered populations,
based upon animal fur products. This Europe is already dominant, it
already goes beyond its over-narrow confines, it is already taking
advantage of its geography, with its topography structured by the land,
the sea, fjords, lakes and rivers, and lastly by its islands and peninsulas,
which serve as so many staging points to venture further afield. Alfred
the Great, starting from the geography of Isidore of Seville, enlarges this
on the basis of his own knowledge, in a remarkable work; Adam of
Bremen, following the account of a Scandinavian prince, tells of Norman

activities as far away as Byzantium, and these are confirmed by Byzantine authors, by Scandinavian sagas and by Arabic coinage. Now, these same Norsemen constitute a homeland for themselves in Normandy, where they learn French, and carry out the conquest not only of England but also of southern Italy, finding themselves, by western routes, confronting again the Byzantines and the Arabs, waging fierce battles with them within the framework of the Crusades, whose privileged inspirers they were, both on the religious plane and as regards the economy, navigation and booty. Ranke (1888: 128) had already seen that the age of discovery is the direct continuation of the Crusades, of a Mediterranean and Anglo-Baltic world that has been awakened, and has at its disposal – by its contacts with regions and men up to then unknown – the knowledge and courage necessary to go ever farther. They could avail themselves not only of technical means of navigation, but also of financial resources.[1] Where, in all that, can one find stagnation?

A comparable dynamism characterizes the evolution of population and, within this framework, that of the towns (Genicot, 1953; Braudel, 1984: 92ff.). Confronted with the dynastic struggles of the Merovingians, it has been forgotten that these hardly affected the mass of the population, which enjoyed greater peace than at any time since the third century. Thus the seventh century brought about the first appreciable increase in population and more extensive land settlement. After the Carolingian wars of expansion and the ravages of the onslaughts by the Normans, Arabs and Hungarians, from the tenth century onwards there begins a demographic upsurge that changes the face of the West. For France it has been estimated that the population had trebled by the thirteenth century, before the setback brought about by the Great Plague of the fourteenth century, which was followed by stagnation. For England, the increase in population has already been emphasized, but there was also, from the tenth century onwards, a relatively remarkable state of well-being. Saxony, equipped with economic structures (towns, markets, the coinage of money and roads) by the Carolingians and taking advantage of its silver mines and the commercial trends of the Ottonian era, unleashes its demographic forces to such an extent that it becomes the scene of a spectacular urban development, and at the same time the point of departure for a great colonizing movement towards the east.

During the twelfth and thirteenth centuries more than a thousand towns are created in Germany – most of them fairly small, it is true, but all the same constituting local centres, stimulating exchange and favouring the social improvement of a not inconsiderable section of the population (Schlesinger, 1963: 4–67). The appeal for settlers from

1 Ranke underlines the involvement of 'propagatio fidei' in a movement which was first directed by the leading Catholic powers.

Flanders, the Rhineland and Saxony by the Slavonic princes, and the propagation of types of customary urban law, such as that for example of Magdeburg, throughout central and eastern Europe attests to the success of this evolution, as does the remarkable development of commerce and navigation in the Baltic, which will be the origin of the great 'Hanseatic' league of towns from Bruges to Novgorod. An urban world appears with a new social role, that firstly of *mercatores*, then of traders, which not only ensure for themselves a share in urban government but indirectly succeed in playing a political role within the framework of the towns granted privileges by the Emperor (*Reichstädte*) from the twelfth and thirteenth centuries onwards. Now, the political authorities had favoured the development and the activities of merchants for a long time – there has rightly been emphasized the political and military role of the early commercial centres (seventh to ninth centuries) such as Würzburg, Erfurt, Magdeburg, and Hamburg, as well as the fact that commercial centres could become episcopal cities such as Utrecht, Merseburg and Bamberg. The differentiation between *burgliute* (Burgleute) and *landliute* (Landleute), the former living according to *burgreht* (Burgrecht) – which means 'urban customary law' and not 'castle law', since the word *burg* (Burg) only evolved later from its meaning of 'town' to that of 'castle' – appears in the year 1000 in Notker of St Gallen, demonstrating that the Germanic countries had achieved the structures that had characterized up to that time only those countries that had formed part of the Roman Empire. A comparable evolution can be noted in the Slavonic countries, where the designation for *civis*, *gorzane* derives from *gord*, *gorod*, *grad* (town), as does in the Germanic countries the word *burger* (*Bürger*), from *burg* – *civitas*.

Now, the expansion in forms of life originating in the Mediterranean world to the east and north of Europe is indissolubly linked to the propagation of the Catholic faith in those same countries. We have therefore the right to ask, as did Ernst Troeltsch in 1922 (748ff.) when he was already using the term *Strukturgeschichte*, whether the bases for this European history of structures are not to be found in Hebrew prophesying, the Greek *polis*, Roman imperialism and 'medieval civiliz-ation that still awaits adequate historical portrayal' (Oexle, 1984: 332). Recent research has brought so many new proofs of the spiritual dynamics of the long-neglected centuries of the 'High Middle Ages' that we do not hesitate to assign them a key position in an essay of explanation of the 'European miracle'. Our thesis would therefore be that this 'miracle' did not take place after the 'Middle Ages' or in spite of the 'Middle Ages', but because of the existence of a Christian world dominated in the west by Catholic doctrines, a world we have become accustomed to calling the Middle Ages.

It is true that in human history there is never one single *prima causa*. But if we had to choose one word that, by itself alone, were capable of expressing an essential factor in what we understand by the 'European miracle', we would choose the philosophical term which the Nuremberg inventors of the portable mechanical watch gave to its main part, namely, the balance wheel: *Unruh*, which means 'in perpetual movement', but also anxiety, agitation – the English word 'unrest', but also 'restlessness' (German *Ruhelosigkeit*, a word lacking in French, where one has to resort to a paraphrase such as 'agitation continuelle'). Whilst Asia and its wisdom and, in its train, the great religions and philosophies, strive towards the art of the recollection of self, of seeking out the centre of the soul and of the world, and of resting in God, of having *arrived*, the European of the Europe miracle is a man who is always ready to take-off once more, once he has arrived somewhere. Even for the poet, freedom is always 'to go whither thou willst' (Hölderlin). The *Aufbruch* is thus as profoundly European as is the French term *élan*, which links style to the act, to the activity that is characteristic of the man who truly lives the beauty of gesture. This urge is one that we find in a form that is as concrete as it is remarkable in the *peregrinatio*, the sublime ideal of the Irish, and then of the English, who gave themselves over body and soul to the *propagatio fidei* among the heathen. Now the whole idea of the pilgrimage, which causes Anglo-Saxon kings, Frankish nobles, priests and monks, whole populations, and even children, to venture on to roads that are difficult and dangerous, is the expression of the duty not to stay still, to achieve the path to God, that is to the Jerusalem in the heavens, of which the Jerusalem on earth is the palpable symbol. A medieval historiographer said of Geoffroy de Bouillon, '*decertat de hac (sc. Ierusalem), ut vivat in illa*' (Parente, 1983: 316; Löwe, 1983: 327–72; Labande, 1973). But where must be sought the *causa causans* of this mentality?

The spur to anxiety is to be seen in the pangs of sin, with its consequences of repentance, doubt and redemption, in the search for pardon and grace. The importance of the deliverance of every soul gave an hitherto unheard-of prominence to the individual, independent of his social rank, the individual who, seen from this viewpoint, is in no way swallowed up in the masses nor founders by abandoning himself to destiny. The value put on free will and responsibility is a factor whose multiple consequences must be perceived, even more so because the responsibility for the souls of others exists both for Charlemagne as well as for St Louis. Now, the sense of responsibility seems to me to be one of the strengths of the Europeans that are to accomplish the 'miracle'. Likewise redemption does not only concern what one must do for one's own soul, but also what one can do to mitigate the fate of souls that are dear to one. Jacques Le Goff (1981), in his very thought-provoking book on purgatory, wanted to site chronologically in the twelfth century onwards the decisive effect of this important religious motivation. It is sufficient to look at the magnificent volume recently published by the centre for medieval research at Munster, concerning the *Memoria*, to be convinced that on this point Le Goff mistook the era.[2] The essential premises – namely the fact that the immense majority of human souls do not constitute a part of those who will be damned for all eternity without any possible recourse, nor of those whose saintliness places them from the outset in Paradise, close to God, as well as the conviction that something can and must be done for these souls held 'in suspense' – these premises are to be found in St Augustine. They were developed in such a way that the entire Carolingian upper clergy meet solemnly from 762 onwards in the Attigny palace in an association of prayer for the dead, and gifts for the souls of the departed reach unbelievable proportions in the ninth and tenth centuries, constituting, among other things, the basis for the rise of the Cluny monks in Europe (their prayers being considered as particularly pure and effective before God and those saints interceding between God and man). In the Frankish Empire and its successor states a fortune in property that was truly immense had been amassed in this way by the church, and its economic effects were considerable. On the one hand, there was an incentive to build up a patrimony because it was necessary to own something in order to be able 'to do something' on behalf of souls; on the other hand, the estates of the monasteries reformed by the Cluny order were veritable model undertakings, favouring the economic and demographic take-off of the surrounding areas, and giving rise to the foundation of *burgi* – settlements of merchants and tradespeople around abbeys and priories. Finally, the church lands constituted an enormous fund of capital, into which dipped the powerful and the rich, as well as the small entrepreneurs, by soliciting land grants. What Le Goff is talking about is not the beginning, but a second wave that arose from the anxieties men felt about the fate of their soul and those of their neighbours, an effect that from the twelfth century onwards reflects the new world of the towns, and of money available in large amounts. This new form of 'capitalism of prayers for the remission of sins' will lead to the greatest concentration of capital ever seen, at the same time as the rise of the

2 For the *Memoria*, see Schmid and Wollasch (1984: 437). For the 'Munsterer Sonderforschungsbereich "Mittelalterforschung" (Bild, Bedeutung, Sachen, Worter und Personen)', see the review 'Fruhmittelalterliche Studien. Jahrbuch des Instituts fur Fruhmittelalterforschung, Munich (Wilhelm Fink)' with regular 'Bericht', giving important bibliographic information. See also Gurjewitsch (1978: 250–305), Chiffoleau (1980), Murray (1978), Tellenbach (1936).

papacy and the organization that it was able to give to a church that henceforth was 'Roman'. This first process of 'fiscalization' on a grand scale in the West, preceding that of the great states, with France and England at their head, originates at the Italian bank, which laid the institutional and instrumental bases for the first capitalism that Antiquity had never known. The spiritual roots of the phenomena that, at first sight, belong to the take-off of the 'modern world' appear just as clearly in the beginnings of printing: there was need for the mass production of a particular text, first of all for tracts designed as propaganda for the great places of pilgrimage, which threw themselves into redoubtable competition with one another – it is the entrepreneurs dominating this market who financed the first printed books. All in all, the behaviour of men, as well as their mentality at the moment of the take-off of Europe, are inseparable from the Catholic world and the impulsions it had given to the faithful. As for Protestantism, it was not the initial force that set off this upsurge, but it too was a second wave, surpassing the effects of the first because it no longer accepted either the dominant role of the church in temporal affairs (thereby profiting from the wave of anti-clericalism that was then sweeping over Europe), nor the 'tranquillizers' that the Catholic Church in the very last period before the Reformation had doled out, against payment in cash, to anxious souls. Let us not forget that a few centuries earlier the Roman Church had been on the side of the *Libertas* of consciences and faith. By abusing its power, by regimenting too strictly the world, even the most powerful princes, it provoked a violent reaction, not only in those countries that became of Protestant obedience, but also in those which remained Catholic, where the state would radically reduce the authority of Rome, even in ecclesiastical matters, and *a fortiori*, in the political sphere.

The Reformation, and the Catholic Counter-Reformation that it sparked off, first unleashed the religious forces in Europe: 'the conversion of millions of people to a demanding spirituality and to the practices of the religious elite constituted a considerable transformation in the psychology of the masses, to the benefit of a written culture, of a message founded upon a Book and an education increasingly based upon printing' (Delumeau, 1978 – an author who knows the *real* limits of the period). Here are views based upon meticulous, quantified research that are refreshing after the clichés of a pious and naïve 'Middle Ages' and of a 'Modern Age' that is enlightened and sceptical: the age of Christianity, that of 'princes and priests', as Victor Hugo expressed it,[3] an age that

3 Victor Hugo: 'Dieu offre l'Afrique a l'Europe. . . . Versez votre trop plein dans cette Afrique et du même coup résolvez vos questions sociales . . . et que sur cette terre, *de plus en plus dégagée de prêtres et de princes*, l'esprit divin s'affirme par la paix et l'esprit humain par la liberté ' quoted by Elwitt (1975: 275).

began in the fourth century and whose predominance was abolished in
the eighteenth or even the nineteenth century, is marked by two phases,
the first of which is characterized by a greater homogeneity, the second
by an intensity of faith that was more widespread, of which the terrible
wars of religion were a striking expression. To these two phases there
correspond two kinds of somewhat different religious sentiment. We
shall outline that of the first phase, placing the emphasis on its social and
political consequences. It is essentially based upon the Old Testament,
which dominates the thinking of Constantine and his successors no less
than that of Charlemagne. They all took David as their model and were
called 'new Davids'. God guides the wars of Israel, thus those of the new
chosen people, the Christians whose head is the Emperor, and thus those
of the Franks who were designated by the popes, in letters piously
preserved by the Carolingians, as the new chosen people. God crushes
the enemies of Israel: the armed people that fights the enemies of God is
the people of God (Judges, V, 11–13: *populus Domini; . . . Dominus in
fortibus dimicavit*) (Werner, 1987a, 1987b; cf. Jaspers, 1947: 28). The
measures taken by Charlemagne in Saxony are incomprehensible save in
this context. Kings – good ones and bad – are the instruments of God
whereby he directs the affairs of the world. The destiny of kings, good
and bad, is the sign and warning that God gives to his people; such signs
must be carefully noted, but also interpreted by Christian historiography,
and thus by the church, as must also be the signs made up of celestial
apparitions and miracles (*signa!*). All the decisive conflicts – for example
the changes of dynasty – therefore become judgements of God: God
makes and unmakes kings, which implies that reigning kinds owe their
authority directly to God. The church, which with the *Historiae* of
Orosius was the examplar and guide for understanding the history of
Rome and the world (manuscripts about it were countless and were to be
found everywhere), was thus throughout history the educator of young
princes, the counsellor of kings and of their counsellors also: it does not
hesitate to blame and even to castigate the powerful when they, in its
view, depart from the way prescribed by God. Right up to the
seventeenth century and beyond, this is what will be the *Haupt- und
Staatsaffairen* that are played out on the stage of the *Theatrum Europaeum*:
kings are important because they are installed by God and because the
action of God can be observed carefully by men who at the same time see
in the destiny of kings the image of the risks that they themselves are
running, and this has a moralizing effect.

It is patently obvious that Protestantism, through its radical separation from the faith and the affairs of the world, by its rejection of the
church as the privileged interpreter of the permanent action of God in
the world, and finally by its quest for the authenticity of the divine

message solely in the text of the revealed Book, sounded the knell for this kind of religious sentiment in ancient Christian Europe. Protestantism destroys the continuation of the story of God and men, which had begun with the Creation and had been told in the Bible, by refusing to accept the interpretation of the signs of divine activity in the world given by the Catholic Church, considering it to be inauthentic and made up by fallible men. The involuntary consequence was that Protestantism put an end to the palpable presence of God in the present time, relegating him solely to the origins of the world and of Christianity, in the far distant past, with all its well-known consequences: God might have created the world and have saved humanity, but afterwards left the world to its fate. The idea that the sagacity of men could develop outside the wisdom of a framework of a world and a history that had been revealed, and thus known in advance, could make headway; certainty could give way to research.

The world directly ruled by God was, in spite of the tumults introduced into it by the Lord's will, necessarily a fairly stable one, in which everything had its place. What was true for the king was also true for the aristocracy – its destiny was to rule over men in the world, as moreover in the church which, after some timorous precursory signs in the ninth and tenth centuries, only accepted from the eleventh century onwards, particularly in France and Italy, and under the impulsion of reform movements, bishops not of aristocratic origin. The ecclesiastical and politico-social hierarchies corresponded, furthermore, to the heavenly hierarchies, with the whole being ordained by God.

Beside the religious foundations of a strongly conservative approach to the social and political world there must be seen, particularly in the institutions, the role played by the legacy of Rome, which, according to the most recent research, goes far beyond what many historians have thought, still influenced by the humanist fiction of 'the end of the Roman Empire through the barbarian invasions'. Here I can only touch briefly on the matter. The politico-social hierarchy of the 'Middle Ages' rests almost exclusively upon the foundations laid down by the Christian Empire in the fourth and fifth centuries. The top officials appointed by the Empire clearly did not pass on their functions to their descendants, although they did pass on the rank they had reached. In this way was formed what was henceforth the only authentic *nobilitas*, that of the different ranks of the Roman senators. In Gaul the senatorial nobility was recognized by the new Frankish king who, for his part, had been recognized as *rex praecellentissimus* and *nobilissimus* by the emperor at Constantinople; the latter remained, without any shadow of dispute, at the head of the political hierarchy of the Roman world. All this not only implied the acknowledgement of the king's superior rank by the senators, but also that of the appointments that the king, recognized as *princeps et dominus* in the place of the emperor, could make to the highest posts in the hierarchy. As with the Romans, except for some simplifications, a Frankish count, appointed by the king, was *vir illuster*, his wife was *illustris matrona* and his children would belong to the authentic *nobilitas*. Evidently, in order to exercise high office personally it was always necessary to enter the prince's service, the *militia*, to receive as the outward sign the *cingulum militiae* and exercise the prerogatives of the function to which one had been appointed and which was called – all this totally unchanged since the Roman Empire – the *honor* (Werner, 1985: 186–200).

This continuity is all the more important because it corresponds entirely to a large number of other politico-administrative continuities that have been brought to light by recent research (Witthöft, 1983: 457–82; Durliat: 1982, 67–77). Hence the Roman origin of the detailed weights and measures of the Frankish world, and the astonishing duration in this kingdom of the use of Roman roads, or new roads that were, however, absolutely parallel to the Roman ones, which had avoided the villages, whereas the new ones linked them with one another. More important are the proofs recently advanced concerning the survival and development of taxes under the Merovingians and the Carolingians, with the active participation of the church, whose integration into the state administrative apparatus had begun from the era of Constantine the Great onwards.

Thus one should not be too astonished at the definite traces of a 'rationality' of the high Middle Ages which, for example, is shown by the preservation of linear boundaries 'in the Roman fashion' and, in most cases, also, of Latin names for the administrative units. State rationality existed also under Charlemagne who, for example, forbade the abuse which consisted in avoiding army service by becoming a monk. There is a rationality that we find in the will to create or impose norms for ecclesiastical rules and juridical laws, for singing and the service of God in the churches, and for the construction of monasteries and the administration of estates.

This regulation of public life did not disappear with the Carolingian Empire; it merely shifted the framework in which it was applied, as effective power also shifted to the regional and local. Thus we find regulatory arrangements in the tenth century in Bavaria and Normandy, made on the authority of the prince or the duke, in the eleventh century with the Domesday Book, which was inspired by the registers of the Carolingians, in the twelfth century with not only the remarkable legislation made by the Counts of Barcelona, but also a *ratio de curtibus comitis* for Flanders, and also in Catalonia. It is this same twelfth century which brings us the *dialogus de scaccario* of the English court, which surprises as much by the rationality of a practical mind that is none the less systematic, as by a pedagogical wisdom in the teaching of that subject. Now, it must be realized that a whole world of practical literature has remained unknown because of a lack of interest on the part of modern historians, who discovered it only a score of years ago. This *Fachliteratur*, once it is published and better known, will revolutionize our ideas about the 'Middle Ages' and will show us the lengthy preparation there was for what is destined to be the strength of Europeans in the achievement of the 'European miracle', namely the systematic and practical side, developing for every subject a doctrine that is able to be improved upon and to serve as an introduction for any who had need of it (Eiss, 1967). About 1100, Theophilus Presbyter writes the *Schedula diversarum artium* for the production of textiles in the monasteries. Writings deal with weavers, dyers and tailors, and later, furriers. Naturally this literature is increasingly written in the vernacular, and the same holds good for the art of war, fencing, arms production, fortifications, hunting and so on.

All these activities reveal more and more innovations, in spite of the often very ancient models that they follow. The Lombardy jurists, carrying out their duties in the king's law-court at Pavia, in the imperial law-court at Rome and elsewhere, continue to note down scrupulously the *novellae* to be added to Lombard law in the tenth and eleventh centuries (Sohm, 1919: 155; Koschaker, 1947; Coing, 1973: 122ff., 365ff.). They then create the *Liber Papiensis*, which is of utmost importance since it gives rise to a commentary. The *Expositio* (*c.*1070) will lead, at about the end of the century, to the *Lombarda*, the first systematic collection of the subjects contained in the whole of Lombard legislation. This new method will be applied by Irnerius to Roman law, at the time of the discovery of a precious manuscript of the Digests, and this will be the glory of the Bologna school. Now, this same method will be at the origin of the work of the compilers of glossaries of church law and, finally, of the *Corpus juris canonici*. Antiquity is likewise surpassed in the methods – somewhat crude, it is true – of scholastic education, which, however, as we know today, has been the necessary condition for modern systematic thought and for several of its methods. A long time previously, innovations in the technical field had multiplied. Advantage was taken of mills that had been known in Antiquity, but which had been little used, to develop and increase their number; a new method of harnessing animals was invented, allowing the use of a large number of horses to draw very heavy vehicles that had been unknown in previous times, and allowing also the use of more powerful ploughs. Thus, according to Robert S. Lopez, the rigid shoulder-collar for the horse, with the harrows, hoes and more solid pitchforks, and with more rationally constructed carts, constitute 'in the system of transportation the greatest metamorphosis that it had undergone between the age of the Babylonian chariots and the age of steam' (1982: 143). All this occurs – and this must be emphasized – in the most unrewarding times, in the ninth, tenth and eleventh centuries.

To conclude, let us return to the role of the state, the political entities and the changes they have undergone through the effects of the ecclesiastical reform in the eleventh to the thirteenth centuries, the most important for the genesis of modern Europe before the Reformation.

The historian of modern times learns and teaches that the state, with a word *stato*, is a creation of modern Europe. I have a letter from Gaines Post, who has done so much in discovering the antecedents of the state in the Later Middle Ages, in which he thanks me for having pointed out the *status regni nostri* in an act of a Breton duke at the end of the High Middle Ages. The word used for state was *regnum*. The presumption that the *regna*, which are none other than the kingdoms of modern times and belong to the same Roman tradition of the *res publica*, a tradition which was never lost, may not have possessed the character of a state between the sixth and the fifteenth centuries is one of numerous scientific legends (Werner, 1980a: IX–XXXIV). On the other hand, there have indeed been changes in the character and significance of these notions that clearly must be studied with the greatest care. The same is true for 'nations', which, it goes without saying, have existed in both 'ancient' and 'medieval' times, with virulent forms of nationalism (it is enough to mention those of the Jews, the Roman and the Franks), but which are different (simplifying a complex matter) in two respects: they are not our present-day nations – and this is why modern nations have had difficulties in recognizing them as true nations – and they are not yet aware of the self-determination (real or pretended) of contemporary nations after the revolutions of the contemporary era (Werner, 1970: 285–303; 1987c). This said, from the sixth century onwards one knew, and it was said, that a people that is not politically, or as a state, embodied in a *regnum* is condemned to disappear. Today we know that even the period of the migrations was followed immediately by an act of 'territorialization' that gave to the mixed populations resulting from these large-scale movements a political identity in a precise territory, namely the ability to be a *gens* in a *patria*. The name of *gens* could be that of the *patria* that had existed geographically beforehand, but also that of the people, or rather that of the migrating group. In any case it was the nucleus of the creative myth that laid claim to be the original community of all the inhabitants bearing that name, which was now accepted by everybody. The legends that modern nations have created for themselves in their respective historiographies are not essentially different in the production of corresponding myths of common origin.

What to us seems characteristic of the period on which we are reporting here is the fact that the maintenance of the supposedly absolutely authentic tradition of the Christian Empire, first appearing in concrete form with the Empire of Charlemagne, with its ideal of the *unanimitas* of all Christians, regulated by church and state, under the leadership of the emperor/king, and later in the Holy Roman Empire, could not in any way prevent the vigorous growth of particular *regna* which will clearly be the source of the wealth and liberties of Europe and the nuclei of modern European nations. What constitutes the difference between their character in the heyday of Catholic Europe and that of more recent times?

We look for it in the domain of 'desacralization'. In order to think with profit about this, we must first recall that every supreme authority, the one that decides matters of life and death, has had a more or less sacred character since the origins of societies that have been politically organized, and above all, we must emphasize, in the ancient 'pagan' world, before the advent and victory of Christianity. Pagan Rome was a sacred Rome; one had to worship, as well as all the 'individual' gods, *Roma*, and then also the genie of the Emperor. Friedrich Klingner (1941: 54) saw clearly by 1941 that the first desacralization of the state was that extolled by Christianity, which could not admit its sacred character. This character was reserved exclusively for God, the Trinity and, in varying degrees, to everything attached to it in heaven and upon earth by the bonds of the Holy Spirit. We know perfectly well that the persecutions were provoked by the radicalism of Christians, who refused to show any respect for all other cults – in their contemporaries' eyes it was clearly they who were lacking in tolerance. St Augustine, in his *De civitate Dei*, has drawn up the indictment against the *civitas terrena*, which could at best only attempt not to be 'a haunt of brigands', by respecting justice and enforcing respect for it.

Such desacralization was not successful (Werner, 1980b: 151–98, 1987d). On the contrary, the Christian Empire, by making the Emperor Constantine the 'saviour' of the church, the first of its bishops and in effect the president, in his palace, of the synods decisive for Christian dogma, ended up by enhancing the sacred character of the palace, the divine origin of power (St Paul against St Augustine), and the unity of the men of the Christian Empire under the leadership of the Emperor. It was not by chance that the ideas of St Augustine persisted in Rome, and in the Latin world that would become the Catholic world and that of the Roman Church. Ambrose of Milan and Pope Gelasius are the first to bear witness to a struggle about the basis of the absolute sovereignty of the faith, represented on earth by the Church alone, and this last represented, in the unity absolutely necessary for it, by the papacy. It is through the latter, therefore, that the second desacralization of the state was to come about. It was expressed in the Gregorian movement and the struggle of Gregory VII for the *Libertas Ecclesiae*, which was immediately transformed into a claim for the domination of the church, represented by the papacy. The fact that the unity of a Christian world of all men reunited under God was first broken by the church, with the aim, it is true, of protecting the purity of conduct of Christians from the claims of the powerful upon this earth, is deserving of the closest attention. The state reacted on several occasions, in stages that lead from Philip the Fair and Edward I right up to the separation of the church and state at the beginning of the twentieth century, by securing for itself the control of the church in the temporal sphere, whilst still leaving it 'its liberty'. The state free from any ecclesiastical and spiritual guardianship, society creating, at the instigation of the state, the careers of men (as lawyers, administrators, technicans, economists, publicists) outside any influence of the churches – this very sign of modern European society has its origin in the 'annulment' of the ancient close communion between the prince and the Catholic Church, by the latter; this event is peculiar to the Latin and Catholic West and distinguishes it from the Christian East and the Orthodox Church. Would any stronger proof be required to show how much Europe, whilst becoming 'secularized' during the centuries of the greatest success of its 'miracle', owes to the decisive 'changes in direction' given in its history, which represent so many markers in its religious history, linked for ever to the names of Constantine, Gregory VII and Luther?

References

Braudel, F. 1984: *Civilization and Capitalism, 15th–18th Century*, vol. 3, *The Perspective of the World*, London.
Chiffoleau, J. 1980: La comptabilité de l'au-delà. Les hommes, la mort et la religion dans la région d'Avignon à la fin du Moyen Age. *Ecole Française de Rome*, 47.
Coing, H. (ed.) 1973: *Handbuch der Quellen und Literatur der neueren europäischen Privatsrechtsgeschichte*, vol. 1, *Mittelalter, 1100–1500*, Munich.
Delumeau, J. 1978: *La Peur en Occident (XIVe–XVIIIe siècles Une cité assiegée)*, Paris.
Durliat, J. 1982: Du 'caput' antique au manse médiéval. *Pallas*, 29.
Eiss, G. 1967: *Mittelalteriche Fachliteratur*, Stuttgart.
Elwitt, S. 1975: *The Making of the Third Republic. Class and Politics in France, 1868–1884*, Baton Rouge.

Genicot, L. 1953: Sur les témoignages d'accroissement de la population en Europe occidentale du XIe au XIIIe siècle. *Cahiers d'histoire mondiale* 1.

Gurjewitsch, A. J. 1978: *Das Weltbild des mittelalterlichen Menschen*, Dresden.

Jaspers, K. 1947: *Vom europäischen Geist*, Munich.

Klingner, F. 1941: *Vom Geistesleben des ausgehenden Altertums*.

Koschaker, P. 1947: *Europa und das römische Recht*, Munich.

Labande, E.-R. 1973: Essai sur les hommes de l'an mil. In *Concetto, storia, miti e imagini del medioevo*, Florence.

Le Goff, J. 1981: *La naissance du Purgatoire*, Paris.

Lopez, R. S. 1982: *Naissance de l'Europe*, Paris.

Löwe, H. 1983: Westliche Peregrinatio und Mission. Ihr Zusammenhang mit den länder- und völkerkundlichen Kenntnissen des frühen Mittelalters. In *Popoli e paesi nella cultura altomedioevale. Settimane di studio del Centro italiano di studi sull'alto medioevo*, vol. 39, Spoleto.

Mommsen, W. 1974: *Max Weber. Gesellschaft, Politik und Geschichte*, Frankfurt.

Murray, A. 1978: *Reason and Society in the Middle Ages*, Oxford.

Musset, L. 1979: La Scandinavie intermédiare entre l'Occident et l'Orient au Xe siècle. In *Occident et Orient au Xe siècle*, Publications de l'Université de Dijon, vol. 17.

Oexle, O. G. 1984: Sozialgeschichte-Begriffsgeschichte-Wissenschaftgeschichte. *Vierteljahrschrift für Sozial- und Wirtschaftsgeschichte*, 71.

Parente, F. 1983: Terra santa come esperienze religiosa. In *Settimano di studio del Centro italiano di studio sull'alto medioevo*, vol. 39, Spoleto.

Ranke, L. von 1888: Ueber die Epochen der neueren Geschichte. In *Weltgeschichte*, vol. 9, Leipzig.

Sawyer, P. H. 1982: *Kings and Vikings. Scandinavia and Europe, AD 700–1100*, London.

Schlesinger, W. 1963: *Beiträge zur deutschen Verfassungsgeschichte des Mittelalters*, vol. 2, Göttingen.

Schmid, K. and Wollasch, J. (eds) 1984: *Der Geschichtliche Zeugniswert liturgischen Gedenkens*, Munich.

Sohm, R. 1919: *Institutionen. Geschichte und System des römischen Privatsrechts*, Munich.

Tellenbach, G. 1936: *Libertas. Kirche und Weltordnung im Zeitalter des Investiturstreits*, Stuttgart.

Troeltsch, E. 1922: *Der Historismus und seine Probleme*, Tubingen.

Werner, K. F. 1970: Les nations et le sentiment national dans l'Europe médiévale. *Revue historique*, 244.

—— 1980a: Histoire comparée de l'Administration. Une introduction. In W. Paravicini and K. F. Werner (eds), *Histoire comparée de l'Administration, IVe–XVIIIe siècles*, Munich.

—— 1980b: L'Empire carolingien et le Saint Empire. In M. Duverger (ed.), *Le Concept d'Empire*, Paris.

—— 1984: *Les Origines jusqu'à l'an mil, Histoire de France*, vol. 1, Paris.

—— 1985: Du nouveau sur un vieux thème. Les origines de la 'noblesse' et de la chevalerie. *Académie des Inscriptions et Belles-Lettres. Comptes rendus*, Paris.

1987a: Les structures de l'Histoire a l'âge du christianisme. In *Storia della storiografia*, Milan.

1987b: Gott, Herrscher und historiograph. In *Deus qui mutat regna. Festschrift für Alfons Becker*, Sigmaringen.

1987c: Volk, Nation, Masse (Mittelalter). In O. Brunner et al. (eds), *Geschichtliche Grundbegriffe. Historiesches Lexikon zur politisch-sozialen Sprache in Deutschland*, vol. 6.

1987d: Hludouuicus Augustus. Gouverner l'Empire chrétien – idées et réalités. In P. Godman and R. Collins (eds), *Charlemagne's Heir. New Perspectives on the Reign of Louis the Pious*.

Witthöft, H. 1983: Mass und Gewicht im 9. Jahrhundert. Fränkische Traditionen im Übergang von der Antike zum Mittelalter. *Vierteljahrschrift für Sozial- und Wirtschaftsgeschichte*, 70.

11

The Cradle of Capitalism: The Case of England

Alan Macfarlane

For Marx, Weber and many others it has been evident that capitalism is a peculiar social formation. Its birthplace was in western Europe. Within this region there was a particular area which was precocious in its development, where the new social formation emerged in its purest and earliest form. Marx noted that in the early dissolution of the preceding 'medieval' property system 'England [was] in this respect the model country for the other continental countries' (Marx, 1973: 277). It was, as Brenner puts it 'classically in England' that we have 'the rise of the three-tiered relation of landlord/capitalist tenant/free wage labour, around which Marx developed much of his theory of capitalist development in *Capital*' (1977: 75). For Max Weber also, England was 'the home of capitalism' (1961: 251); it was in England above all that the Puritan outlook 'stood at the cradle of the modern economic man' (1970: 174). Since England was the cradle and nursery of capitalism, it is not surprising that later writers have concentrated on that country. For instance, Polanyi takes England's history as the central example of the 'Great Transformation' (1944). It is not unreasonable to suppose that if we could explain why capitalism emerged and developed in England, and specifically what differentiated it from other parts of Europe and allowed this growth, we would have moved some way towards understanding the 'European miracle'.

We may look at some of the more outstanding attempts to solve this problem. Marx's treatment of the causes for the emergence of capitalism is intriguing but ultimately unsatisfying. He skilfully shows how the transition may have occurred, and a few of the preconditions. But he totally avoids giving any solution to the questions of why then and why there. He analyses the central features of the supposed transition; the creation of a 'free' labour force through the destruction of a dependent peasantry is the central one. This was linked to the expansion of market forces, money, production for exchange rather than for immediate consumption. Thus growing trade and commerce is seen as one of the major propelling forces: 'the circulation of commodities is the starting-point of capital. . . . The modern history of capital dates from the creation in the sixteenth century of a world-embracing commerce and a world-embracing market' (1954: vol. 1, 145). But long-distance trade had been present for centuries and had centred on the Mediterranean. Why should trade suddenly have had this shattering effect, and why should its prime target be north-western Europe? Unsatisfied with the analyses in *Capital* with its mystic theories of internal contradictions which were bound to lead to inevitable dissolution of the previous social formation, we may look to his other writings.

In *Grundrisse* Marx outlines various combustible elements that would explode into capitalism. There is money and more specifically 'mercantile and usurious wealth'. But money, urban craft activity and towns had been present in many civilizations. Why in western Europe did they alone lead to the growth of capitalism? Marx does provide some further hints. One central foundation for capitalism was the pre-existence of a rural social structure which allowed the peasantry to be 'set free'. In other words there was something particularly fragile in the pre-existing relations of production. The substratum of feudalism, arising from its origins in the 'Germanic system' was particularly vulnerable to the new urban craft development and accumulation of wealth. The crucial feature of the Germanic system was its form of property. In the Ancient and Asiatic civilizations, there was no individual, private, property. But in Germanic society something new and odd emerged. In this period no land remained in the possession of the community or group. People had moved half-way, according to Marx, from communal property, to half-individualized property based on the household. It would take another thousand years for the second half of the movement to be made. In other words, there is something within feudalism, some hidden spirit, which is special. This is implied in other remarks, for example that 'the economic structure of capitalist society has grown out of the economic structure of feudal society. The dissolution of the latter set free the elements of the former' (1954: vol. 1, 668). The metaphor of 'setting free' suggests that Marx believed that the spirit of capitalism was already present before the emergence of capitalism.

Weber considered a number of possible explanations for the emergence of capitalism. He rejected the crudely technological and materialistic ones: colonial trade, population growth, the inflow of precious metals. He then isolated some of the necessary but not sufficient 'external conditions', the particular geography of Europe with its cheap transportation by water, the favourable military requirements of the small states, the large luxury demand from an unusually prosperous population. Ultimately it was not these external factors, but something more mysterious that was important. It was the ethic, the justification of the pursuit of profit. He found the roots of this in a paradox. The new attitudes were waiting to escape. The paradox is summarized by Weber himself. 'The final result is the peculiar fact that the germs of modern capitalism must be sought in a region where officially a theory was dominant which was distinct from that of the east and of classical antiquity and in principle strongly hostile to capitalism' (1970: 162). This region was medieval Christendom.

We may note the use of 'officially' here with its implication of the submerged, unofficial, practice. Judaism was an important background feature in giving to Christianity 'the character of a religion essentially free from magic' (Weber, 1961: 265). But what was most important was the presence of Protestantism. Protestantism was not the cause of capitalism, but it gave older and deeper tendencies a necessary protection. It was the enabling force. This view of Protestantism as a kind of wind-break which allowed the young plant to grow is well shown in numerous places by Weber. For instance, when writing that the Puritan outlook 'stood at the cradle of the modern economic man' (1970: 174), the image is not of a mother giving birth, but of a friend, perhaps a godparent, who gives support and blessing to the new infant. More specifically, Weber wrote that 'We have no intentions whatever of maintaining such a foolish and doctrinaire thesis as that the spirit of capitalism . . . could only have arisen as the result of certain effects of the Reformation, or even that capitalism as an economic system is the creation of the Reformation' (1970: 91). Many aspects of capitalism were much older. As Bendix summarizes Weber's position, 'this world historical transformation, then, was not the product of Puritanism; rather, Puritanism was a late development that reinforced tendencies that had distinguished European society for a long time past' (1961: 71–2).

Weber provides some suggestive clues as to why England should be the cradle of capitalism. There was the peculiar position of the peasantry. In England the peasants were particularly weak and vulnerable because, being an island, they were not needed by the king and nobility as a necessary fighting force; 'hence the policy of peasant protection was unknown in England and it became the classical land of peasant eviction' (1961: 129). In England, Weber noted, no legal emancipation of the peasants ever took place.

The medieval system is still formally in force, except that under Charles II

serfdom was abolished. . . . In England, the mere fact of the development
of a market, as such and alone, destroyed the manorial system from within.
In accordance with the principle fitting the situation, the peasants were
expropriated in favour of the proprietors. The peasants became free but
without land.

In France, however, 'the course of events is exactly the opposite. . . .
France, in contrast with England, became a land of small and medium
sized farms' (1961: 85–6). Not only was this a reflection of the different
power of the peasants, the pressures of wealth in England were greater.
Because of the rapid development of a particular means of production,
the English woollen industry with its division of labour and commerce,
the large-scale stock raising, Weber argued, made the tenant weak and
redundant. The massive growth of the English cloth industry from the
fourteenth century onwards meant that a new capitalist class emerged.
This was combined with the growth of the 'bourgeoisie', the free
dwellers in the peculiar towns and cities of northern Europe.

Having subtly interwoven some of the religious, economic and social
factors, Weber does not omit the political and legal dimension. He
argues that 'the State, in the sense of the rational state has existed only in
the western world' (1961: 250). He contrasts this western state with the
charismatic, patrimonial and other traditional systems of government in
China, India and Islam. The state is essential to capitalism; 'very
different is the rational state in which alone modern capitalism can
flourish'. The basis of the rational state is rational law. Here Weber
recognizes another paradox. The most 'rational', that is the most
carefully worked out and logically coherent of legal systems, was that of
Roman Law. Yet, ironically, capitalism flourished most in the one area of
Europe without Roman Law, namely England. Weber resolves the
contradiction subtly. He distinguishes between the formal side, in
modern terms 'procedural' or 'adjectival' law, and its content or
'substantive law'. Thus the 'rational law of the modern occidental state
. . . arose on its formal side, though not as to its content, out of Roman
law'. Yet, since 'England, the home of capitalism, never accepted the
Roman law' (1961: 251), it is clear that 'in fact all the characteristic
institutions of modern capitalism have other origins than Roman law'.
Weber gives a list of these devices.

The annuity bond . . . came from medieval law, in which Germanic legal
ideas played their part. Similarly the stock certificate arose out of medieval
and modern law . . . likewise the bill of exchange . . . the commercial
company is also a medieval product, so also the mortgage, with the security
of registration, and the deed of trust. (1961: 252)

I have dwelt on Marx and Weber at some length because they anticipate almost all the theories that have come later. Though they failed to solve the problem, it is doubtful whether any subsequent writer has reached as close to a solution. A few recent attempts, concentrating specifically on the question of why the miracle occurred in north-western Europe can be considered. Braudel in his majestic surveys of capitalism and material life has in general accepted the inevitability of the transition, falling back on those material and technological factors which Weber dismissed (1973). The seeds were assumed to be present and we just watch them growing. The sense of marvel and uniqueness which Marx and Weber possessed has gone. A recent voluminous attempt by Anderson to solve these problems does not reach further than the great theorists. The treatment of the central case of England, for instance, is not satisfactory. Anderson admits that the 'feudal monarchy of England was generally far more powerful than that of France', and yet 'the strongest medieval monarchy in the West eventually produced the weakest and shortest Absolutism' (1974: 113). That England should go through an 'Absolutist' phase, seems to be essential for Anderson; it is a precondition of capitalism. Yet he signally fails to show that such a phase occurs. As he admits, most of the more extreme measures of the Tudors were not put into practice and they lacked a standing army. Despite what he believes was an 'inherent tendency' of the Tudor monarchy towards 'absolutism' on the continental model, the Crown was surrounded by a peculiar landowning class which was 'unusually civilian in background, commercial in occupation and commoner in rank'. The result was that this was a state which 'had a small bureaucracy, a limited fiscality, and no permanent army' (1974: 127). Yet a large bureaucracy, heavy taxation and a standing army are the three central criteria of absolutism as defined by Anderson. An England where 'the coercive and bureaucratic machinery of the monarchy remained very slim' (1974: 129) hardly seems suited to the Absolutist mantle. (These criticisms, I recently discovered, have also been made by Runciman, 1980.)

The failure to show that England had either of the two essential prerequisites of the capitalist revolution according to his general model, namely Absolutism and Roman Law, forces Anderson to fall back on a rehashed version of Marx's theory about the expropriation of the peasants, combined with a certain amount of 'natural tendency' thrown in. Trade and manufactures grew, the peasantry were socially differentiated and weak and were destroyed, both from without and within. We are no further forward.

One of the most interesting developments in the discussion has been in two articles by Brenner. In the first he showed the inadequacy of demographic explanations of the rise of capitalism, particularly in the work of Ladurie and Postan. By cross-comparative analysis Brenner showed that the same major demographic pressures led to entirely different results in western and eastern Europe. Nor can the explanation lie in trade and commercialization in themselves. The solution lies, as Marx thought, in the relations of production: 'it is the structure of class relations, of class power, which will determine the manner and degree to which particular demographic and commercial changes will affect long-run trends in the distribution of income and economic growth – and not vice versa' (1976: 31). What, then, is his theory? It is that the different trajectories of western and eastern Europe arose out of the fact that in western Europe the peasantry were already strong and could not be re-feudalized, as they were in the East. But this general approach leads him into problems with the test case of England.

It has normally been held, as we saw with Weber, that it was the weakness of the English peasantry which led to its destruction. Brenner's thesis leads him into a contradiction. In England the peasantry were both weak and strong. Their strength led them to eliminate themselves. They vanished and conquered at the same time. 'In England, as throughout most of Western Europe, the peasantry was able by the mid-fifteenth century, through flight and resistance, to break definitively feudal controls over its mobility and to win full freedom' (1976: 61). Yet, strangely, in England, they did not win economic security, as they were to do in France. They did not manage to attach themselves to the land and become a strong landholding peasantry: 'it was the emergence of the classical landlord–capitalist tenant–wage labour structure which made possible the transformation of agricultural production in England, and this, in turn, was the key to England's uniquely successful overall economic development' (1976: 63). Brenner is here trying to get the best of both arguments. The peasants were strong and resisted the landlord and did not become serfs again, on the other hand they were weak and were eliminated. 'The contrasting failure in France of agrarian transformations seems to have followed directly from the continuing strength of peasant landholding into the early modern period while it was disintegrating in England' (1976: 68). As well as the inconsistency of this explanation, it is unsatisfying because it does not begin to tackle the reasons for the peculiar nature of the English relations of production. How had this situation emerged and in what, precisely, did the peculiarities lie?

Reactions to this first stimulating essay have pointed out the weaknesses, but failed to go further. Thus in a thoughtful response Croot and Parker agree that Brenner has pinpointed the significant variable, the differences in social structures, but believe that 'the explanation offered for the emergence or non-emergence of such relations is unconvincing' (1978: 45–6). Unfortunately, these authors, besides laying stress on one or two factors such as the importance of the small farmer (yeoman) in England, are unable to offer a better solution. Likewise Bois agrees that 'the decisive part in the transition from feudalism to capitalism is played out in the countryside' (1978: 62n.), but provides no more plausible explanation than Brenner. He points to the divergences between English and French 'feudalism', which differed from at least the thirteenth century according to Bois (1978: 65), but this important insight is not followed up.

In a second important article Brenner then demolished another group of theorists, namely the 'Neo-Smithian Marxists': Frank, Sweezy and Wallerstein. He shows that the basic premise of all these accounts is the view that capitalism was already there before it emerged. The profit motive was already present. For instance, we are told that 'Sweezy's mistake was obviously to assume the operation of norms of capitalist rationality, in a situation where capitalist social relations of production did not exist, simply because market exchange was widespread' (Brenner, 1977: 45). Likewise 'the Smithian theory embedded in Sweezy's analysis . . . is made entirely explicitly, and carried to its logical conclusion in Wallerstein's *Modern World System*' (1977: 53). Brenner has much innocent fun showing that these Marxists are at heart followers of Adam Smith. What he fails to point out is that they are also Marxists. As we saw earlier, Marx himself needed to believe that the capitalist profit motive existed, that the germ was present, before the existence of capitalism. Brenner has again cleared the decks, but provided no alternative. His later reply to his critics elaborates the earlier position but takes us no further towards a solution (1982).

Two further more recent theories are worth noting. The first is that the development of the West was made possible by the political fragmentation of Europe. Whereas the unified empires of India and China crushed all economic progress, 'the constant expansion of the market . . . was the result of an absence of political order extending over the whole of western Europe' (Baechler, 1975: 73). Thus Baechler's main conclusions are that the 'first condition for the maximization of economic efficiency is the liberation of civil society with respect to the State. This condition is fulfilled when a single cultural area is divided into several sovereign political units', as in Europe (1975: 113). This thesis has been forcefully restated by Hall. He adds to it the important role played by Christianity which 'kept Europe together . . . the market was possible because people felt themselves part of a single community' (1985: 115, 123). Again these are necessary, if not sufficient, explanations.

We are thus in a position where we have a clearer idea of the problems.

These are: why did capitalism emerge and triumph in a part of western
Europe in the early modern period? Why this area, and particularly why
in England? We also know what not to pursue: towns, population growth,
overseas trade, colonialism, the growth of trade and the market,
technology were necessary but not sufficient causes. We know that a
particular strand of religion, an integrated and rational state and new
kind of law, were all important. The common culture of Christianity
holding together several small sovereign political units was also
important. Above all, we know that it was not in a single one of these
features, but in the way in which economy, politics, law and religion were
linked together that the solutions are likely to lie. Furthermore we have
hints that there were some crucial differences here within Europe, and
especially as between England and other continental countries. We may
now turn to a possible solution to some of these problems.

There is a very widely held belief that the emergence of capitalism was
linked to a pre-existing social formation known as 'feudalism'. Two of
the most influential proponents of this view were Maine and Marx. For
Maine, feudal ties formed the basis for the most momentous of all
changes, from relations based on status (kinship) to those based on
contract. In feudalism, he wrote, 'the notion of common kinship has been
entirely lost. The link between Lord and Vassal produced by Commen-
dation is of quite a different kind from that produced by Consanguinity'
(1875: 86). He traced the origins of private property of a modern kind to
the new feudal ties (1875: 115). Feudalism was connected to what Maine
considered to be the central feature of modern society, the idea of
indivisible, inheritable, individual property symbolized and enshrined in
primogeniture: 'in the ancient world, and in the societies which have not
passed through the crucible of feudalism, the Primogeniture which
seems to have prevailed never transformed itself into the Primogeniture
of the later feudal Europe' (1890: 237). Maitland picked up the
implications of Maine's fundamental insight. 'The master who taught us
that "the movement of the progressive societies has hitherto been a
movement from Status to Contract" was quick to add that feudal society
was governed by the law of contract. There is no paradox here' (Pollock
and Maitland, 1968: vol. 2: 232–3).

Marx, we have seen, also saw that only out of a dissolved feudalism
could capitalism emerge. In the feudal system (as opposed to the Asiatic
and primitive), the essential divorce which is a precondition of private
property of the few had taken place. 'Feudal landed property is already
essentially land which has been disposed of, alienated from men' (1963:
133). While Maine and Marx stressed the changes in property concepts,
Weber noted other ideological changes. No longer was the kinship
sentiment dominant; loyalty to the family based on status was changed to

a bond based, ultimately, on contract, the political decision to serve a lord. According to Bendix, Weber argued that 'in western Europe and Japan the specifically feudal combination of loyalty and status honour was made the basic outlook on life that affected all social relationships' (1966: 364). It is on the basis of these views that most of the major theorists of the rise of capitalism – Anderson, Brenner, Barrington-Moore – see feudalism as a vital transitory state. Yet if this is true, some puzzles remain. Two of these are particularly relevant to this essay. Firstly, why did feudalism have such different consequences in different parts of Europe, and particularly as between England and much of the continent? Secondly, how was it that feudalism dissolved?

In order to proceed further we need to set up an ideal typical model of what feudalism is, or was. For Maine, the central feature was the nature of proprietorship. Put very crudely, the economic and the political were not split apart, unlike capitalism which keeps them in separate spheres. Feudalism 'mixed up or confounded property and sovereignty' (1883: 148), for in a certain sense, every lord of a manor was a king as well as a landholder. Political power and economic power were both delegated down the same chain. A second feature, more narrowly economic and legal, was the ability to conceive of different layers of ownership or possession within feudal tenures: 'the leading characteristic of the feudal conception is its recognition of a double proprietorship, the superior ownership of the lord of the fief coexisting with the inferior property or estate of the tenant' (1875: 295).

Marx's characterization of feudalism in his various writings is a fairly conventional and largely economic picture of an immobile, mainly self-subsistent, 'peasant' society, with a hierarchy of owners. There was little division of labour, production was mainly for use, and the serfs were chained to their lords (1963: 128; 1954, vol. 1: 316; 1964: 46). Perhaps Weber's most important insight was his recognition that feudalism constituted a different political system. His views have been summarized by Gerth and Mills thus:

> feudalism is characterized by Weber in terms of private property of the means of military violence (self-equipped armies) and in the corporate appropriation of the means of administration. The 'ruler' could not monopolize administration and warfare because he had to delegate the implements required for such a monopoly to the several privileged groupings. (1948: 47)

In other words, there is political and legal decentralization; the centre cannot hold and mere anarchy is loosed upon the world. There is again reference to the fusion of military, political, legal and economic power down a chain of delegation. A feudal society in this sense is a pre-state society; people are not citizens, but vassals of particular lords.

The most influential model of feudalism is that presented by Bloch. Again his stress is mainly on the military, political and legal features of feudalism, rather than on the economic and property aspects. He summarizes the central features of the model thus:

> a subject peasantry; widespread use of the service tenement (that is the fief) instead of a salary; the supremacy of a class of specialized warriors; ties of obedience and protection which bind man to man and, within the warrior class, assume the distinctive form called vassalage; fragmentation of authority, leading inevitably to disorder; and, in the midst of all this, the precarious survival of other forms of association, the family and State. (1965: vol. 2, 446)

The fragmentation is well illustrated in his description of the judicial system in Europe in about AD 1000. 'First, we may note the tremendous fragmentation of judicial powers; next, their tangled interconnections; and lastly, their ineffectiveness (p. 359). In some ways feudalism is best defined negatively. It was not based on kinship: 'feudal ties proper were developed when those of kinship proved inadequate' (p. 443). Although modelled on family ties, this was a relation of contract, not status. Nor was feudalism a state system. 'Again, despite the persistence of the idea of a public authority superimposed on the multitude of petty powers, feudalism coincided with a profound weakening of the State, particularly in its protective capacity' (p. 443). In Bloch's view this strange and unique system was a transition phase, the turbulence of the Germanic invasions led to a fusion of Roman and Germanic that broke the old mould. Ganshof, likewise, stressed political fragmentation. One of his four defining features of feudalism was 'a dispersal of political authority amongst a hierarchy of persons who exercise in their own interest powers normally attributed to the State and which are often, in fact, derived from its break-up (1964: xv).

We may provide one final description of feudalism. Maitland lamented the difficulty of defining feudalism: 'the impossible task that has been set before the very word *feudalism* is that of making a single idea represent a very large piece of the world's history, represent the France, Italy, Germany, England, of every century from the eighth or ninth to the fourteenth or fifteenth' (Pollock and Maitland, 1968: vol. 1, 67). The result is confusion. Maitland attempted to clarify the situation. The central feature of feudalism, as Maine had stressed, was the strange mixture of ownership, the blending of economic and political. The feud, fief or fee was

> a gift of land made by the king out of his own estate, the grantee coming under a special obligation to be faithful (Maitland, 1919: 152)

> To express the rights thus created, a set of technical terms was developed: the beneficiary or feudatory holds the land of his lord, the grantor – *A tenet terram de B*. The full ownership (*dominium*) of the land is as it were broken up between A and B; or again, for the feudatory may grant out part of the land to be held of him, it may be broken up between A, B, and C, C holding of B and B of A, and so on, *ad infinitum*. (p. 153)

Maitland believed that 'the most remarkable characteristic of feudalism' was the fact that 'several persons in somewhat different senses, may be said to have and to hold the same piece of land' (Pollock and Maitland, 1968: vol. 1, 237). But there are equally characteristic and essential features. In some mysterious way power and property have been merged. Feudalism is not just a landholding system, but also a system of government. While many have seen 'the introduction of military tenures' as the 'establishment of the feudal system', in fact, when 'compared with seignorial justice, military tenure is a superficial matter, one out of many effects rather than a deep seated cause' (1921: 258). He describes as 'that most essential feature of feudalism, jurisdiction in private hands, the lord's court' (Pollock and Maitland, 1968: vol. 1, 68). The merging of power and property, of public and private, is well shown elsewhere in Maitland's work. The English lawyer Bracton knew of the distinction of 'private' and 'public', yet 'he makes little use of it'. This was because

> feudalism . . . is a denial of this distinction. Just in so far as the ideal of feudalism is perfectly realized, all that we call public law is merged in private law: jurisdiction is property, office is property, the kingship itself is property; the same word *dominium* has to stand now for *ownership* and now for *lordship*. (p. 68)

Although we have already quoted extensively from Maitland, it is helpful to summarize his views of the ideal typical model of feudalism in one further description. This is an elegant synthesis of the essence of feudalism against which particular systems can be measured. It shows the two strands of the economic and political held together. Feudalism is

> a state of society in which the main bond is the relation between lord and man, a relation implying on the lord's part protection and defence; on the man's part protection, service and reverence, the service including service in arms. This personal relation is inseparably involved in a proprietary relation, the tenure of land – the man holds lands of the lord, the man's service is a burden on the land, the lord has important rights in the land, and (we may say) the full ownership of the land is split up between man and lord. The lord has jurisdiction over his men, holds courts for them, to which they owe suit. Jurisdiction is regarded as property, as a private right which the lord has over his land. The national organization is a system of these relationships: at the head there stands the king as lord of all, below him are his immediate vassals, or tenants in chief, who again are lords of tenants, who again may be lords of tenants, and so on, down to the lowest possessor of land. Lastly, as every other court consists of the lord's tenants, so the king's court consists of his tenants in chief, and so far as there is any constitutional control over the king it is exercised by the body of these tenants. (1919: 143–4)

This completes our attempt to sort out in ideal typical terms the social formation out of which capitalism was born.

Various things are now clear. The emergence of capitalism required not only a particular geographical, religious and technological complex, but, above all, a particular politico-economic system. This was provided by feudalism. Yet there remain many puzzles. One lies in a general paradox. In many ways feudalism as described in the Bloch/Maitland model seems a very unpropitious ground for capitalism. Firstly, it rests on that very fusion of economic and political which has to be broken if capitalism is to triumph. Of course, the modern market has to rest on a particular political framework; but for capitalism to flourish the economy must be granted a great deal of autonomy. It must be set free. If economic relations are merely a sub-aspect of devolved power, capitalism cannot emerge. Secondly, the political system must be integrated and centralized. The modern 'state' is a necessary concomitant to capitalism; to this extent Anderson's stress on the necessity of absolutism is correct. Yet the overriding and defining feature of feudalism is the dissolution of the state, the loss of power at the centre. These puzzles are linked to a more specific one. Feudalism is widely held to be a phenomenon which covered most of western Europe. Why was it then that in England it first dissolved into capitalism? Fortunately, the answers to all these puzzles seem to lie in the same direction.

Many observers past and present have assumed that all of Europe, and particularly most of north-western Europe, went through a similar 'feudal' phase. David Hume, after giving a sketch of feudal anarchy consistent with the 'dissolved state' description, pointed to 'the great similarity among the feudal governments of Europe' (1975: 20). De Tocqueville described how 'I have had occasion to study the political institutions of the Middle Ages in France, in England, and in Germany, and the greater progress I made in this work, the more was I filled with astonishment at the prodigious similarity that I found between all these systems of law'. Having elaborated the similarities he concluded that 'I think it may be maintained that in the fourteenth century the social, political, administrative, judicial, economic, and literary institutions of Europe had more resemblance to each other than they have perhaps even in our own days' (1955: 15). Marx broadly accepted this view, arguing that England was a truly feudal society, indeed it was the most feudal: 'the feudalism introduced into England was formally more complete than the feudalism which had naturally grown up in France' (1964: 88). If this view is correct, then the puzzles remain. But there are reasons for doubting it.

Weber seems to have realized that the English feudal system was in some way different. Having distinguished between two major forms of government in traditional societies – patrimonialism and feudalism – Weber recognized that England did not fall exactly into either. We are told that 'he took England as a borderline case in which patrimonial and feudal elements were inextricably mixed' (Bendix, 1966: 358). England had a powerful, decentralizing force in the old baronial families, through whom the Crown governed, but the Normans had also imposed a powerful central force and the king's ministers and judges were also powerful.

The suspicion that England had a peculiar form of feudalism is made stronger by Bloch's work. Read superficially, Bloch could be taken to argue that England was an ordinary 'feudal' state in the early Middle Ages. Writing of vassalage, Bloch noted that England was 'already feudalized on the continental model' (1965: vol. 1, 232). He states that it was one of the countries with 'an exceptionally close feudal structure' (vol. 2, 383), 'in certain respects . . . no state was more completely feudal' (p. 430). Yet if we look more closely at the context of these remarks, we can see that Bloch was aware of the peculiar nature of English feudalism.

Bloch noticed the centralization and uniformity of the English political and social system. This was totally opposed to his major feature of feudalism, devolution, disintegration and the dissolution of the state. The contrasts come out when he compared England and France.

In England there was the Great Charter; in France, in 1314–15, the Charters granted to the Normans, to the people of the Languedoc, to the Bretons, to the Burgundians, to the Picards, to the people of Champagne, to Auvergne, of the *Basses Marches* of the West, of Berry, and of Nevers. In England there was Parliament; in France, the provincial Estates, always much more frequently convoked and on the whole more active than the States-General. In England there was the common law, almost untouched by regional exceptions; in France the vast medley of regional 'customs'. (pp. 425–6)

Thus England was uniform and centralized, France varied and regionalized. Because 'the public office was not completely identified with the fief', Bloch argued, 'England was a truly unified state much earlier than any continental kingdom' (p. 430). Furthermore, the English parliamentary system had a 'peculiar quality which distinguished it so sharply from the continental system of "Estates" '. This was linked to that 'collaboration of the well-to-do classes in power, so characteristic of the English political structure' (p. 371).

Bloch noted central differences. The 'distinction between high and low justice always remained foreign to the English system' (p. 370). The allodial estates common on the continent which prevented the final penetration of feudal tenures to the bottom of society were totally extinguished in England where all land was ultimately held of the king and not held in full ownership by any subject. England was exceptional in not having private feuding sanctioned after the Norman Conquest; it therefore avoided that disintegrated anarchy which was characteristic of France (vol. 1, 128). Indeed, English feudalism, we are told 'has something of the value of an object-lesson in social organization', not because it was typical of feudal society but because it shows 'how in the midst of what was in many respects a homogeneous civilization certain creative ideas, taking shape under the influence of a given environment, could result in the creation of a completely original legal system'.[1] It is this 'completely original legal system' which provides the key to the emergence of capitalism. But what is the secret of this system? For the solution to this puzzle it is necessary both to understand perfectly the nature of feudalism and to have a deep knowledge of how the English system worked. It needed Maitland to state the essential paradox of English feudalism and to resolve it.

Maitland commented that 'we have learnt to see vast differences as well as striking resemblances, to distinguish countries and to distinguish times' when we discuss feudalism. Thus 'if we now speak of the feudal

1 For a subsequent recognition of some of the peculiarities of English feudalism, see Ganshof (1964: 67, 164–6).

system, it should be with a full understanding that the feudalism of France differs radically from the feudalism of England, that the feudalism of the thirteenth is very different from that of the eleventh century' (1919: 143). For England 'it is quite possible to maintain that of all countries England was the most, or for the matter of that the least, feudalized' (p. 143). The paradox is resolved when we remember that there are two central criteria whereby we measure feudalism. In terms of land law, England was the most perfectly feudalized of societies, as Bloch also noted. All tenures were feudal. Maitland wrote, 'in so far as feudalism is mere property law, England is of all countries the most perfectly feudalized' (Pollock and Maitland, 1968: vol. 1, 235). Thus

> owing to the Norman Conquest one part of the theory was carried out in this country with consistent and unexampled rigour; every square inch of land was brought within the theory of tenure: English real property law becomes a law of feudal tenures. In France, in Germany, allodial owners might be found: not one in England. (Maitland, 1919: 163–4)

For instance the 'absolute and uncompromising form of primogeniture which prevails in England belongs not to feudalism in general, but to a highly centralized feudalism in which the King has not much to fear from the power of his mightiest vassals' (Pollock and Maitland, 1968: vol. 2, 265). Thus, in terms of tenure, England was the most feudal of societies and Marx was right.

On the other hand, in the even more important sphere of public and private law and political power, that is in terms of government, England went in a peculiar direction, towards centralization of power, rather than the dissolution of the state. Maitland points out that

> our public law does not become feudal; in every direction the force of feudalism is limited and checked by other ideas; the public rights, the public duties of the Englishman are not conceived and cannot be conceived as the mere outcome of feudal compacts between man and lord. (1919: 164)

Maitland outlines the major features of this limitation of public feudalism.

> First and foremost, it never becomes law that there is no political bond between men save the bond of tenure . . . whenever homage or fealty was done to any mesne lord, the tenant expressly saved the faith that he owed to his lord the king. (p. 161)

Thus a man who fights for his lord against the king is not doing his feudal duty; he is committing treason. Over-mighty subjects could not draw on justification from this system. This point is so important that Maitland elaborates it in various ways.

'English law never recognizes that any man is bound to fight for his lord. . . . Private war never becomes legal – it is a crime and a breach of the peace' (p. 161). A man can hardly 'go against' anyone at his lord's command without being guilty of 'felony'. As Maitland wrote, 'Common law, royal and national law, has, as it were occupied the very citadel of feudalism' (Pollock and Maitland, 1968: vol. 1, 303). To bring out the full peculiarity of this, Maitland tells us, 'you should look at the history of France; there it was definitely regarded as law that in a just quarrel the vassal must follow his immediate lord, even against the king' (1919: 162). In England, 'military service is due to none but the king; this it is which makes English feudalism a very different thing from French feudalism' (p. 32).

There are a number of other differences which make this central feature possible and flow from it. There is an alternative army for the king, which helps to protect him against an over-dependence on his feudal tenants.

> Though the military tenures supply the king with an army, it never becomes law that those who are not bound by tenure need not fight. The old national force, officered by the sheriffs, does not cease to exist. . . . In this organization of the common folk under royal officers, there is all along a counterpoise to the military system of feudalism, and it serves the king well. (p. 162)

Another source of strength for the centre is the fact that 'taxation is not feudalized'. Maitland tells us that 'the king for a while is strong enough to tax the nation, to tax the sub-tenants, to get straight at the mass of the people their lands and their goods, without the intervention of their lords' (p. 162). Thus he is not entirely dependent on powerful lords for soldiers or money.

Nor is he entirely dependent on them for advice. We are told that 'the *Curia Regis*, which is to become the *commune concilium regni*, never takes very definitely a feudal shape. . . . It is much in the king's power to summon whom he will. The tradition of a council of witan is not lost' (p. 163). Finally, the king is not forced to delegate judicial power to the barons. 'The administration of justice is never completely feudalized. The old local courts are kept alive, and are not feudal assemblies.' As a result of this:

the jurisdiction of the feudal courts is strictly limited; criminal jurisdiction they have none save by express royal grant, and the kings are on the whole chary of making such grants. Seldom, indeed, can any lord exercise more than what on the continent would have been considered justice of a very low degree.

Starting with considerable power, the king 'rapidly extends the sphere of his own justice: before the middle of the thirteenth century his courts have practically become courts of first instance for the whole realm' (pp. 162–3).

The contradiction is thus resolved. By taking one aspect of the feudal tie, the idea that each person is linked to the person above him both in terms of tenure and power, to its logical limits, the English system developed into something peculiar. By the standards of Bloch's French model of feudalism, England was both the most and the least feudal of countries. Looked at another way, England was the ideal typical feudal society, with an apex of both landholding and justice and power in the chief lord, and it was other feudal systems which, through the devolution of too much power, were defective. Both are tenable views. Despite some minor modifications, Maitland's vision is still acceptable, certainly there 'can be no doubt that by the end of the period covered by his books', in other words the end of the thirteenth century, 'the world was as Maitland saw it' (Milson, in Pollock and Maitland, 1968: vol. 1, xlvii).

The argument very briefly stated and summarized is as follows. No single factor explains why capitalism emerged. We do know some of the necessary causes, as outlined by Maine, Marx and Weber. All of them are important. But to proceed further we need to concentrate on hints from all these writers, as well as Brenner and others, that as well as geography, technology and Christianity, there was needed a particular form of political and economic system. This was broadly provided by 'feudalism'. But the variant of feudalism which finally allowed the 'miracle' to occur was a rather unusual one. It already contained an implicit separation between economic and political power, between the market and government. While it was not absolutism in Anderson's sense, it was a firm and centrally focused system which provided the security and uniformity upon which trade and industry could be based. If we accept the view attributed to Adam Smith by Dugald Stewart that 'Little else is required to carry a state to the highest degree of opulence from the lowest barbarism, but peace, easy taxes, and a tolerable administration of justice; all the rest being brought about by the natural order of things' (1980: 322), then the English political system provided such a basis. It guaranteed peace through the control of feuding, taxes were light and justice was uniform and firmly administered from the thirteenth to eighteenth centuries. This offered the framework within which there developed that competitive individualism whose later history I have tried to analyse elsewhere (Macfarlane, 1978).

Yet it would clearly be foolish to overstress any evolutionary necessity in this process. It could at any time have been reversed; the victory of the Spanish Armada, for instance, might well have changed the direction. Nor is it sensible to overstress the uniqueness of England. There was clearly much that overlapped with northern France, the Netherlands and Scandinavia. Yet Marx, Weber and others were not wrong to see England as the cradle of capitalism. If Protestantism was one of those who stood at the cradle, an unusual politico-economic system which Bloch and Maitland have so clearly described for us, is another guest at the baptism. Indeed it may even be that it was this guest who lay in the cradle. Who brought it there, and when, is, of course, another story.

References

Anderson, P. 1974: *Lineages of the Absolutist State*, London.

Baechler, J. 1975: *The Origins of Capitalism*, Oxford.

Bendix, R. 1966: *Max Weber: An Intellectual Portrait*, London.

Bloch, M. 1965: *Feudal Society*, 2nd edn, 2 vols (trans. L. Manyon), London.

Bois, G. 1978: Against the neo-Malthusian orthodoxy. *Past and Present*, no. 79.

Braudel, F. 1973: *Capitalism and Material Life*, London.

Brenner, R. 1976: Agrarian class structure and economic development in pre-industrial Europe. *Past and Present*, no. 70.

    1977: The origins of capitalist development: a critique of neo-Smithian development. *New Left Review*, no. 104.

    1982: The agrarian roots of European capitalism. *Past and Present*, no. 97.

Croot, P. and Parker, D. 1978: Agrarian class structure and economic development. *Past and Present*, no. 78.

Ganshof, F. L. 1964: *Feudalism*, 3rd English edn, London.

Hall, J. A. 1985: *Powers and Liberties: The Causes and Consequences of the Rise of the West*, Oxford.

Hume, D. 1975: *The History of England*, abridged by R. Kilcup, Chicago.

Macfarlane, A. 1978: *The Origins of English Individualism*, Oxford.

Maine, H. 1875: *Lecture on the Early History of Institutions*, London.

    1883: *Dissertations on Early Law and Custom*, London.

    1890: *Ancient Law*, 10th edn, London.

Maitland, F. W. 1919: *The Constitutional History of England*, Cambridge.

    1921: *The Domesday Book and Beyond*, Cambridge.

Marx, K. 1954: *Capital*, 3 vols, London.

    1963: *Selected Writings*, eds T. B. Bottomore and M. Rubel, London.

    1964: *Pre-Capitalist Economic Formations*, trans. J. Cohen, London.

    1973: *Grundrisse*, trans. M. Nicolaus, London.

Polanyi, M. 1944: *The Great Transformation*, London.

Pollock, F. and Maitland, F. W. 1968: *The History of English Law: Before the Time of Edward I*, 2nd edn, 2 vols, Cambridge.

Runciman, W. G. 1980: Comparative sociology or narrative history? *European Journal of Sociology*, 21.

Stewart, D. 1980: Account of the life and writings of Adam Smith Ll.D. In *The Glasgow Edition of the Works and Correspondence of Adam Smith. Volume Three: Essays on Philosophical Subjects*, Oxford.

Tocqueville, A. de 1955: *The Old Regime and the French Revolution*, Garden City, New York.

Weber, M. 1948: *From Max Weber: Selected Writings*, eds H. H. Gerth and C. W. Mills, Oxford.

—— 1961: *General Economic History*, trans. F. H. Knight, New York.

—— 1970: *The Protestant Ethic and the Spirit of Modern Capitalism*, London.

12

The European Tradition in Movements of Insurrection

René Pillorget

The history of Europe comprises a host of movements of insurrection that have assumed degrees of violence and spatial dimensions whose extent has been markedly unequal. In this respect it summons up the image of a continent prey to almost permanent seismic tremors, certain of which would cause very damaging eruptions, but the immense majority of which would register only a weak reading on the Richter scale. Movements of insurrection – those political and social tremors – certainly not only present differences in intensity, but also differences of a qualitative order, particularly as regards their antecedents, their protagonists and circumstances. Not all of them have been studied in depth – far from it. Nevertheless it is possible today to discern in their origins a limited number of patterns and psychological mechanisms.

The Genesis of Movements of Insurrection

Whatever may be their later development, all have been preceded by a period of mental distress. Thus, in a time of scarcity, or merely one of expensive bread, the poor person looks upon the rich with greater envy and more sullenness than usual, and perhaps also makes out the authorities to be responsible for the general situation. Such an attitude of mind may be even more marked in the case of an epidemic. In the same way, during the times of the liturgical feasts or when funeral ceremonies take place, the religious majorities suffer less than usual from the proximity or sight of dissident minorities. Finally, certain circumstances, certain pieces of news, whether exact, distorted or false, can exacerbate a certain latent hostility towards the foreigner. Spontaneous manifestations of collective anger are unleashed according to permanent lines of cleavage: poor and rich, governed and governors, the little people and the more prominent, the orthodox and the dissidents, fellow-countrymen and foreigners. Such lines of cleavage become all of a sudden more acute.

However, there exist psychological tensions that are in no way spontaneous, but are excited by various notables who enjoy great esteem among the inhabitants of their town or the countryside surrounding their estates. These notables play a capital role in the information they give out, particularly at times and in areas where the media are either insufficient or non-existent. The psychological tension can be the result of an ideological, political or religious preparation of the ground, of a propaganda that can assume varied forms, or, quite simply, that of a series of made-up tales.

Four models – in part identified and defined by Neil Smelser (1962) – account for all uprisings, whether they have broken out spontaneously or been provoked: panic; an explosion of hostility; the move towards norms; the move towards values.

Many uprisings begin by the fear of hunger, or the fear of such and such a person seen to be approaching as he gallops along the highway. Panic may be defined as collective flight, which itself can be divided into three stages: an uncertainty, an anxiety, a new conviction which, however pessimistic it may be, gets rid of the uncertainty and anxiety by joining men to one another in an identical and new conviction. Pascal expressed it very well in a striking epigraph: 'They hide themselves amid the throng and call upon numbers to help them. Tumult' (1965: section IV, 260).

A panic can very easily die down of its own accord. But it can happen that it gives rise to a more complex phenomenon: an explosion of hostility. Everything occurs as if the crowd were furious with itself for having taken fright. Abruptly roused to anger, it bears down upon the person or the group that set off the wave of fear – or upon another person or group. The movement can cease after the massacre, flight or disappearance of the object of this explosion of hostility.

But it can also happen that this explosion in turn gives rise to a more complex phenomenon – the third of our models. The movement becomes more rational, in the sense that it directs itself towards norms, that is towards the way in which local problems are resolved: the election of magistrates, salaries, prices, food supply, the mode of tax collection and so on. It directs itself towards these norms either in order to control their modification, or on the contrary, in order to defend them against an innovation. It can happen that some result or concession, even a partial one, on the part of vested authority gives satisfaction to the crowd, restores calm to it and causes it to disperse.

Nevertheless it can happen that those in revolt are lifted far above the problems of daily existence; they continue their action by directing their acts either to the defence or – more rarely – to the modification of values, that is to the highest interests of the community to which they belong: their religion; the respect due to their dead; their conception of the relationships between their province and the central authority; their privileges, that is the status of their province, town, village or ethnic group.

We must insist that each of these four models can, in the history of Europe, be met with in isolation. There are panics provoked by the approach – or the announcement of an approach – of armed troops, which cause the workers in the fields to rush inside the city walls, which cause the city to sound the tocsin for its defence, but which have no further consequences. There are explosions of hostility that appear not to be preceded by the slightest panic – at least no trace of it is apparent in the documents – and there are moves directed towards the norms in which there is not to be discerned any antecedent happening such as a panic or explosion of hostility. Yet it is more frequent to encounter two, three or even four of these phenomena associated in a cumulative process, unfurling more or less rapidly, in a four-stage pattern: panic gives rise to an explosion of hostility, the latter engendering a movement directed towards the norms, and this then broadening out into a movement for the defence of values. A cumulative process, particularly significant examples of which can be singled out in certain great days in the history of France: 14 July 1789 and 18 March 1871.

The birth of panic and its transformation into an explosion of hostility can – like later developments – be entirely spontaneous, as can also the action of individuals who, all of a sudden, through their speeches, succeed in unleashing enthusiasm and setting themselves up as leaders. But a panic can be artificially provoked, notably by the tocsin. An explosion of hostility may have been prepared for by means of placards, through the dissemination of true or false news, or by organized rumours. Finally, those holding the reins of power can bring into play in their favour the links of dependency, and in particular mobilize their servants, their farmers and tenants, their clients.

The Typology of Movements of Insurrection

Yet whereas a four-stage pattern that is relatively simple allows us to account for the genesis of all movements of insurrection – at least it appears to do so – the same is not true as regards the participation of the different social groups. A typology must comprise three groups, or, more precisely, three main types, each of which present a certain number of varieties or subtypes.

The first type is the movement that takes place within a community, which sets at loggerheads with one another the inhabitants of the same town or village, where one of the two parties has control of public offices within the municipality. This internal conflict can assume the classical form of an opposition by the poor to the domination of the rich, or by the common people to that of the nobility. But it can correspond equally well to a 'vertical' cleavage, with each party including within it rich and poor, nobles and commoners, united either by common interests, by an ideology, or by belonging to the same church. The internal conflicts of Mediterranean towns or those of English towns at the time of the Great Rebellion as studied by Alan Everitt (1973) are very characteristic in this respect.

The second type is the movement that expresses the hostility of the community to an outside element, considered to be an intruder or an enemy, suspected of wishing to attack the life of its members, either through their property or their rights. Its reaction can appear at the same time to be unanimous, spontaneous and brutal. And in fact this view of the matter can be valid in accounting for the crises of anger that occasionally cause a revolt in a population outraged by the violence of soldiers in the Europe of modern times. But this is only one case among many. Taken as a whole, the reality reveals itself to be much more complex. Firstly, it does not seem that any community appears to be perfectly unanimous in its action. Side by side with the leaders and the daring and violent elements, there always exist the prudent and the timid, who are content to be spectators or even take flight as soon as they feel an incident is about to occur. Secondly, there can exist within certain communities persons or families who are favourable to the adversary, such as officials or tenants of the lord, clients or party that he himself sustains. Thus it can happen that uprisings which one might be tempted – basing oneself upon their external characteristics – to classify as struggles between local clans, in reality constitute episodes in the struggle of the majority of the population against a neighbouring lord or against a rich neighbour attempting to win control of the town or village through his puppets.

The third type is the mobilizing of forces beyond the framework of the community, the narrow confines of the town or village, and against the interventions of a central authority in the life of the inhabitants of a canton, province or larger territorial entity. It appears to be both a variation and, as it were, an enlargement of the preceding type. It can include movements of a certain size and complexity that in France pit themselves against the central authority; these are bodies representing a province or a region and habitually speaking in its name, as well as a certain number of communities that both urge them on and follow them. It can happen that the greater part of the province or region remains calm and contents itself with affording tacit approval to the declarations and acts of its representatives. It may happen that acts of violence are committed against the persons of the agents of the central authority or that threats or various means of constraint are used against them. Certain inhabitants of the canton, province or region may be treated in the same way because they are suspected of going along with or even conniving with the central authority – or simply because their enemies depict them as such. In several French provinces before 1660 one can pick out clusters of events, spread over periods of very different length, that bear the mark both of a provincial revolt against the central authority, the episodes in which are more or less frequent and spaced out, and the mark of multiple local quarrels. Each of the four sets of events that occurred in Provence in 1630, in 1634, from 1649 to 1653, in 1658 and 1659 – sets of events that are especially characteristic – appear to be made up of a certain number of movements of insurrection that relate either to the first or second types defined above; they are entangled with one another, and, in the last analysis, indissociable. The violence suffered by urban factions at Aix in 1630, at Marseilles in 1634, in those two towns and elsewhere – in particular at Arles and Draguignan, during the Fronde and the Second Fronde – might appear *a priori* to be very far removed from the object of the conflict that opposes certain local authorities and the central government, geographically far apart. Yet, in fact, the link is direct between the conflict of Paris and Provence and the internal struggles of communities. The theme of the defence of the status of the province is used, either rashly or skilfully, by certain local factions because they know that it is capable of rallying round them more numerous and determined supporters – and because they think themselves able in this way to triumph over their opponents, classed as 'traitors to the region'. Legal opposition takes place in the public forum and reawakens local struggles that can be of very ancient origin.

In the twentieth century instances exist of the same solidarity of claims and the same federative characteristic of violence. Thus in 1907 in Languedoc there is to be seen emerging, and growing in strength, a coalition against the measures taken by the Clemenceau government. This coalition gathers round itself very different political and social elements, but these share the common characteristic of living by winegrowing: large-scale owners, agricultural workers and merchants.

Such a typology may appear somewhat complicated. But this arises from the fact that these movements of insurrection, however modest in size they occasionally may be, are rarely very simple. After all, it seeks to interpret relationships between the elements provided by the documents, and not those between pure inventions of the mind. It is therefore normal that they should present neither the austere beauty nor the perfect symmetry of *a priori* constructs.

Movements of Insurrection and Spatial Area

Is this typology valid for continents other than that whose history has served to elaborate it? One might incline to think so, and to confer upon it a universal value. Now, it seems that movements of insurrection in a country as vast as Russia present certain features that clearly differentiate them from those of Europe proper. In particular, they extend over much vaster areas and, above all, they spread with astonishing speed, almost from one end of the territory to the other. This was the case at the beginning of the seventeenth century, with the uprisings known as those of the false Dimitri and Bolotnikov, the 'Time of the Troubles' that ends in 1613 with the accession of the Romanovs. It is even more so at the time of the revolt of Stenka Razine and his Cossacks. After a whole series of towns – Saratov, Samara, Simbirsk – had fallen under his power in a few weeks, in September and October 1670, there occurred an immense uprising that was both urban and peasant in nature, a host of simultaneous, uncoordinated revolts within the entire bend of the middle Volga, and beyond, at Nijni-Novgorod, Tambov and Penza. The insurrection began in the towns. When they saw the emblem of Stenka Razine – the horse's tail on the end of a lance – being brandished by some Cossacks, the *strelsi*, the artisans, the small traders, the serfs of the outlying districts massacred the administrators and opened the gates to the lieutenants of the rebel leader. From the towns the revolt spread to the countryside like a light set to a trail of gunpowder. In the villages the peasants rose up, killing the lords, pillaging the houses, forming gangs which linked up with Stenka Razine or isolated detachments who claimed to be on his side. The racial minorities, the peoples that have been colonized, the Finnish tribes, the Mordvinians, Tchouvaches and Tcheremisses, whether they are rich or poor, made common cause *en masse* with the Muscovite rebels against the colonizing state. The Cossacks appeared no more than the fomentors of a vast insurrection that brought together against the state and the nobility all those oppressed.

The popular uprisings of western and central Europe contrast greatly with those of Russia. Thus, whilst in the seventeenth century – and even in the eighteenth – Russia had several times been covered by vast areas of dissidence, France experienced only a few insurrections of any great territorial size – and that without losing their provincial character: those of the Croquants of the Saintonge, the Anjou and Poitiers areas (1636), the Périgord area (1637), the Va-nu-Pieds of Normandy (1639), the Sabotiers of Sologne (1638), the Torrében of Brittany, of the Camisards (1702–4), and finally that of the Vendée (1793–9). The other movements of insurrection appear sporadically, scattered both in space and time.

Curiously, the peasant revolts of medieval and modern Japan cannot fail to evoke those that occurred during the same eras in western and central Europe. The year 1428 is marked by Jacquerie-style revolts (*doikki*), by attacks on storage depots and *sake* stores, and by pillaging. In the following year the revolt of the *Eikyō* era effects the union of peasants and warriors and is the expression of a fierce hostility to the local lord more than of any material demands. In 1485 the revolt of the Yamashiro region, whose inhabitants are weary of being the victims of the struggles of the two contestants for power, ends in the proclamation of the autonomy of the western part of that territory. In the seventeenth century, at the beginning of the *Edo* epoch, the rural areas are sacrificed to the towns, and the weight of taxation bears down upon the peasants. This aggravation in their condition is expressed in an increasing number of revolts (*Hyakushō ikki*) that question the authority of the direct administrators, who were on occasion confiscators and distributors of land, as the land registers show. In 1637 the revolt against the lords of Shimbara presents a character of even greater violence because the majority of the peasants and the former samurai who take part in it are Christians. But from the eighteenth century onwards the reasons for the Jacquerie-style revolts are much more patently fiscal, or, in a more general way, financial: the price of rice, fixed legally by the Shōgunate, arouses the rage of the country-dwellers more than once. In these special cases the peasant revolts have their counterpart in the towns, where the people violently sack the rice and *sake* stores. It is inappropriate to magnify such movements: in many cases only a few peasants, ranged behind a leader, come to give vent to their despair, threatening the town-dwellers and rocking with their tumult the small towns whose houses are clustered round a castle. In these revolts, provoked by misery, fear and hunger, and physical and moral weakness, it would undoubtedly be fruitless to seek to discover any kind of organization, a programme, or other motives than mere aspirations.

These differences between Russia – and probably China and India – on the one hand, and Japan and western and central Europe on the other, have behind them reasons of a geographical nature. In Japan and Europe the distances are less, the land is divided up into units of medium, small or even minute size, whereas in Russia, from the north-west to the south-east, are to be discerned wide strips of land with uniform vegetation. There do not exist in Russia those little 'homelands', those strongly knit territorial communities whose very minuteness contributes in uniting all the inhabitants, and all social groups, in order to defend the local status – but in the same way localizes any revolt. The great Russian revolts tended to take place over vast areas, covering land masses that are scarcely differentiated, over hundreds of kilometres.

The reasons for the smaller territorial extent of the European and Japanese insurrection should likewise be sought in the distribution of the population and the social and institutional structures. Whereas the density of the French population in the seventeenth century is about 40 per square kilometre, that of Russia is only three or four, with its population of some twelve million inhabitants extending over more than three million square kilometres. Moreover, at the beginning of the century, following the deportations organized by Ivan I, the Tartar invasions, the headlong scramble of peasants fleeing from the pressure of taxation and seeking new lands, there exists within the Russian people a large proportion of 'rootless' persons, and even a whole floating population. Furthermore, there exists a 'frontier', an indecisive zone situated to the very south of the country, before the line of fortifications and in the steppes, between the Muscovite state and the Tartars, in which there develops the Russian equivalent of 'folk without home or place' or 'vagabonds': the Cossacks.

Moreover, the typology of movements of insurrection that has been set out above is founded upon the *community*. Now, are there any real communities in Russia, Japan, China and India? Or indeed in the rest of the world, save in those countries where Europeans have settled? By community we mean of course a cluster of houses, generally grouped around a castle, most certainly around a Protestant or Catholic church, a group of families of peasants, artisans and tradesmen, but also and above all a moral, affective and political unit, a little democratic or aristocratic republic, possessing its privileges, namely its statutes, its constitution, whether this is written or not, and a long practice of self-government – in short, an autonomous centre for decision-making. Allowing for the fact that phenomena resulting from collective enthusiasm can occur, the decisions generally appear to be taken after a thoughtful discussion in which the voice of the prudent has been able to make itself heard. When in 1630 the community of Draguignan, then the size of a large village, decided to revolt, not indeed against the king, but against the government of Richelieu, and to purchase arms, the decision was taken after a vote of its council, noted – and later covered up as best as could be – in its record of its proceedings. The plebeian masses of Russia appear much more gregarious.

In Japan, as in Europe, there is to be found a host of towns and villages
that constitute so many legal entities, enjoying real autonomy. Likewise
there are regions or provinces whose population has been attached to the
land for many generations, who have fashioned the landscape and
developed multiple links with the earth that have made it for them the
soil of their ancestors – these factors incite every social group to defend
its status, but at the same time make it mistrustful of outside intervention.

Similarly one finds in Europe very many strata that are intermediate
between the very rich and the very poor; different categories of
bourgeois, among them a real bourgeoisie, at different stages of
development in the countries, it is true, but generally considerable in
number, and rich; activities that are more numerous and more
diversified, and more resources than in the other continents; finally, a
large number, at least relatively so, of state officials and king's officers,
generally well organized in hierarchical bodies – as in France. And
Germany, in this respect, appears even more characteristic. It only
experienced one flare-up of anger on the part of the peasants; this, the
great uprising of 1524, embraced a considerable portion of its territory.
But the event was an ephemeral one, lasting only a few weeks and,
depending on the territories involved, unequal in violence. Furthermore,
it appears that the structures of the Empire had a determining influence
upon the behaviour of the population; a much tighter administrative
framework than elsewhere – in the Empire there were some 350
territories, each enjoying *Landeshoheit*, and in consequence the prince is
never far removed – helped to stimulated wisdom.

Movements of Insurrection and European Values

European movements of insurrection take place in the context of a
civilization that, technically at least, is more advanced than that of other
continents, and certain of these movements reflect this. To cite only one
example: revolts broke out, in the medieval and modern periods,
following currency changes. Outside Europe, such revolts can be found
only in very limited areas.

By their social composition, which is astonishingly varied, as well as in
their causes and the way they develop, particularly through the combined
participation of the gentry, notables, the officer corps, artisans and
peasants of different social status, other movements of insurrection, of
differing size, reveal institutional and social structures of a complexity for
which there appears to exist no equivalent on the other continents. Yet
more movements demonstrate the basic values to which Europeans were
and remain attached.

Thus, when an execution takes place in public, the crowds may jeer the condemned person, or feast upon the spectacle with unhealthy pleasure. Yet it can happen also that the crowd is moved, that it riots and tries to snatch the man or woman from the executioner and the guards. In the same way, when a policy of 'shutting away the poor' is set in motion from the end of the sixteenth century, and when it leads to provoking a hunt for beggars by state or town officials, in order to incarcerate them in hospices that bear a strong resemblance to prisons or penitentaries, riots may break out to preserve their liberty. These riots break out because Europeans, deeply steeped in Christianity, tend to consider the human person – every human person – to be the prime value, that which, above all others, undoubtedly possesses a sacred character. This state of mind has its clearest manifestation in the conception of the Rights of Man.

It can certainly happen in Europe that the condemned, before being put to death, are subjected to horrible tortures: the wheel or the stake are surely as bad as Ottoman impalement. But it seems that such punishments are applied much less frequently than in Russia or China. And repression of popular uprisings in seventeenth-century France was of astounding moderation. A poor wretch who was foolish enough or simple enough to let himself be caught or to confess is hanged; so too are those pitiful creatures whose past weighs heavily upon them, who should already have been convicted for previous crimes. All sentences are, above all, pronounced *in absentia*. In comparison, the repression of uprisings in the Russia of that time – that of Stenka Razine in particular – appears to be marked by extraordinary atrocities. Finally, one cannot fail to recall that it was in eighteenth-century Europe that there arose, in particular with Beccaria, a movement of ideas that led, after following a lengthy path, to a relaxation in the penal law and even to the abolition of the death penalty.

Nothing in Indian or Chinese civilizations seems comparable to these Rights of Man, as they are conceived by Europeans. For scholars of China and India, they appear to be a specifically European conception. A basic reason for this difference seems to lie in the fact that those civilizations – whose basis is either materialist or pantheist – did not work out any clear concept of the person.

In Europe the sense of justice can move crowds, and the same is true for the sense of liberty. Revolutions bear witness to this, in 1688, 1789 and 1830, sometimes accompanied by wars of independence, as in the Low Countries at the end of the sixteenth century. Nevertheless, well before they fought for liberty, conceived of as a basic value, the Frenchmen of the Middle Ages and the *ancien régime*, as the Greeks and Romans before them, had affirmed that they were free men. Great theorists such as Jean Bodin and Charles Loyseau contrasted – and this theme is destined to become a commonplace in the literature of politics – the liberty that their compatriots enjoyed under an absolute monarch to the servitude of the Turks under their Sultan, or that of the Muscovites under their Tsar. They emphasize this in their works: the Sultan and Tsar can dispose freely of the persons and property of their subjects. This is not true for the King of France. He cannot deprive a subject of his own property, or confiscate it, save as a consequence of a crime committed by the subject, and after a trial by due process of law. In this country, as in other European states, absolutism in no way signifies tyranny, nor even dictatorship. His sovereignty does not allow an absolute king to violate the privileges, that is the rights, of his subjects. On the contrary, it is a guarantee of them. There exist – and this again is a characteristic of Europe – the sphere of the sovereign's rights, and the sphere of the subject's rights. And the one is not permitted to encroach upon the other. By so doing in 1685, through the Revocation of the Edict of Nantes, Louis XIV committed a grave error. He acted as a tyrant. The revolt of his subjects in the Cévennes was therefore perfectly understandable.

The most absolute kings of Europe derive their powers from God, it is true, but also from the law. China, despite its level of social organization, did not know this notion of law. Its Emperor's paternalist power had a tendency to despotism, and was based upon principles very different from those common to European states. Similarly the motives that prompted the Chinese to rock and topple a dynasty appear very different from those of European revolutionaries or insurgents.

Chinese action is based upon principles of a cosmic order. If there were epidemics, famines, earthquakes, storms of extraordinary violence and tidal waves, if military disasters piled up, if banditry increased, if nepotism, favouritism, excessive pressure from taxation, and waste – if these turned the state and its apparatus into a band of exploiters so that it no longer was the organism unifying the wills of everybody in the common good; if the state no longer controlled the interplay of social relationships, if it no longer prevented landowners from exacting ever higher rents, coupled with gifts and presents in time of scarcity, and let the conflicts between social groups worsen, then, so it was thought, there was no shadow of doubt: Heaven had withdrawn its mandate, its 'commission', from the Emperor. The monarch was not found, or no longer found, to be on the path of virtue. He no longer followed 'The Path of Heaven'. No longer was he in harmony with the order of the universe. He had failed in his duties as the prince. He had not respected the conventions, the *Ki*, the foundations of social order. By this very fact he had plunged the cosmos into disorder and unhappiness. He was no longer worthy of the Empire. Mencius (*c.*372–289 BC), the grandson of Confucius said that, in such conditions, the people must revolt and change their prince. If the rebellion was successful, it showed that it had done nothing more than carry out the will of Heaven.

Periodically – upon the expiration of a period of time whose length varies between 250 and 400 years – such a conjunction of circumstances came about once more. It constituted, for the Chinese, a sign: it signified to them that not only their Emperor, but also his family, had lost 'the mandate of Heaven'. Then they gathered round some fortunate soldier, a claimant to the Empire, who did not delay in dethroning the sitting sovereign and in founding a new dynasty. The latter reigned, benefiting from obedience to traditional rules until the recurrence of a concomitance of circumstances such as that which presided over its foundation.

In this way the 'Dynastic Cycle' unfolded. Revolt provoked a change of ruler. But it preserved the same regime, the same form of government, as well as the principles on which both were based; revolt was therefore not really a revolution. On the contrary, in some respects it was even a part of the established order. For its function was periodically to re-establish that order, in a succession of dynastic cycles, in accordance with an 'Eternal Return'. This is a conception suitable for an agrarian society, which lives in the belief that there exists a bond, a relationship, between cosmic phenomena and the conduct of men.

In Europe, during the Middle Ages and in modern times, and even later, astrology was resorted to in order to interpret events and to predict the future. But it appears that it has never been used, at least as a principal factor, to stir up crowds to action. Other means have been, and are still used. To spark off the masses it is not enough that certain conditions of a political, economic and social order are fulfilled, or for a doctrine to be spread among a more or less considerable section of the population, even if it be presented with undeniable skill. In order to move the crowd, something else is necessary – as Georges Sorel realized:

> use must be made of a body of images which, *by intuition alone*, and before any considered analyses are made, is capable of evoking as an undivided whole the mass of sentiments which corresponds to the different manifestations of the war undertaken [against the regime in power]. (1961: 122–3)

Among these sets of images some may correspond to realities; others may be mere constructs of the mind or the fruit of imagination, hypothetical reconstructions of the past, or imaginative visions of the future. Sorel continues:

Experience shows that the *framing of a future, in some indeterminate time*, may, when it is done in a certain way, be very effective, and have very few inconveniences; this happens when the anticipations of the future take the form of those myths, which enclose with them, all the strongest inclinations of a people, of a party or of a class, inclinations which recur to the mind with the insistence of instincts. . . . A knowledge of what the myths contain in the way of details which will actually form part of the history of the future is then of small importance; they are not astrological almanacs; it is even possible that nothing which they contain will ever come to pass. . . . In our own daily life, are we not familiar with the fact that what actually happens is very different from our preconceived notion of it? And that does not prevent us from continuing to make resolutions. (pp. 124–6)

For a long while it was held that the most precious rights of a subject were his liberties – conceived as privileges of an order, a body, or an individual – and that it was legitimate to resist, and even to revolt, when a prince, beyond the sphere of his own rights, encroached upon that of the rights of his subjects. But from the time of the first English revolution this notion gave way, very slowly, to one of liberty, conceived of as a set of universal rights that must be those of all men – the liberty of each individual being indissolubly linked to the liberty of the whole, and the liberty of the whole to the liberty of each individual. And it is also in England, during that tragic century of revolutions, that property was made one of the foundations of individual liberty – thus, however, expressing the thinking of many Europeans. Men are free, it was argued, because they are the owners of their goods. They must also therefore be free bodily, as they are regarding their property. Liberty flows from ownership. One of the bases for resistance to state taxation – which brought about, not hundreds, but thousands of popular uprisings, and which was accepted so slowly and with such great difficulty – resides in the fact that the state removes by tax a portion of property, and that this constitutes an unbearable violation of the right to property. State taxation is only accepted in the case of absolute necessity, in wartime, for example, and when it is consented to by the owners.

On this point Europe appears once more to be very different from other parts of the world, and in particular from Russia, its neighbour, where the Tsar is the eminent and sole owner of all Russian soil. Europeans also manifest a real horror of collective ownership, as is borne out, for example, by the reactions of Bernier (1830), a French doctor who in the seventeenth century resided for a long while in India.

Europeans seem to have the capacity to receive from men of other continents objects, forms, ideas and techniques and to be able happily to turn them into something European. In return, they seek to make converts everywhere, and tend to win over the rest of the world by propaganda, preaching and persuasion. Everywhere they seek to accomplish what they esteem to be a step forward, whether it be greater or improved production, or the realization of the human type of which they dream. They do not succeed everywhere. Thus, from the seventeenth century onwards, Asia as a whole rejected Europe. In any case, through its own people Europe began to export overseas its discoveries, beliefs, books and ideas. Europeans built churches and schools, started clubs and rationalist societies imbued with its tradition of contestation, and even of revolution.

Most insurrections that have taken place in overseas countries and that have led to a radical renewal of structures have directly, or at the very least indirectly, sprung from Europe. It will be objected that the Great Revolution at the end of the eighteenth century began in North America, that it passed to the Low Countries, and then to France and Switzerland. But it would be fair to recall that an Atlantico-British political world existed – or rather what was vaguely called an empire – that stretched from the North Sea to Ohio, and that the sequence of events that led to the Declaration of Independence of 1776 took place within an exclusively British framework, based upon ideas imported from the mother country. The cluster of revolutions that led to the independence of Iberian America is located among the consequences of Napoleonic imperialism, which constitutes merely an extension of that of the French Revolution. The revolution of 1917 was only able to triumph because of the involvement of Russia in a European war, and the Chinese Revolution that achieved victory in 1949 constantly referred to an ideology that had been worked out in Europe.

Europe is movement and evolution. It is the critical spirit, to such an extent that self-criticism constitutes a constant element in its thought. It is not vouchsafed to all peoples periodically, or continuously, to call into question their ideals and lifestyles, to compare them among one another, and with those of other cultural areas, to discern the contradictions in them, their illogicalities, and weaknesses, and to imagine better systems.

References

Auty, R. and Obolensky, D. (eds), 1976: *An Introduction to Russian History*, Cambridge.
Baechler, J. 1970: *Les phénomènes revolutionnaires*, Paris.
Bernier, F. 1830: *Voyages*, vol. 1, Paris.

Blickle, P. (ed.) (1980): *Aufruhr und Empörung. Zwei Studien zum bäuerlichen Widerstand im Alten Reich*, Munich.

Blum, J. 1961: *Lord and Peasant in Russia from the Ninth to the Nineteenth Century*, Princeton.

Burke, P. 1980: Did Europe exist before 1700?. *History of European Ideas*, 1.

Cobb, R. 1970: *The Police and the People: French Popular Protest, 1789–1820*, Oxford.

Eliseef, D. and Eliseef, V. 1974: *La civilisation japonaise*, Paris.

Elliott, J. H. 1984: *The Revolt of the Catalans: A Study in the Decline of Spain*, new edn, Cambridge.

Everitt, A. 1973: *The Community of Kent and the Great Rebellion, 1640–1660*, new edn, Leicester.

Forster, R. and Greene, J. P. (eds) 1970: *Preconditions of Revolution in Early Modern Europe*, London.

Franz, G. 1976: *Geschichte des deutschen Bauerstandes vom fruhen Mittelalter bis zum XIX Jahrhundert*, Stuttgart.

Gaxotte, P. and Tulard, J. 1975: *La révolution française*, Paris.

Gernet, J. 1983: *Le Monde Chinois*, rev. edn, Paris.

Godechot, J. 1970: *The Taking of the Bastille*, trans. J. Stewart, London.

Koenigsberger, H. G. 1971: *Estates and Revolutions*, Ithaca.

Lefebvre, H. 1954: *Etudes sur la Révolution française*, Paris.

   1973: *The Great Fear of 1789: Rural Panic in Revolutionary France*, trans. J. White, London.

Lindley, K. 1982: *Fenland Riots and the English Revolution*, London.

Lui, J. T. C. 1961–2: An administrative cycle in Chinese history. *Journal of Asian Studies*, 21.

Maier, P. 1973: *From Resistance to Revolution: Colonial Radicals and the Development of British Opposition to Britain, 1765–1776*, London.

Meadows, T. T. 1856: *The Chinese and their Rebellions*, London.

Merriman, R. B. 1938: *Six Contemporaneous Revolutions*, Oxford.

Mollat, M. and Wolff, P. 1970: *Ongles bleus et Ciompi: les révolutions populaires en Europe au XIVème et XVème siecles*, Paris.

Mousnier, R. 1970: *La plume, la faucille et la marteau*, Paris.

   1971: *Peasant Uprisings in Seventeenth Century France, Russia and China*, trans. B. Pearce, London.

   1973: *Social Hierarchies: 1450 to the Present*, trans. P. Evans, London.

Mousnier, R., Livet, G. et al. 1980: *Histoire générale de l'Europe*, 3 vols, Paris.

Palou, J. 1958: *La peur dans l'histoire*, Paris.

Pascal, P. (ed.) 1971: *La Révolte de Pougatchev*, Paris.

Pascal, R. 1965: *Pensées*, London.

Pillorget, R. 1966: Les problemes monétaires de la France de 1602 à 1689. *XVIIeme Siecle*, 70–1.

   1975: *Les mouvements insurrectionels de Provence entre 1596 et 1715*, Paris.

   1976: Genèse et typologie des mouvements insurrectionels d'après une étude régionale. *Francia: Forschungen zur westeuropaischen Geschichte*, 4.

   1984: Del Absolutismo a las Revoluciones, 1660–1776. In *Historia Universal*, Pamplona.

Pocock, J. G. A. 1980: *Three British Revolutions. 1641, 1688, 1776*, Princeton.

Schulze, W. (ed.) 1982: *Europäische Bauernrevolten der frühen Neuzeit*, Frankfurt.

Skalweit, S. 1967: *Reich und Reformation*, Berlin.

Smelser, N. 1962: *Theory of Collective Behaviour*, London.

Sorel, G. 1961: *Reflections on Violence*, London.

Tulard, J. 1985: Les révolutions. In J. Favier (ed.), *Histoire de la France*, vol. 4, Paris.

Zagorin, P. 1982: *Rebels and Rulers, 1500–1660*, 2 vols, Cambridge.

13

Republics of Merchants in Early Modern Europe

Peter Burke

In the mid-1970s, a conference of economic historians at Montreal discussed Renaissance Italy and seventeenth-century Holland as examples of 'failed transitions' to industrialization (Krantz and Hohenberg, 1975). In this essay, however, I shall examine the other side of the coin, the relatively successful economic performances of these two societies and the reasons for that success. The emphasis will be on the wider political and cultural factors which encouraged this success rather than on economic explanations. We have been warned to expect a debate between Marxists and non-Marxists: there may also be some degree of controversy between those who think (like Eric Hobsbawm) that 'economic explanations of economic phemonena are to be preferred if they are available', and those who believe (like Fritz Stern), that 'Capitalism is too serious a subject to be left to the economic historian alone' (quoted in Wiener, 1981: ix, 4). My own preference, which this chapter attempts to justify, is for treating economic growth and decline as part of total history.

It will be argued that the economic performance of late Renaissance Italy and seventeenth-century Holland (especially that of the major cities) is not fully intelligible unless non-economic factors are taken into account. The economic efficiency of these two regions depended on the activities of a group of talented and ruthless entrepreneurs, classic examples of what Pareto called the 'speculator' type, whose pursuit of profit at once encourages and is encouraged by economic development (1935: paragraph 2233ff.).

Entrepreneurs of this kind can be found in a number of regions and periods, but they found an unusually favourable micro-environment for their activities in the cities of Italy and the Netherlands in the late medieval and early modern periods. The environment was favourable both politically and culturally. The political advantage to them was the fact that these cities were relatively autonomous, relatively free from control by kings or nobles. They were in fact sometimes taken over by merchants, but 'freedom from' (from interference with trade by powerful individuals or groups with different priorities) was probably even more important than 'freedom to' (to administer themselves), or, to put the point a little differently, the value of 'freedom to' was essentially that it guaranteed 'freedom from'. The regime which frustrated entrepreneurs the least was the best – not only for them but for economic growth.

These cities also offered a relatively favourable cultural environment for entrepreneurs by virtue of their traditional stresses on such values as achievement, competition, toleration, industry, thrift and calculation. They were pro-enterprise cultures, where the value-system had been shaped by entrepreneurs but in turn shaped others.

This central argument is little more than a development of certain famous ideas of Montesquieu and Adam Smith. Montesquieu implies, if he does not formally assert, that the 'virtue' associated with republics is better for prosperity than the 'honour' associated with monarchies (1949: Book 20), while Adam Smith suggests a relationship between 'the progress of opulence' moral qualities such as punctuality and both political and economic liberty (Smith, 1976: Book 3; on Smith, see Winch, 1978). All these assertions require more justification than can be given here (or perhaps anywhere), but they can at least be illustrated with historical examples. The economic importance of the cities of Italy and the Netherlands goes back a long way into the Middle Ages, but a division of labour with Professor Jacques Heers, no less than my own research interests, suggests a concentration on the sixteenth and seventeenth centuries. I shall discuss two cities in detail, Genoa and Amsterdam, but attempt to place them in their regional context.

In north and central Italy there were, around the year 1200, between 200 and 300 city republics, although only a handful of them contained more than 20,000 inhabitants apiece (Waley, 1969: 11). In the course of the fourteenth and fifteenth centuries, the number fell sharply but the survivors included cities of great commercial importance, notably Genoa, Venice and Florence. They were republics of merchants in which the ruling class did not disdain trade but actively engaged in it.

The culture of these Italian cities has been well described by Jacob Burckhardt, who stressed their 'individualism', meaning competitiveness as well as self-consciousness (1944: chapter 2). This competitiveness is not difficult to document. The leading humanists Leonardo Bruni and Leonbattista Alberti both described life as a race (a boat-race in the latter case, in which one must 'sweat to be the first'; Alberti, 1969: 167). The

Florentines seem to have been especially competitive. The buildings of Florence identified their builders in particularly conspicuous ways, with the usual coat of arms joined by names incised in huge capital letters or even the bust of the owner (Goldthwaite, 1980: 86). There was an open pride in wealth which is likely to strike twentieth-century European scholars as quite American in style. 'The marble alone cost 4000 florins' runs the inscription on a tabernacle commissioned by Piero de'Medici, father of the 'magnificent' Lorenzo (Wackernagel, 1981: 239n.). The tomb of Filippo Decio, professor of law at Pisa in the sixteenth century, boasts of his salary of 1500 ducats a year; a striking example of competitive attitudes and love of money carried to the grave and also of a culture which permitted such attitudes to be expressed in such a setting. (The inscription is printed in Terrasson, 1750: 418. The tomb is still to be seen at Pisa.)

As for literacy, it cannot easily be measured but the practical uses of literacy in early modern Italy seem well established in four different domains: the family, business, religion and politics (Burke, 1987). The numbers of Florentine *ricordi* in particular (combined account-books, diaries and chronicles), testify to a literate, and numerate mentality. So does the famous *catasto* or census of 1427, a Tuscan Domesday Book (Bec, 1967; Guglielminetti, 1977; Herlihy and Klapisch, 1978). There is also evidence of a new sharp sense of time – merchant's time, measurable time, time as money – in this culture, where clocks were beginning to proliferate (Le Goff, 1980: 29–42; Cipolla, 1967).

In Venice there were fewer signs of open competitiveness; as in Japan today, the appearance of cohesion and consensus was highly valued. There were fewer private diaries than in Florence (though one of the exceptions, that of the patrician Marin Sanudo, is a truly gigantic one, running to 58 volumes and covering the years 1496–1533 in print: see Sanudo, 1879–1903). There was a long tradition of state intervention in economic affairs – the Arsenal was a state-run enterprise which went back to the early twelfth century. But in Venice as in Florence there was a tradition of numbering the people, and by the sixteenth century the census-takers were issued with printed forms to ensure comparability of information.[1] Venice was also famous – or notorious – for its toleration of diversity and its ethnic and religious mix, which included Orthodox Greeks and Slavs, Muslim Turks, Jews, and, in the sixteenth century, northern Protestants as well. An English visitor of the mid-sixteenth century was quite amazed at Venetian permissiveness. 'No man there marketh another's doings or . . . meddleth with another man's living', he commented. 'No man shall ask thee why

1 Discussed in Burke (1986). The forms are still preserved in the Archivio del Stato in Venice.

thou comest not to church ... to live married or unmarried, no man shall ask thee why' (Thomas, 1549). Another Englishman found it surprising that the Venetian nobility 'keep no honourable hospitality, nor gallant retinue of servants about them, but a very frugal table', although some of them were extremely wealthy (Coryat, 1905: 397, 415 – he visited Venice in 1608).

By the sixteenth century, Venice was losing her commercial pre-eminence even if she was not, in absolute terms, in economic decline (Woolf, 1968; Tucci, 1973; Pullan, 1973). The patricians were withdrawing from trade and buying land on the *terraferma*, from Verona to Friuli. It is likely that these purchases were originally made because land was a good investment at that point, but in the long term the ownership of landed estates encouraged a change in values. In the seventeenth century, if not before, the Venetian patricians – once among the leading European entrepreneurs – were turning into rentiers. (Burke, 1974; but see the criticism of Burke and Tucci in Rapp, 1979). They were even coming to despise the patricians of Florence as mere merchants. However, Florence was not the great trading city it had once been. For an early modern example of an Italian republic of merchants it is best to look at Genoa.

By 1500 Genoa already had a long commercial past. The Genoese had set up their trading post at Caffa on the Black Sea in the thirteenth century. They had pioneered maritime insurance; they had fought Venice for economic supremacy, and one of them had discovered America (Heers, 1961; cf. Lopez, 1963). Genoa, like Venice and Florence, was a city-state ruled by a merchant patriciate but it was run in a somewhat different way.

In Florence and Venice, the state had tamed the magnates by the end of the thirteenth century, but not in Genoa. The state was poor and weak, the magnates, such as the Doria, the Spinola and the Grimaldi, were rich and powerful. They kept private armies and treated some of the public spaces of the city as their private territory. *Publice egestas, privatim opulentia.* Sallust's verdict on Rome, applied by J. K. Galbraith to describe the USA in the 1950s, is equally applicable to late medieval and early modern Genoa. A weak state which included a rich city was of course a temptation for neighbouring powers. In the fifteenth century Genoa became a satellite of Milan and in the early sixteenth century a satellite of France. But in 1528 – one of the most famous dates in Genoese annals – Andrea Doria, a naval condottiere in the service of François I, went over to Charles V and, as his supporters put it, 'liberated' the city. It is the following century, 1528–1627, with which we are most concerned here; the so-called 'age of the Genoese' which might also be described as the century of the 'Spanish connection' (Braudel,

1979, following the still unpublished work of F. Ruiz Martin, *El siglo de los genoveses*; cf. Grendi, 1976: 181ff.).

After 1528 some Genoese magnates began to lend money to Charles V and after him to Philip II, Philip III and Philip IV. The sums were large – a million ducats at a time was not unusual. The terms to the royal borrowers were relatively generous; more exactly, the Genoese financiers showed themselves prepared, time after time – until, in 1627, enough was enough – to accept the renegotiations of terms in the borrowers' favour which go by the name of Spanish 'bankruptcies' (Castillo, 1963; cf. Lapeyre, 1953). To compensate the bankers they received commercial concessions, and much of the Genoese patriciate became involved with the Spanish economy. There were Genoese in Seville (the port through which American silver was funnelled into Spain), and in such major cities of the Spanish empire as Antwerp, Milan and Naples. The Genoese controlled the exchange transactions at the fairs of Piacenza and profited from the fact that silver was worth more in Italy, where they sold it, than in Spain, where they bought it. The magnates made fortunes, part of which they spent on the magnificent palaces of the Strada Nuova (palaces which have now, appropriately enough, been taken over by banks). The Spaniards did not care for the 'gnomes of Genoa', who took the blame for Spanish inflation. Quevedo's famous poem about 'Mr Money' is bitter as well as witty.

> Poderoso caballero es Don Dinero
> Nace en las Indias honrada
> Donde el mundo le acompaña,
> Vien a morir en España
> Y es en Génoa enterrada.

These gnomes, however, were also a military nobility; the tradition of the condottiere was not yet dead. To borrow another phrase from the America of the 1950s, we may speak of the Genoese 'military–financial complex'; appropriately, because the same families and even on occasion the same individuals, were involved in military and financial operations (McNeill, 1982). From about 1550 onwards, there was a Genoese squadron in the Spanish galley fleet, financed by Spain but fitted out by the Dorias and their like. On land, the most famous examples of the links between war and finance was that of Ambrogio Spinola. Spinola was a Genoese patrician who entered the service of Archduke Albert (governor of the Spanish Netherlands) with 9000 men raised at his own expense and became Commander-in-Chief (Low Countries) a year later, in 1603. His best-known exploit was the capture of Breda. His military success had a financial explanation; unlike other Spanish commanders he was able to pay his troops and so prevent mutinies. (See Parker, 1977, on the background of mutinies.)

Let us look a little more closely at the political framework and the cultural background of this golden age – or better, this age of silver – of the Genoese economy.

The political system was not ideal. Its faults were described in some detail by a number of Genoese writers of the sixteenth and seventeenth centuries in a remarkable literature of political analysis which circulated mainly in manuscript (the *samizdat* of the day).[2] They drew attention to two main problems. The first was the conflict between the 'old' nobility (the powerful families I have been calling 'magnates') and the 'new', a conflict which nearly turned into civil war in 1575–6, when there were barricades in the streets and the *vecchi* enlisted their rural vassals into private armies. Supporters of the 'new' faction criticized the old for preventing social mobility, while supporters of the 'old' made fun of the social origins of their opponents. The second problem was that of relations with Spain. The Spaniards felt that they were under the economic domination of Genoa, exploited (in contemporary terms 'skinned' or 'fleeced') by the Genoese. On the other hand, the Genoese felt that they were under the political domination of Spain, in danger of being incorporated (in contemporary terms, 'swallowed') by the Spanish Empire (Costantini, 1978).

These writers (most of them anonymous or pseudonymous) may have exaggerated the defects of the political system under which they were living. While contemporary Venetians were rather too much inclined to celebrate themselves, their stability and cohesion (the 'myth of Venice', as scholars now call it), the Genoese were self-critical to a fault. There was no 'myth of Genoa' or if there was it was negative rather than positive, a sign of the Genoese lack of 'public spirit'. Even this criticism is not mine but comes from a fascinating minor writer of the early seventeenth century, Andrea Spinola, nick-named 'the philosopher', a distant relative of Ambrogio Spinola, the general (Spinola, 1981).

Andrea Spinola was an outspoken man (indeed he was on occasion imprisoned for speaking out). He was a 'civic humanist' in the sense that Hans Baron (1955) and John Pocock (1975) have given to that term. He was a moralist in the tradition of Juvenal, Seneca and Tacitus, who believed that Genoa had had a public or civic spirit but that it had been lost. I cannot find this political golden age in the past. I am inclined to think that Spinola and his friends were the first representatives of this

2 Among the more important of these are the anonymous dialogues between Philip II and the Duke of Alba and between 'Genovese' and 'Romano' and the Relazione dello stato politico ed economico della serenissima republica di Genova – besides the work of Andrea Spinola, discussed below.

civic spirit; stimulated, perhaps, by the threat from Spain just as, according to Hans Baron, the threat from Milan had encouraged the rise of Florentine civic humanism two hundred years earlier. It is tempting to compare both situations with the threat from Persia for the Greeks at the time of Marathon; the threat from Spain at the time of the Armada; the threat from Germany at the time of Dunkirk. The reason for calling Andrea Spinola into the witness-box at this point is for him to testify to the general lack in Genoa of the values in which he passionately believed.

Spinola wrote no treatise but many brief essays or notes on topics such as 'discipline', 'equality', 'parsimony' and so on. What he opposed was 'corruption', 'tyranny', 'luxury' and formality, including the 'ridiculous ceremonial' which some Genoese citizens had caught from absolute monarchs; in other words, the 'Spanish disease'. Spinola was aware of the connection between Genoese luxury and American silver, but he placed less emphasis on the economic explanation of changes in behaviour than he did on political and cultural factors. He criticized private 'palaces', for example (the word no less than the thing), on the grounds that they gave the children brought up in them 'vain opinions' of themselves – an obvious reference to Strada Nuova and its denizens. He opposed magnificent funerals (if they were really necessary, he wrote with characteristic irony, the poor would not be able to afford to die). What Spinola favoured was the triad of liberty, equality and frugality, which he associated with ancient Rome and Sparta and modern Switzerland. He wanted to see more respect for the mechanical arts and also for public buildings.

The watch, he thought, should police the Loggia dei Banchi to prevent youths from sleeping out and playing football there while money should be spent on the Palazzo Publico (the town hall) for the sake of *maestà publica*. He also wanted a statue of Columbus to be erected at public expense. Spinola failed and his failure is instructive, illustrating the prevalence of private and individualistic values in Genoa at the age of its financial miracle.[3] However, these values and the associated weakness of the state are part of the explanation for Genoese economic success.

The concept of a 'weak state' is actually a rather clumsy analytic tool. It would be useful, for example, to distinguish military weakness from internal political divisions. The Genoese were well able to defend themselves against Venice in the fourteenth century, and against Savoy in the seventeenth. However, they had a state which was less highly centralized than most in Europe. It did not interfere with individual entrepreneurs and it even allowed the development of what has been called (in a phrase which is useful though imprecise), a 'state within a

3 This summary draws on the unpublished Ricordi rather than on the texts published in Spinola (1981).

state', or rather several different ones, from the main aristocratic clans to the Bank of S. Giorgio.[4]

It is not surprising to find that Spinola admired the Netherlands, the principal commonwealth of merchants in the Europe of his day. Like northern Italy, it was a region which had long been highly urbanized and commercially successful, and in the early modern period the Netherlanders at last overtook their Italian rivals. In Braudel's sequence of four dominant urban economies, the second is Antwerp and the fourth is Amsterdam – a judgement shared by many economic historians.

Antwerp is said to have emerged as the 'metropolis of western Europe' about the year 1500, at the expense of Venice as well as Bruges. Its rise to this position was fuelled initially by Portuguese spices, but the city also became, in the 1520s, the 'financial metropolis of the west', a money market in which important loans to princes such as Charles V and Henry VIII were negotiated. Local industries such as the finishing and dyeing of cloth also flourished and the population of the city rose from some 50,000 in 1500 to 100,000 fifty years later (Van der Wee, 1963: vol. 2, 199ff.; cf. Braudel, 1979: 118ff.).

It is clear that the rise of Antwerp owed a good deal to economic factors in the strict sense. The discovery of Amsterdam changed the pattern of international trade and gave north-west Europe a new advantage over the south. However, political and cultural factors also helped Antwerp become a metropolis. It was made the Portuguese spice staple in 1499 thanks to the aid of the Emperor Maximilian, as a reward for support against the towns of Flanders. Like the other towns of the Low Countries it was relatively autonomous, 'quasi-independent' as a foreign observer, Lodovico Guicciardini (1567: 90), noted (as a Florentine patrician he would have been a connoisseur of urban liberty). The municipality did little to restrict the freedom of such able, thrusting, ruthless, successful entrepreneurs as Gilbert van Schoonbecke or the Italian financier Gaspar Ducci. Foreigners were welcome and the religious atmosphere of the Netherlands was relatively mild. The attitudes of Erasmus of Rotterdam seem to have been shared by many of his countrymen, as the resistance by Catholics to Philip II's persecution of Protestants would show. Like northern Italy, the Netherlands seems to have been a relatively literate and numerate culture at the end of the Middle Ages, and it was in Antwerp that the first Dutch treatise on double-entry book-keeping was published in 1543 (Ympijn, 1543; on the cultural background, see Voet, 1973).

Like its rise, the decline of Antwerp cannot be explained in purely economic terms. The city joined the general revolt of the Netherlands

4 Heers (1961) denies that S. Giorgio was a state within a state, but he does use this term to describe the aristocratic clans.

against Spain but was recaptured in 1585, after which date the rebels in the north destroyed Antwerp's trade by blockading the mouth of the Scheldt. The economic recession and the persecution of Calvinism which followed the city's recapture encouraged emigration on a massive scale, to Amsterdam in particular.

Not all Antwerp's loss was Amsterdam's gain, for cities such as London, Rouen and Leiden also profited. Not all Amsterdam's gain was Antwerp's loss, for the 'mother trade' of Amsterdam, the first stage of the economic rocket, was the Baltic trade. However, the migration of capital and skills from Antwerp did give the rocket a powerful boost.

The economic rise of the Dutch Republic (or 'United Provinces') and of Amsterdam in particular is one of the two great economic success stories of the seventeenth century, the other being the rise of Tokugawa Japan. The Dutch success is all the more striking because of the Republic's lack of basic commodities such as grain and wood and because this economic 'golden age' coincided with a period of 'crisis' (or at best stagnation) in most other European economies. The story of this 'miracle' has often been told (Schöffer, 1966; Swart, 1969). The Dutch dominated the European carrying trade. The Dutch East Indian Company, or VOC, was the most successful commercial company in Europe. Industries such as cloth production in Leiden, shipbuilding in the Zaanstreek, and soap-boiling, sugar-refining and printing at Amsterdam all prospered. Amsterdam replaced Genoa and Antwerp as the European money market. Agriculture was highly specialized, highly commercialized and highly successful (Barbour, 1950; Boxer, 1965, Vries, 1974).

From that day to this many attempts have been made to explain the 'Dutch phenomenon'. Envious foreign contemporaries such as Sir Josiah Child pointed to low interest rates as the key to Dutch success. Others have emphasized the importance of the *fluit* (a low-cost, high-capacity transport ship, the container of the seventeenth century). Some historians see the 'agricultural revolution' as the key to Dutch prosperity; others point to low wages or to the Republic's economic 'hegemony' over its rivals and trading partners, whether 'core states' such as England or 'peripheries' such as the East Indies (Aymard, 1982; Wallerstein, 1980: chapter 2). My purpose here, however, is not to evaluate the rival economic explanations but to point to the possible relevance of political and cultural factors.

To begin with politics. In an age of centralizing monarchies, the Dutch lived in a decentralized republic, a federal system which (despite the existence of a 'Governor' or *Stadhouder*) was dominated by the towns and in particular by Amsterdam. The defence of urban privileges or 'liberties' had in fact been one of the main aims in the Dutch revolt against Spain, a movement which has been shrewdly described as 'the revolt of medievalism' against Philip II's attempt to introduce a more modern centralized state (Renier, 1950). The federal system which emerged might be described, like the Genoese system, as a 'weak state', with the proviso that their performance in the so-called 'Eight Years War' against Spain showed that the Dutch were eminently capable of defending themselves. Once again the phrase 'state within a state' may have its uses. The VOC was compared by an acute foreign observer, Sir William Temple, to a 'Sovereign State' which was able to make war or peace in the East Indies; so the decentralized state may have been no mere 'indicator' of economic strength (as if the Dutch could afford this handicap), but a factor positively favouring economic efficiency (Temple, 1932; Wallerstein, 1980: chapter 2 – contrast with Braudel, 1979: 169). Not too much state (as in France); not too little (as in the case of fragmented Italy, which might have benefited from federation, had that been politically feasible), but a golden mean.

There was, in other words, a good 'fit' between this form of state and the interests of the leading Dutch entrepreneurs, the Bickers, De Geers, Trips and the rest. The links between business and politics were closest in the most decentralized decades, the so called 'period without a *Stadhouder*' from 1650 to 1672. In these years the most powerful man in the Dutch Republic was Jan de Witt, a lawyer by training but a man close to the business community, as his collaboration in *The Interest of Holland* (1662) shows; for this pamphlet was a plea for freedom of trade as well as for political and religious freedom (1702: Part 1, chapter 14; Part 2, chapter 15; Part 3, chapter 3). It argues, incidentally, that since the days of Sidon and Tyre 'Trade has flourish'd most under Republican governments.' As a reminder of the human costs of economic freedom, however, it should be added that the clothiers of Leiden (one of whom, Pieter de la Court, had a large part in writing this pamphlet) employed children of eight to work fourteen hours a day for low wages (Posthumus, 1939: vol. 2, 573ff.).

President Calvin Coolidge is said to have remarked that 'The business of the United States is business', while Charles Wilson (Chairman of General Motors and Secretary for Defense in the 1950s) declared that 'What's good for General Motors is good for the United States.' In the seventeenth century, it might equally well have been said that 'The business of the United Provinces is business' and that 'What's good for the VOC is good for the Dutch Republic.' Witness the notorious 'trade with the enemy' during the Eighty Years War, when Dutch entrepreneurs supplied Spain not only with food but even with munitions (Kernkamp, 1931–4)! When war finally came to an end in 1648, this was 'almost entirely' due to 'the pressure of the great commercial centres of

Holland' who had decided by this time that peace suited them even better than war (Israel, 1977). There would seem to be a modicum of truth, despite the distinct whiff of sour grapes, in the contemporary English and French observation that the Dutch were a 'petty commonwealth' guided by 'commercial advantages' alone, in other words a nation of shopkeepers (Viner, 1969).

Dutch culture was also such as to encourage a high level of economic performance. In suggesting this I do not intend to underwrite the 'Weber thesis' about the links between Calvinism and capitalism, a thesis which has long been pounded by the batteries of historians, who have scored at least a few palpable hits (Samuelsson, 1961). At the direct level, it seems clear that Calvinist clergy were unsympathetic to capital accumulation, which they denounced as 'avarice' (Boxer, 1965: 113). At a more indirect level, however, it might still be argued that the Calvinist ethic encouraged the hard work and frugality which foreigners noted as particularly Dutch characteristics and which help explain their economic success. Temple is only one of a number who commented on 'the great simplicity and modesty in the common Port or living' of even the richest and most powerful citizens of the Republic (1932: 76; cf. 60, 79, 141ff.). The absence of a court doubtless made it more difficult for the common European habit of competitive conspicuous consumption to infect the Dutch ruling class, but the Protestant ethic made this frugality respectable. Frugality was not the only element in Dutch culture of the seventeenth century which is relevant to their economic efficiency. The Hollanders and Zealanders at least were relatively literate and numerate, with a sharp sense of time which may be illustrated from canal-boat timetables (Vries, 1978) as well as from clock-making. Dutch culture seems to have been as relatively receptive to innovation as it was to foreign elements. As historians pointed out long ago, the toleration of religious diversity encouraged the immigration to the United Provinces of many individuals with capital and skills, not least the Spanish and Portuguese Jews who became so prominent in Dutch financial circles.

This chapter has suggested that northern Italy and the Netherlands might both be described as pro-enterprise cultures in which governments did relatively little to frustrate the designs of merchants or hinder economic growth, a negative characteristic which all the same gave those countries an important advantage over their competitors. A few concluding observations about these competitors may therefore be of

For a classic example of an anti-enterprise culture we may turn to early modern Spain and in particular to Castille, where politico-religious values took precedence over economic ones. Merchants were despised and the government expelled the industrious Moriscos and Jews for a combination of religious and political reasons (Lapeyre, 1960; Elliott,

1961). France provides a similar if less extreme contrast to the commonwealths of merchants with which this essay has been concerned. The kings of France like the kings of Spain took little personal interest in trade or industry. The Protestant 'state within a state', the 'United Provinces' of the south-west, was dismantled in the seventeenth century and the expulsion of the Huguenots, like that of the Moriscos, reveals the priority of political and religious aims over economic ones (Scoville, 1960; Garrisson, 1985). When the government did found commercial companies on the Dutch model, they were unable to find sufficient investors because capital was diverted into the purchase of offices in the *parlements* and elsewhere. These offices carried high social status and even tax exemptions, so that merchants with money to spare were in effect rewarded for doing the opposite of what Richelieu and Colbert thought best for the economy. At the end of Louis XIV's reign, the failure of an official attempt to create a *noblesse commerçante* suggests that anti-enterprise values were rooted in French culture (Grassby, 1960). In England, where the value-system seems to have been more favourable to merchants, the governments of James I and Charles I managed to hinder their activities, notably by the creation of monopolies (Ashton, 1979).

These comparisons suggest that the most efficient economies in early modern Europe were those where the culture and the regime hindered entrepreneurs least. This is not a plea for private enterprise. I am not arguing that government intervention in the economy is always bad for economic growth and still less that economic growth is the highest human value. However, the examples examined here do support Baechler's thesis of the importance of political and cultural factors in the history of capitalism and even his assertion that 'The less that politics meddles in the economy . . . the more the economy will prosper' (Baechler, 1975).

References

Alberti, L. B. 1969: *Libri della famiglia*, eds R. Romano and A. Tenenti, Turin.
Ashton, R. 1979: *The City and the Court*, Cambridge.
Aymard, M. (ed.) 1982: *Dutch Capitalism and World Capitalism*, Cambridge.
Baechler, J. 1975: *The Origins of Capitalism*, Oxford.
Barbour, V. 1950: *Capitalism in Amsterdam in the 17th Century*, Baltimore.
Baron, H. 1955: *The Crisis of the Early Italian Renaissance*, Princeton.
Bec, C. 1967: *Les marchands écrivains*, Paris.
Boxer, C. 1965: *The Dutch Seaborne Empire*, London.
Braudel, F. 1979: *Le Temps du Monde*, Paris.
Burckhardt, J. 1944: *Civilization of the Renaissance in Italy*, London.

Burke, P. 1974: *Venice and Amsterdam*, London.
1987: The uses of literacy in early modern Italy. In P. Burke and R. Porter (eds), *The Social History of Language*, Cambridge.
Castillo, A. 1963: Dette flottante et dette consolidée en Espagne de 1557 a 1600. *Annales E.S.C.*, 18.
Cipolla, C. 1967: *Clocks and Culture*, London.
Costantini, C. 1978: *La Repubblica di Genova nell'età moderna*, Turin.
Coryat, T. 1905: *Crudities*, vol. 1, Glasgow.
Elliott, J. H. 1961: The decline of Spain. *Past and Present*, no. 20.
Garrisson, J. 1985: *L'Edit de Nantes et sa revocation*, Paris.
Goldthwaite, R. A. 1980: *The Building of Renaissance Florence*, Baltimore.
Grassby, R. B. 1960: Social status and commercial enterprise under Louis XIV. *Economic History Review*, 13.
Grendi, E. 1976: *Introduzione alla storia moderna della republica di Genova*, Genoa.
Guglielminetti, M. 1977: *Memoria e scrittura*, Turin.
Guiccardini, L. 1567: *Descrittione di tutti i paesi bassi*, Antwerp.
Heers, J. 1961: *Gênes au 15e siècle*, Paris.
Herlihy, D. and Klapisch, C. 1978: *Les Toscans et leurs familles*, Paris.
Israel, J. 1977: A conflict of empires: Spain and the Netherlands, 1618–1648. *Past and Present*, no. 77.
Kernkamp, J. H. 1931–4: *De handel op den vijand*, 2 vols, Utrecht.
Krantz, F. and Hohenberg, P. (eds) 1975: *Failed Transitions to Modern Industrial Society: Renaissance Italy and 17th century Holland*, Montreal.
Lapeyre, H. 1953: *Asientos*, Paris.
1960: *Géographie de l'Espagne Morisque*, Paris.
Le Goff, J. 1980: *Time, Work and Culture in the Middle Ages*, Chicago.
Lopez, R. S. 1963: Quattrocento genovese. *Rivista Storica Italiana*, 75.
McNeill, W. H. 1982: *The Pursuit of Power*, Oxford.
Montesquieu, C. 1949: *The Spirit of the Laws*, trans. T. Nugent, New York.
Pareto, V. 1935: *The Mind and Society*, ed. A. Livingston, London.
Parker, G. 1977: *The Dutch Revolt*, London.
Pocock, J. G. A. 1975: *The Machiavellian Moment*, Princeton.
Posthumus, N. W. 1939: *De Geschiedenis van de Leidse Lakenindustrie*, vol. 2, The Hague.
Pullan, B. 1973: The occupations and investments of the Venetian nobility. In J. Hale (ed.) *Renaissance Venice*, London.
Rapp, R. T. 1979: Real estate and rational investment in early modern Venice. *Journal of European Economic History*, 8.
Renier, G. 1950: *The Dutch Nation*, London.
Samuelsson, K. 1961: *Economy and Religion*, London.
Sanudo, M. 1879–1903. *I Diarii*, Venice.
Schöffer, I. 1966. Did Holland's Golden Age coincide with a period of crisis? *Acta Historiae Neerlandicae*, 1.
Scoville, W. 1960: *The Persecution of the Huguenots and French Economic Development, 1680–1720*, Berkeley.
Smith, A. 1976: *The Wealth of Nations*, Oxford.
Spinola, A. 1981: *Scritti scelti*, Genoa.

Swart, K. W. 1969: *The Miracle of the Dutch Republic as seen in the 17th century*, London.

Temple, W. 1932: *Observations upon the United Provinces*, Cambridge.

Terrasson, A. 1750: *Histoire de la jurisprudence romaine*, Paris.

Thomas, W. 1549: *History of Italy*, London.

Tucci, U. 1973: The psychology of the Venetian merchant in the 16th century. In J. Hale (ed.) *Renaissance Venice*, London.

Viner, J. 1969: Power versus plenty as objectives of foreign policy in the seventeenth and eighteenth centuries. In D. Coleman (ed.), *Revisions in Mercantilism*, London.

Voet, L. 1973: *Antwerp: The Golden Age*, Antwerp.

Vries, J. de. 1974: *The Dutch Rural Economy in the Golden Age*, New Haven.
  1978: Barges and capitalism. *AAG Bijdragen*, 21.

Wackernagel, M. 1981: *The World of the Florentine Renaissance Artist*, Princeton, New Jersey.

Waley, D. 1969: *The Italian City Republics*, London.

Wallerstein, I. 1980: *The Modern World Economy*, vol. 2, New York.

Wee, H. van der 1963: *The Growth of the Antwerp Market and the European Economy (14th to 16th Centuries)*, 2 vols, The Hague.

Wiener, M. 1981: *English Culture and Decline of the Industrial Spirit*, Cambridge.

Wilson, C. 1968: *The Dutch Republic*, London.

Winch, D. 1978: *Adam Smith's Politics*, Cambridge.

Witt, J. de 1702: *The Interest of Holland*, London.

Woolf, S. J. 1968: Venice and the terraferma. In B. Pullan (ed.), *Crisis and Change in the Venetian Economy*, London.

Ympijn, J. 1543: *Consten des Rekenboecks*, Antwerp.

14

The European Family and Early Industrialization

Peter Laslett

The case argued here is that the remarkable difference between Europe and the rest of the world in matters of industry, commerce and perhaps political aggrandisement may have been to some extent due to an entirely individual familial system. Before the coming of the factory the family was the site and instrument of production as well as of reproduction. Family and kinship, moreover, are almost universally assumed to be at the heart of every social structure. Therefore it may be granted that in pre-industrial societies familial traits must have been important to comparative progress in economic and industrial life. I am not myself convinced of the simple, rather mechanical model, Aristotelian in origin, of the family as the centre and building block of society. I do believe, however, that it is not much of an exaggeration to call the family the great multiplier, its importance in the socialization process making its form and structure a determinant, though to varying degrees, of every distinguishable influence and circumstance which can be called social.

The uniqueness of the European familial system of production and reproduction is not to be grasped in one variable. It is a bundle of attributes which concerns us.[1] Its relevance to general social development, to exceptional European social development particularly, is multiplex rather than single-stranded. We begin with *procreative activity*

---

1 The defining variables of the European, specifically the English and north-west European, familial system were first listed in Laslett (1977a) and extended, with comparisons for other European areas and, along with a discussion of its work group characteristics, in Laslett (1983a, 1983b, 1984). They are further discussed in Macfarlane (1978, 1981), and, with particular reference to marriage, in Macfarlane (1986). A preliminary attempt at assessing the potentialities of Western familial forms for economic progressiveness was made by Laslett (1975).

in relation to resources and with the particular attributes of the European system in this respect.

It can be shown, I think, that the specifically European system of ensuring that procreative activity only takes place between spouses who are required to create their own households ensured that European populations were sensitively and stably related to their economic and physical environment. We now have good reason to believe that such a system goes a long way back in European development. It was the stability and sensitivity of the interconnection which accounted for the fact that European history was not marked to the same extent as that of Asia, and no doubt of Africa and other areas if we had the record, by famines, plagues and crises of population, in so far as these were induced by imbalance between population and resources.

To say to the same extent is not to deny that crises occurred in the European past, nor is it to play down the influence which such lugubrious events must have had on European progress. It is to claim in comparative terms that the Europeans were insulated to some degree against vicissitude – endogenous and exogenous. Population increase never seems to have raised numbers to such a level that mass extinction became necessary if the balance with the environment was to be restored.[2]

To pursue this point a little further with illustrations, one could say that the extremest form of crisis ever known to have affected historical European populations was the Black Death in the fourteenth century. This did not, as earlier scholarship supposed, debilitate Europe in subsequent centuries, certainly not to the degree that epidemic mortality affected the populations of Asia and other parts of the world lacking the familial characteristics we are discussing. Bubonic plague is to a large extent an exogenous threat to the survival of a population, though not one which defies all human intervention because a society can, and medieval Italy did, take fairly effective measures against the spread of the contagion (Cipolla, 1973). The manner in which Iceland survived the eruptions of its volcanoes in the eighteenth century (Guttormson, 1984) illustrates how resilient a European society could be under exogenous attack from its physical environment.

The details of the demographic contrast between Europe, or more particularly west and north-western Europe, perhaps especially England, are now well known to historians, especially through the famous volume on *Population History of England* by my two colleagues at the Cambridge

2 For the comparative infrequency and mildness of population crises, especially those due to famine, in England since the sixteenth century at least, see Wrigley and Schofield (1981: esp. chapters 8, 9, appendix 10). On France, compare Laslett (1983c: chapter 6). On China, India and Asia, see Jones (1981).

Group: E. A. Wrigley and R. S. Schofield. England, and to a rather lesser extent and to different degrees, the Low Countries, northern France and Scandinavia, do not appear to have been at any recoverable point in their histories areas of high-pressure demographic regimes, characteristic as those regimes seem to be of agrarian peasant society generally. That is to say collective survival was not the outcome of very large numbers of births and a very large population increase being maintained in normal times, so as to ensure numbers sufficient to survive catastrophes. Rather the European familial/procreative system ensured that at all times because of *late marriage and high proportions of the non-marrying there was fertility unused, fertility which could be brought into operation as vicissitudes demanded,* by the simple mechanism of the age of marriage going down and the proportions marrying increasing (Hajnal, 1965, 1983; Macfarlane, 1978, 1986). Marriage choices are social variables. It is a nexus of social connections which an individual must respect, but may exploit, which is at issue when a person marries, and not biological circumstances. It is finally through choice and deliberation, then, that the European system ensured harmony of environment, procreation and population change.

It is usual at this point in such arguments to cite T. R. Malthus, the quintessentially European analyst of population in relation to resources, and my comment on his position has to be this. Malthus got wise to the European system as he did because he thought he saw it failing to work in his own generation (Wrigley, 1983, 1986; Laslett, 1983a, 1985; Macfarlane, 1986). This generation happened to be one of maximum marriage, for England anyway, of very high fertility and of fairly stable mortality. It was marked by the fastest population growth for the three or even five preceding centuries, at least in England. Even in the lifetime of Malthus, however, rates of fertility and of increase were well below what is still common in developing countries, and what must have been very widespread indeed there in earlier times.

Had Malthus been able to reconstruct the previous two centuries of the population history of his own country, which has now been done for him, he would no doubt have appreciated that what he saw in his own time was the high point of what I should boldly claim was a secular sine-wave of population increase and decrease. He might even have been able to see that an earlier peak had come in the late sixteenth century and a yet earlier one in the late thirteenth century, with troughs in the mid-seventeenth century and in the mid-fourteenth century too. In fact Malthus predicted such oscillations as a theoretical construct and claimed that they kept Europe free of really extreme conditions, those whose presence have been demonstrated elsewhere in the world and especially in China, Europe's possible rival in the developmental race.

Historical demographers indeed are having considerable difficulty in precisely demonstrating examples in the European story of those acute crises of population which stand out so clearly among Asians and Africans, past and present (Laslett, 1983c: chapter 6; Rotberg and Rabb, 1985).

The second individual feature of the European familial system may have been responsible for a whole series of features conducive to economic progress, and perhaps innovation. The conditions laid down for marriage and procreation imposed on all individuals, but especially on the very large majority who were poor, the necessity of saving, accumulating. If they were to set up independent households of their own they had to find a means to do so, generally, though not always, with help from their parents, but for the most part by their own efforts. This required (again of the whole population, but especially of the worst-placed) a long period of discipline and training in youth and in early adulthood. Everyone had to have a vocation and qualify for placement.

Accordingly the established arrangements bore hard on the young and the nubile, in a society where marriage was the only way to full citizenship and assured personal status. This was so because individuals in the relevant age groups had a fair proportion of the product of their labour taken from them, but were required nevertheless to accumulate a fund of their own from what was left. In this way the European familial system fostered the spirit of hoarding and parsimony, beloved of Weber and his followers as conducive to capitalism, at the same time as it sanctioned a degree of personal exploitation, by the father of those children of working age who remained with him, and especially by the master of his life-cycle servants, women as well as men.

Moreover, this system in ways not quite so clearly discernible promoted a high level of geographical mobility amongst young people. At the age of secondary socialization, of skill acquisition, and of their greatest strength and productivity, a majority of English youths and maidens were in service and changed their servants' places almost every year. They moved within a small area for the most part, but into, out of and within the cities, especially the capital. Their migratory habits only came to an end when they finally married and 'settled down', a phrase highly characteristic of the marriage pattern which we are distinguishing from others elsewhere in the world (Laslett, 1977b: chapter 2; Kussmaul, 1981; Wrigley, 1967).

In the European system, therefore, procreation was reserved to those successful enough under the prevalent economic circumstances to create their own households. This required sufficient resources for them to live on their own, not with their parents or other relatives, and, in principle anyway, not at the expense of the collectivity, at least during the earliest years of the marital careers. Procreation was not so restricted in Asia and in Africa, where marriage was early and universal, where the married might remain in the households of their parents and need not found households of their own.

All this was assured in Europe by marriage being late for both sexes; by marriage being to some degree companionate; by the marriage decision being largely that of the spouses concerned and not that of their families; by the relative unimportance of dowries, that is to say a right to a part of the savings of the parents; by the requirement that most young people should leave the household of their parents at the beginning of their economic usefulness to work in other productive units as servants, that is as trainees, but also as surplus-producing subordinates hoarding for marriage. *Life-cycle service of this kind was unique to Europe,* and *especially characteristic of the European north-west.* Being bound to be trained and to save until reaching the head of the marriage queue was, then, the crucial element of the particular quality of the European familial system in relation to production (Hajnal, 1983; Laslett, 1977a, 1983; Macfarlane, 1986).

Service gave rise, as has been said, to labour mobility on a scale whose extent amazes everyone when it is encountered in a wholly traditional society. Servants moved from household to household throughout the whole period of service, that is to say up to ten or twelve times in an ordinary career. If they belonged to the minority who never married at all, they would circulate throughout their working lives. The inter-relationship between the small village settlements characteristic of north-west Europe could thus become one of economic and productive symmetry. The creation of concentrations of industrial populations or of urban centres in that part of Europe, which in the end became economically the most progressive, was a straightforward matter under such circumstances. It has to be insisted, however, that though urban areas, particularly when successful, retained a surprising number of the immigrants in northern Europe, the migration and turnover pattern made the movement reciprocal between village and town or city. This ensured that a degree of information, technical awareness and training should be fairly constant over the whole surface of predominantly rural societies (Wrigley, 1967).

To this can be added the ease with which north-west Europeans could move across the ocean to North American colonies, or could take ship and spend much of their productive period of youth in the commercial centres overseas which finally became the nodal points of the European empires. Such a familial system facilitated the recruitment of armies, and especially navies. Because of the society's insistence on training, it kept skill levels high and rising. Because of its individualistic, competitive, capitalistic character, as I have called it, this system and outlook make the work of Adam Smith as well of Malthus understandable as quintessentially European, each to be read from our present point of view as a commentary upon the unique European familial system.

The final feature of this system in relation to European social and particularly administrative life is difficult to convey or to describe within the present compass. Although the set of arrangements described was individualistic, since it rested firmly on the independent procreative responsibility of each individual, it did not, and could not, grant to all individuals enough resources to ensure against all the procreative eventualities which marriage might give rise to. If a couple at the lower social levels had more than four surviving children under fifteen years old who were living at home, their individualistic domestic autonomy was threatened. If a mother was widowed or deserted at any time, or a single woman saddled with a child, such autonomy was out of the question on the resources usually available to the family (Laslett, 1985: esp. 361). These recurrent circumstances, together with the final dependency of the non-earning elderly, brought about a relationship between family and collectivity in Europe which is a present preoccupation of many theorists of these issues. It led to extensive transfers, transfers on a considerable scale, from families in surplus to families in deficit, transfers which were organized by the collectivity – locally and nationally.

The English Poor Law is the most obvious and most easily understood of the European institutions imposing and administering this flow of resources. Its provisions more or less guaranteed to the least favourably placed couple that, once having succeeded in finding a slot and getting married, they would survive if they happened to become responsible for more children than the current population economy balance required of the average marital union. Some large families might be needed in any case so as to recoup the population after vicissitudes of a social character, when the whole society was being threatened by epidemic, or by such natural catastrophes as came about in early eighteenth-century Iceland.

Then there was the hazard of growing old and incapable, of being orphaned, or illegitimate, or disabled. The dependent elderly and other casualties were badly placed in the European familial system because the simple family household discouraged co-residence of dependent parents or of other kin. To compensate for such hardships as were imposed by nuclear family rules, the typical European state evolved a country-wide, inter-local redistributive system which may have something to do with the superior administrative efficiency of European society in contrast to that of their Asian and African counterparts.

These are inadequate descriptions, especially in the last paragraph. The final point which has to be made here is to stress that the characteristics I have discussed were particularly concentrated in the north-west European area of maximal productive innovation, that is to say the areas of earliest industrialization, especially England and the Low Countries. They were much less pronounced on the Italian and Iberian peninsulas and these sites of Mediterranean and European aesthetic, intellectual and technical achievement, especially central Italy, were to some degree outside the familial system described. But then industrialization, presumed here to be the most significant of all economic, productive and social achievements in the whole history of the relationship of human populations with their environments, did not occur early in Italy or in Spain.

There is a necessary postscript to this hasty and abbreviated discussion. Social and familial arrangements peculiarly suited to set the industrial system into original motion may not be those best suited to maintain and expand a mature industrial system in being. The Japanese miracle of our day may be symmetrical in some sense, perhaps even a familial sense, with the European miracle of medieval and early modern times.

References

Cipolla, C. 1973: *Christophano and the Plague*, London.

Guttormsson, L. 1984: *Bernska, ungdomur og uppeldi a einveldisold*, Reykjavik (*Childhood, Youth and Upbringing in Iceland in the Age of Absolutism, a Socio-demographic Analysis*, English summary, pp. 220–6).

Hajnal, J. 1965: European marriage patterns in perspective. In D. Glass and D. Eversley (eds), *Population in History*, London.

— 1983: Two kinds of pre-industrial household formation system. R. Wall, J. Robin and P. Laslett (eds), *Family Forms in Historic Europe*, Cambridge.

Jones, E. L. 1981: *The European Miracle*, London.

Kussmaul, A. 1981: *Servants and Husbandry in Early Modern England*, Cambridge.

Laslett, P. 1975: in *Sozialgeschichte der Familie in der Neuzeit Europas*, ed. W. Conze, Stuttgart.

— 1977a: Characteristics of the Western family considered over time. In *Family Life and Illicit Love in Earlier Generations*, Cambridge.

— 1977b: Clayworth and Cogenhoe. In *Family Life*.

— 1983a: Microstructural history in relation to human adaptation. In D. Ortner (ed.), *How Humans Adapt*, Washington, DC.

— 1983b: Household and family as work group and kin group. In Wall et al., *Family Forms*, chapter 17.

— 1983c: *The World We Have Lost Further Explored*, London.

— 1984: The family as a knot of individual interests. In R. Netting et al. (eds), *Households*, Berkeley.

1985: Gregory King, Robert Malthus and the origins of English social realism. *Population Studies*, 39.

Macfarlane, A. 1978: *The Origins of English Individualism*, Oxford.

1981: Demographic structures and cultural regions in Europe. *Cambridge Anthropology*, 6.

1986: *Marriage and Love in England, 1300–1840*, Oxford.

Rotberg, R. and Rabb, D. (eds) 1985: *Hunger and History*, Cambridge.

Wrigley, E. A. 1967: A simple model of London's importance, 1650–1850. *Past and Present*, no. 27.

1983: Malthus's model of a pre-industrial economy. In J. Dupâquier (ed.), *Malthus Past and Present*, New York.

1986: Elegance and experience: Malthus at the bar of history. In David Coleman and R. S. Schofield (eds), *The State of Population Theory*, Oxford.

Wrigley, E. A. and Schofield, R. S. 1981: *The Population History of England*, London.

Index

Index by A. R. Crook

IDEAS is a new Blackwell series which makes available in paperback some of the most adventurous writing in the social and humane sciences in recent years, extending the frontiers of research, crossing disciplinary borders and setting new intellectual standards in international scholarship. Published and forthcoming titles include:

Jean Baechler, John A. Hall and Michael Mann, *Europe and the Rise of Capitalism*

Colin Campbell, *The Romantic Ethic and the Spirit of Modern Consumerism*

William Connolly, *Political Theory and Modernity*

John A. Hall (ed.), *States in History*

Alan Macfarlane, *The Culture of Capitalism*

Derek Sayer, *The Violence of Abstraction*

Michael Peter Smith and Joe R. Feagin, *The Capitalist City*